Parents and Teachers
1 Perspectives on Home–School Relations

Edited by John Bastiani

NFER-NELSON

*Published by The NFER-NELSON Publishing Company Ltd.,
Darville House, 2 Oxford Road East,
Windsor, Berkshire SL4 1DF, England.*

First published 1987

Photoset by Illustrated Arts Limited, Sutton, Surrey.

*Printed and bound in Great Britain
by Billing & Sons Limited, Worcester.*

*ISBN 0 7005 1131 8
Code 8277 02 1*

Contents

Acknowledgements

Acknowledgements are due to the following for permission to publish extracts in this volume.

George Allen and Unwin

Connell, R. W. *et al*. (1982). 'Families and their kids'. In: *Making the Difference: Schools, Families and Social Division*, 52–78.

Newson, J. and Newson, E. (1977). 'Both intermediary and beneficiary'. In: *Perspectives on School at Seven Years Old*, 107–135.

Basil Blackwell

Bridges, D. (1981). '"It's the ones who never turn up that you really want to see:" : the "problem" of the non-attending parent'. In: Elliott, T. *et al*. (Eds) *School Accountability*, 96–108.

The British Sociological Association

Booth, T. A. (1978). 'From normal baby to handicapped child', *Sociology*, 12, 2, 203–221.

Falmer Press

Tomlinson, S. (1985). 'Home, school and community'. In: Craft, M. (Ed) *Education and Cultural Pluralism*, 143–159.

Harper and Rowe

Barton, L. and Moody, S. (1981). 'The value of parents to the ESN(S) school: an examination'. In: *Special Education: Policy, Practice and Social Issues*, 133–148.

Institute of Family and Environmental Research

Rapoport, R. N. (1975). 'Home and school at the launch', *Oxford Review of Education*, 1, 3, 277–286.

Manchester University Press

Batten, E. (1975). 'Attainment, environment and education'. In: Rushton, J. and Turner, J. D. (Eds) *Education and Deprivation*, 23–45.

Routledge and Kegan Paul

David, M. (1980). 'Re-asserting rights to achieve economic efficiency'. In: *The State, the Family and Education*, 185–211.

Introduction

I Background

The study of home–school matters is rapidly coming of age. For significant changes are now taking place both in the conventional wisdom and in widely accepted practice; new perspectives, giving rise to very different views of the key issues and problems, are emerging, which call for different methods of study and inquiry; home–school relations have been brought into the arena of political policy and action; above all, the critical examination of home–school matters is increasingly felt to make a useful contribution to the development of educational thinking and practice and to be a necessary ingredient in the professional development of teachers. All of this makes the study of relations between families and schools, between teachers, parents and pupils, a particularly relevant and challenging task for those who currently work with children and young people.

By contrast, the study of home–school relations in the past appears to have followed rather narrow and separate tracks, each with its own characteristic approaches, literature and followers. First, there was an extensive *research* tradition, which grew in conjunction with the emergence of education as a public service in post-war Britain. Such research, now enshrined in undergraduate texts in chapters called 'Social Background and Educational Achievement', was concerned to monitor the emergence and early development of health, welfare and educational agencies and was clearly located within the context of a commitment to an ideology of equality of opportunity. More recently, this particular tradition has been harnessed to the identification of special needs and the policies that are required to meet them.

Given the profound changes that have taken place in the social climate in the last decade, it would be all too easy to dismiss this work as a hopelessly idealistic attempt to provide a basis for social engineering, which would be doomed to fail. However, it is still useful to remind ourselves of the contribution of such studies in bringing glaring inequalities in our educational system, based on family and class, to the public attention. The failure to develop appropriate policies remains another story!

The second tradition in the study of home–school relations grew not so much out of the development of educational practice as out of its *rhetoric*. Accounts about 'the way things should be' were particularly influential during the late 1960s and early 1970s. These could be located against a background influenced by the rapid expansion of the teaching profession and its developing professionalism, together with a growing public interest in education and a belief in its value, both instrumentally in terms of securing jobs and in its power to enrich the lives of individuals.

Such accounts, which are often written by 'elevated' practitioners, are usually restricted to the level of common sense, practical advice. Their tone is uplifting, if somewhat idealistic, and they tend to play down both actual and perceived problems. They are atheoretical and lack any real empirical support. Above all, such accounts seem very much at odds with the temper of our times.

The third element in the established version of home–school relations as a field of study, derives from the *actual practice* of schools and families, of teachers, pupils and parents. Although in recent years there have been several interesting attempts to collect the *views* of parents on their children's schooling, there has been little attempt to obtain direct evidence of, for example, communication and contact between parents and teachers, or to provide a picture of the actual involvement of parents.

Underlying study and established practice in the field has been a failure to acknowledge openly the rather shadowy and ambiguous place of home–school relationships and responsibilities in the professional lives of teachers. There is almost nothing that is explicit in teachers' contracts, in DES or LEA regulations or school-based policies that spells out the nature and extent of their duties in this area.

This apparent lack of professional commitment has been matched, for parents, by a correspondingly low threshold of expectation of rights concerning their children's schooling, or a clear understanding of how to behave. Wide differences of both belief and practice, reinforced by the absence of formal rules, have characterized the behaviour of parents and teachers alike, and reinforced their marginality. Against such a background, current developments can be seen as both challenging and wide-ranging.

Many of the contributions in this reader draw attention, explicitly or by implication, to the transformation that has been taking place in the study of home–school relations during the last decade. An important ingredient in such an analysis is the way in which relationships between parents and their children's schools, and the issues that stem from this, have become an object of concern for governments, schools and families alike.

A major consideration in any current view of the field has been its recent politicization. The supposed widespread anxiety about educational 'standards', particularly in 'progressive' primary schools and comprehensive secondary schools, has been incorporated into the agenda of all major political parties, where it is seen in the context of a wider debate about the accountability of public services. More recently, however, parental anxiety about the performance of schools has, to some extent, been replaced by a growing concern about the standards of educational provision. Such a change raises some interesting questions about the relationship between government policies and public attitudes.

Taken together, the shared concerns of governments, schools and families have focused attention upon a number of issues:

- the preferences of parents for their children's schools;
- the involvement of parents (and others) in the management of schools;
- discussion of the legal and contractual obligations of teachers and parents;

together with the implications of such concerns for policy and practice. The present government has also sought to clarify some of the rights and obligations of parents in two Education Acts (*Information for Parents*, 1980; *The Education of Children with Special Needs*, 1981) and, at the time of writing, in sections of several White

Papers. The passing of relevant legislation, however limited, coupled with the government's interest in teacher training and 'teacher quality', have also fuelled the rapid development of a variety of courses in the home and school field, in both the initial and in-service sectors. Here, with some honourable exceptions, the absence of a core of empirical evidence and recorded experience is deeply felt.

Another important, but very different, indication of the far-reaching changes that have recently taken place in the field, concerns the way in which home–school relations have come to be regarded as a 'problematic' area, that is, that they concern matters that are not nearly as straightforward as they first appear to be. Such a view, which borrows freely from a sociology of knowledge perspective, identifies a need to examine the *assumptions* upon which thinking and practice have been based. It is also concerned to identify those values which have shaped the definition of key issues and problems, followed by the development of appropriate methodologies and patterns of evaluation.

Such a perspective, which calls for an examination of the 'taken-for-grantedness' of established wisdom and practice, is leading to a need to examine familiar routines and relationships and calls for a considerable refocusing within the field, at all levels. A significant example of this would be the way in which the influential Plowden Report has been critically examined, resulting in its central notions of 'the good home' and 'favourable parental attitudes' being called firmly into question. It has led to a profound shift away from rather mechanistic views of environment and educational achievement towards an emphasis upon:

- the complementary nature of teacher/parent roles, which creates the need to regulate inevitable tension and possible conflict;
- the existence of parental perspectives with characteristic, but differentiated, values, concerns and strategies;
- above all, a concern to examine the experience of parents in their dealings with their children's schools, through a study of the key processes of communication, contact and involvement and their implications for parents, pupils and teachers.

Another consequence of attempting to unravel the problematic nature of home–school relationships is the realization of the extent to which they have previously been dominated by professional perspectives and experience.

More recently, and in spite of the negative effects of the recent dispute between teachers and the government, it has at least become possible to see parents moving from a marginal position on the periphery of professional thought and practice, to a more important position – from an optional extra towards an essential partner.

Such movement, which at least potentially represents a profound shift, might be seen to revolve around three steadily growing beliefs:

(i) Parents, in the wake of the discussion of accountability issues, have a widely-accepted *right* to be consulted about, and involved with, a process that initially affects both the short- and longer-term development of their children.

(ii) Parents have important *knowledge and experience*, which are crucially important to a child's school career and in getting a picture of the effects of policies and practices upon individuals. Their experience is both dynamic and continuous, complementing that of the professional in important ways.

(iii) Parents have an enormous capacity as a *resource* to help and support the education and development of young people, which is largely unrecognized by the school system and almost never utilized.

Taken together these three arguments not only constitute something of a rationale about the role of parents but suggest, in outline, a strategy for action.

So relationships between families and schools are increasingly being seen as an important item on the educational agenda. The fact that a number of key areas of concern are shared by governments, schools and families alike, albeit with important differences between them, has done much to accelerate interest in the field, as a legitimate arena for research, policy and action, as well as for study and investigation.

II Some special features

The main purpose of this reader is to provide a collection of material to illustrate the salient features of issue, perspective and method in a challenging, contemporary account of home–school relations. (A second, linked collection will explore the relationship between policy and practice.) In attempting to provide a broad picture of the field as a whole, the selection draws upon familiar, less well-known and original material, drawn from a range of academic orientations and disciplines. It also draws upon three distinct modes of inquiry and analysis, which are often treated separately, implying ways in which their integration, however incomplete, might be productive:

(i) The study of *parental beliefs and attitudes* has been long-established in the study of home–school relations, drawing attention to the presence of differing but deep-seated views amongst parents. In the present collection, there are a number of parents who operate within a strong ideological frame, which disposes them to see the world in a particular way and to act upon that view. Such a position is relatively impervious to contrary evidence and experience.

(ii) A second, well-established mode of inquiry and analysis seeks to understand home–school relations through a comparison of the *structural characteristics of families and schools* respectively. Such a focus can provide a useful framework for a view of the changing relationships between parents and teachers, and between educational roles and institutions, at both the group and individual levels.

(iii) Finally, although it is less well-established in this area than in others, an *interactionist perspective* draws attention to the actual *experiences* that teachers, pupils and parents have of each other and the ways in which home–school relations are 'made' through contact and negotiation over time. Such a perspective sees relationships between actual teachers and parents as relatively fluid and amenable to influence and change.

In addition to providing a broad and deliberately varied picture, the reader gives emphasis to a number of features consistent both with the concerns of its editor and with the spirit of much of the current work in the field.

So, for example, the reader embodies support for the productive interaction of theory, research, policy and practice. This is particularly visible where the reader attempts to be responsive to contemporary issues and concerns where the theory/research/policy/practice relationships can be *very* varied, in such areas as the accountability of educational institutions, the education of children with special needs, inter-agency co-operation and education in a multicultural setting.

Whilst this is not a principle of selection, the reader embodies the author's own preferences for particular theoretical perspectives and their corresponding methods of study and inquiry. So there is an emphasis given to accounts which embody social action theories in general and interactionist perspectives in particular. Such perspectives are revealed through accounts which use qualitative and ethnographic research methods extensively enabling researchers to provide, for example, close-up views of the actual dealings of teachers and parents and to tap into their experience, rather than merely record their views. It is only in recent work in the home–school field that any real importance has been attached to the exploration of *parental* perspectives and experience and this has not, until now, been adequately reflected in the literature. Here, such an emphasis is embodied in a rather obvious way through the selection of materials which attempts to build up a picture of parental concerns, attitudes and behaviour, based upon evidence *obtained directly from parents themselves*. But it goes beyond this with the value that is attached to the opportunities which are given to parents to speak for themselves, in portraying the world as they see and experience it, and in the extensive use of their own words in many of the published accounts.

The reader sets out to appeal to a range of the people, attitudes and experience that constitute the mainstream of home–school thought and practice. This obviously suggests interested practitioners, particularly those who are actively engaged in the study of home–school issues in a variety of settings.

But although prospective and experienced teachers are likely to form the largest single audience, this should not be interpreted in a narrow or exclusive way. It includes, for example, a wide range of practitioners, for whom the development of 'better' home–school relations transcends the divisions created by providing education for particular age-groups or in particular types of institution, (although there *are* important differences, which several of the accounts acknowledge). It would include those who are concerned with the planning and provision of initial training, in-service work and teacher development; it would also consider a small but significant number of professionals from other agencies who share a concern for relationships between families and schools, and the education and welfare of young people. Finally, it includes a small but growing number of knowledgeable and committed parents who have chosen to become actively involved in educational concerns.

Embedded in a number of accounts in this collection are important and far-reaching criticisms of much of the study and research in the home–school field and of its influence upon the thinking of teachers and parents alike. Taken together, they represent something of a critique of the conventional wisdom, its characteristic perspectives and methods, its salient beliefs and actions. But a critical guard is needed every bit as much to prevent similar weaknesses characterizing contemporary work in the field and subsequent accounts. There is still, for example, a tendency to regard teachers and schools as a rather special case, thus playing down the role of schooling in the wider society or the role of professional authority generally.

Finally, there *are* important gaps in this reader which cannot be rectified since they mirror important gaps in the field and suggest important work yet to be done. There are, for example, important long-term social changes taking place that influence the structure and organization of family life. The spread of long-term structural unemployment, the increase of marital breakdown and the reconstitution of families through cohabitation and re-marriage and the increasing variety of styles of parenting illustrate changes which have important consequences for relations between families and schools. This applies both at the macro level and also at the level of the interaction of individuals. Similarly, there are important changes taking place in the relationships between the major institutions of family, school and work, which are influencing long and deeply-held understandings about the nature of responsibility for socialization, education and training. Both of these examples, however, remain largely unexplored, in both the theoretical and empirical domains and are indicative of the basic work that still needs to be done.

III Content and organization

(i) Selection of contents

The present collection tries to strike a reasonable balance between the competing traditions of academic study that derive from the treatment of complex and problematic educational issues in general, and from a rapidly developing home–school literature, in particular.

On the one hand, we have attempted to provide access to some of the diversity and wide-ranging issue, perspective and method that characterize the area, whilst recognizing that it would be impossible to be comprehensive or definitive in any way; indeed, selection has always been a major problem. We have been obliged to settle for a representative series of illustrations, from a range of academic disciplines that characterize the fruitful study of social and educational issues, such as sociology, social psychology and political economy, together with the academic focus provided by, for example, a developmental approach, an ideological stance or cross-institutional comparisons.

The reader also attempts to represent some of the seminal arguments and more general critiques that have been developed in recent years, together with a consideration of their implications for the continuing study and treatment of home–school issues. Examples here include the revaluation of the Plowden Report's contents and influence or the need to examine the relationship between what we say and what we do in the home–school field.

Some of this work, such as the Manchester Plowden follow-up study or the Nottingham long-term studies of child rearing styles are already fairly well-known, and their influence upon current thinking generally recognized; other materials in the collection are less well-known and in need of a wider audience, or brought together in different relationships or to illustrate different intentions from those of their authors when they were first written. Finally, there is material that has been specially commissioned, which is appearing in print for the first time, as a means of illustrating emerging perspectives and concerns, together with their corresponding ways of working.

It is through the pressures of selection, however, that the editor has been able to endorse a particular stance towards the field of home–school relations. So the selection deliberately includes a leaning towards particular theories, perspectives and the methods that characterize their application, and towards an emphasis upon particular issues and styles of account. This is especially obvious, in the commissioned material, which is drawn from grounded studies in the field and which have their roots in the experience of pupils and parents.

(ii) Structure and organization

The structure of the reader is built around three overlapping parts:

PART ONE FAMILY, SCHOOL AND SOCIETY

This section is concerned with *macro* perspectives and ways of studying them. Such perspectives enable us to examine the place of home–school relations in the wider social system, through their focus upon:

- the structural properties of families, schools and neighbourhoods and their effects upon their dealings with others;
- the continuing influence of family and social background upon educational achievement and its consequences for access to higher education, further training and employment opportunities;
- the changing relationships between the major institutions of family, school and work;
- the general influence of powerful social and political ideologies upon education.

PART TWO RELATIONS BETWEEN PARENTS AND TEACHERS

This section incorporates *micro* perspectives, which become the dominant focus in the field. It gives emphasis to those transactions, often of a face-to-face nature, which characterize communication and contact between families and schools. It corresponds to the frequent use of the close-up lens to counter the wide-angle viewpoints of the first section.

This section is concerned with:

- the day-to-day encounters involving parents, teachers and pupils;
- the empirically-based examination of parental perspectives and experience;
- the exploration of the practice of teaching and parenting, particularly at their interface;
- the examination of educative roles and contexts.

The section begins with a general framework against which policy and practice can be located in terms of general ideologies and their underlying beliefs and attitudes. Further selection here, has been very much sharpened by incorporating two promising areas of contrast and comparison:

(a) The dynamic relationship that is developing between the perspectives, concerns and experience that relate to 'mainstream' schooling and those that grow from the attempt to identify and meet 'special needs', however that is done. Within the current debate about integration, it is possible to see the rich potential of family–school cooperation as both the representation of heightened versions of common concerns, as well as the latter's claims to be considered as 'special' – as separate and distinctive.

(b) By examining a number of assumptions and practices in the field that question their taken-for-grantedness, it is possible to generate a productive comparison, by juxtaposing these accounts which stress the 'making' of home–school relationships in the early, formative stages, with others that are more concerned with the longer-term, cumulative experience and effects of parents' dealings with their children's schools.

The next contribution, drawn from a well-known series of child-rearing studies, demonstrates the untapped potential of parental knowledge, interest and skill and its generally unacknowledged value to a child's schooling. It does so through an approach which integrates research perspectives that are generally kept separate, and through the combination of very different kinds of evidence.

In following an earlier contribution in questioning many of the assumptions and much of the taken-for-granted wisdom in the field of mental handicap, the final account in this section examines their implications for relationships between families and schools and for practical action involving parents and teachers.

PART THREE ISSUES IN HOME–SCHOOL RELATIONS

Finally, the reader gives an airing to a number of current concerns, which not only illustrate, sometimes in a rather more applied form, some of the themes of the collection as a whole, but also illustrate areas which are currently enjoying considerable attention from politicians, academics, practising professionals and committed parents respectively, albeit in different ways.

Such concerns, which have been selected from a wider range of possibilities, incorporate both the general themes which reflect broader preoccupations within the arena of social and educational policy and more particular home–school topics. Examples of the former include:

- the performance of schools and their accountability to external audiences;
- the management of educational institutions and processes;
- special needs; policy, provision and practice;
- education in a multicultural setting;
- co-operation between different agencies concerned with the health, education and welfare of children.

Examples of more particular concerns are bound up with issues that are distinctive to the study and practice of home–school relations, involving policy formation and the allocation of resources, important topics for study and research and issues that concern evaluation and training in this area.

This section opens with an account which draws attention with the pin-point accuracy of case-study techniques and evidence, to the school's preoccupation with the management of the tension and conflict that are an inevitable consequence of academic differentiation, which divides parents just as surely as it divides pupils. Although the account focuses upon the final years of compulsory schooling, where such tensions are heightened, the process is established before children ever *enter* the secondary school.

The second example, in examining family–school relations in a multicultural setting, is drawing attention to an important area which has received scant attention from academics, policy-makers or practitioners alike. It also illustrates some of the potential for a deep clash of culture and values, together with the mutual incomprehension that can be endemic in this area.

The issue of non-communicating or non-attending parents is one that is firmly entrenched in teacher lore and staffroom mythology. It is often used to provide explanations for a wide range of inadequacies and deficiencies that range from family background, with its apparent lack of educational support, through to a child's classroom performance. The contribution of academic study here is to render such explanations problematic, requiring the reader to carefully re-examine the notion itself, together with its implications for policy and practice.

The account of home-visiting, by contrast, is a detailed record of one of a number of allied schemes of parental participation and involvement, harnessed to educational goals. It brings together two issues, each of which can be seen to touch a professional raw nerve, for the issues that relate to home-visiting now divide teacher opinion almost as deeply as parental involvement in their children's reading used to.

The final contribution in this section combines the examination of a special issue, with a reminder of some of the general themes of the collection as a whole. At the particular level, it probes the continuing influence and involvement of families in the educational lives of school leavers, during the passage of young people between school, government training schemes, work or unemployment.

But it also serves to challenge a number of prevailing perspectives and ways of conceptualizing the home–school field. It echoes many of the wider concerns that characterize this collection and, above all, it reopens a number of areas, serving as a reminder of the problematic nature of both the study and practice of home–school relations.

Part One

Family, School and Society

Families and Their Kids

Bob Connell (et al)

Introduction

At the simplest level, home and school are linked by the encounters that family members have with the school's staff. The most important of these, of course, are the daily transactions of the pupil herself. This is the main source of information about the school for other family members, from discussions in the kitchen, over dinner, or around the TV set. Nevertheless there are transactions, formal and informal, which involve other family members.

Some opportunities for this are provided formally. The school is surrounded by a small swarm of auxiliary situations, most designed to tap the voluntary labour or the pockets of parents – Mothers' Clubs, Parents' and Citizens' associations (P & C), working bees, and so on. Some events are intended to inform and involve them with the children's progress – parent–teacher nights, sports days, speech days. And there are bodies with a somewhat wider reach, like Old Boys' and Old Girls' Associations, which hardly exist in working-class comprehensives but can be quite important fund-raisers for the Independent schools.

A good deal of the contact, however, is quite informal. A parent may ring up a teacher or principal about a problem of discipline or academic work. Conversely a parent might get summoned for consultation about a delinquency, as Mrs Siemens was when her son Carl was discovered to have artistically carved graffiti in his desk – though this seems to have been more for psychological effect than for mutual information, as the principal rubbed it into Carl how upsetting this was for her. In the Independent schools, many of the

---

Editorial note: In this account, references to Australian institutions and experience have not been altered, since they do not detract from the striking parallels that exist between family–school relationships in Australia and Britain.

fathers get most of their contact with teachers on the touchlines of football grounds, watching their sons play in the school teams that the teachers coach. Mothers working in the school canteen will talk with teachers and other staff in the course of the day. And at times a teacher may appear at a local organization that parents are members of – a club dinner, or a Sunday School prizegiving.

Transactions, then, are very diverse; but they are far from random. For instance, there are strong conventions about who does what. Work in canteens, and other routine voluntary jobs around infants' and primary schools, are almost entirely done by married women. Most of the contact with school about the kids' academic work is undertaken by their mothers; fathers are more likely to be called in on big decisions or on discipline. Major fundraising committees are likely to be run by men; and fathers who can't find the time for checking homework will often turn out to watch their sons play in school teams.

Links between Independent schools and their families seem to be as strong at secondary level as at primary. Indeed the fathers seem to get more involved as the children move further from infancy and the investment in their education comes closer to pay-off. By contrast, working-class families often tend to lose contact in the transition to high school. Often this is about the point where parents' ability to help with homework ends. Almost always it means a shift from a small institution, the neighbourhood primary school, to a much larger one further away, with a staff of subject specialists and a different way of organizing teaching. We came across a good many parents who had been active in supporting their primary school, but whose involvement fell away almost to nothing after the shift. To the high school staff, the parents therefore appeared to lack interest in their kids' education – one of the commonest complaints we heard in these schools.

Behind the flux of daily transactions, then, we can see more enduring relations that are realized through them. One is a division of labour between parents in childrearing, in which women are defined as having primary responsibility for child care, which carries over to their relation to the other major childrearing institution, the school. Both the organization of families (for example, where husband has a job and wife doesn't) and the practices of schools (for example, setting up 'Mothers' Clubs') sustain this sexual division of labour. It naturally becomes important to the kids, most of whom, boys and girls alike, see their mothers as the parent to take school troubles to in the first instance. On their side, married women usually see it as important to be home when the kids get back from school and this affects the kinds of jobs they look for.

There is also a class pattern of involvement and exclusion. Working-class parents who drop out of involvement with their kids' schooling after the transition to high school have rarely lost interest; it is simply that the school is organized in a way that makes that interest difficult to put into practice. As the research went on, we became very familiar with stories told us by parents of the ways they had been frozen out: promises of action not followed up, phone calls not returned, principals retreating behind bureaucratic rules, insinuations of ignorance and uncouthness, and so on. It is hard to miss the parallel with the experience of their own schooling. There were also many stories of helpful teachers and responsive principals, but it is abundantly clear that working-class families face large difficulties in building a relationship with the high school.

Not that processes of exclusion are unknown in the Independent schools. Indeed quite a complex and subtle dialogue can go on between the school and families of different backgrounds. The relationship between St Margaret's College and the Paton family – mother an Old Girl, father a high-ranking professional, both university-trained and Presbyterians – is noticeably closer and more involving than the relationship between St Margaret's and the Carpenters, who are equally rich but whose money comes from business, who went to state schools and have no university training, and who are members of an unfashionable Baptist church. Nevertheless it is broadly true that the Independent schools are much more open to parents' approaches and that the parents here find it easier to include the kids' schooling as an integral part of the families' collective practices.

How families and schools think about each other

The pleasures of mutual ignorance

Except for those few cases where they are really activists in the life of the school – office-holders in the P&C, for instance – parents have rather limited chances to learn about what goes on inside classrooms, staffrooms, or playgrounds. Their kids may tell them a lot or a little. If a lot, it is of course filtered by what the kids think is fit for their parents' ears. If a little, most parents have only infrequent contacts with teachers, casual discussion with other parents or kids in the neighbourhood, stories told by siblings, and school reports, to fill out the picture.

The schools we studied had an institution designed to overcome this problem, the parent–teacher night, where all the teachers taking a given grade stay back one evening to talk to the parents. In some places this means parents actually queuing up in front of teachers sitting behind tables for a few minutes' quick consultation, while the teacher flips through her book of marks and the rest of the queue breathes down their necks. Opinion is almost universal, on both sides, that this exercise is of little use as an exchange of information. To the parents, the time is far too short; to the teachers, the parents they really want to see are the ones who never come. Yet there is a steady roll-up. Mrs McArthur suggests the main reason:

> It wouldn't matter if you sat there and talked about flying saucers. It's of no consequence to the children what you talk about, but it seems to give them confidence . . . Each time I come home, I get the quiz: 'What did the teacher say?' 'What did this one say?' Well you can't tell the children what the teacher said, but it's of no importance . . . you can see an improvement in their work and in their attitude. Particularly if you hit a teacher you can communicate well with. Some teachers couldn't be bothered.

It's a way for parents to show they care; and that really is crucial in everybody's thinking about schools.

Teachers have even less chance to learn about homes than parents do about classrooms. Apart from very thin indications that might be got from parent–teacher nights, or school record cards (for example, parents' occupations, usually out of date), or staffroom conversation, the only way an ordinary teacher has of learning is if the pupil talks about her family in class or in a private consultation. Most kids don't do that – especially working-class kids who are very wary of saying anything that might make them vulnerable. There are a few teachers who make it their business to find these things out, and put a lot of energy into it. But most secondary teachers effectively know nothing about their pupils' families.

Most people in the education business, including most of the teachers and parents we talked to, would regard this state of mutual ignorance as a bad thing. There are, however, some good reasons for it. School and home do exchange enough information for routine purposes – bearing in mind that secondary schooling is a strongly institutionalized activity, and so are many aspects of parenting. Through report cards, marks on exercises, and so on, the school provides the family with enough information to explain its placement and treatment of the child. Through attendance notes, phone calls and so on, parents provide the school with information about medical events, housing crises, or other things that might disrupt attendance.

To go beyond this level would require expending energy beyond what is normally necessary. And there are some more definite reasons why it isn't usually expended. Working-class parents normally aren't very familiar with the way the high school works, and aren't very confident about approaching it or laying demands on it. Nor does the school as an institution do much to overcome their reservations.

The parents at Independent schools normally know more about what goes on inside them than the parents at working-class comprehensives. Even here, however, there are reasons for a degree of mutual ignorance. There are things such families do not care to have known, notably about their financial affairs. While things are going swimmingly on the academic front, as they usually do in these schools, there is no particular reason for the teachers to wonder about the kids' 'backgrounds'. The very success of the teaching encourages parents to think of teachers as professional experts who can be left on their own to perform their craft. As Mrs Andrews put it:

> You don't go to the doctor unless you've got a problem; why go to the teacher unless you've got one?

On the teacher's side, in the working-class comprehensives things are a little more complex; for here academic work normally isn't going swimmingly, and 'home background' is almost universally thought to be a reason why. It would seem that teachers have a strong reason to find out a lot about the families of the kids they work with. But this would be to reckon without the actual conditions of their work. High schools mix pupils and teachers in proportions of about 13 to 1, which seems almost intimate until one thinks about the way the teachers' work is organized. Between 100 and 150 heads go past in an ordinary working day, and the teacher confronts each new batch alone. Faced with a procession of classes and the turbulence that is normal in these schools, the teacher's first, and continuing, problem is survival as a teacher. Len Johnson, one of the staff at Greenway High, describes a common solution:

> The teacher considers that his job is done in the classroom, and then they nick off home. And you really can't blame them . . . You know, that's what it boils down to. Practicality is the whole thing. And there's a lot of people who've been around long enough to know that you don't take on more than you ought to.

It would indeed be crazy, as things are now, for most high school teachers to try to get close to the family circumstances of even half the kids they deal with. It would be physically and emotionally overwhelming, and would disrupt many of their own survival strategies. To make it possible would require major changes of the circumstances in which the job is done.

Views across the school fence

The fact that parents and teachers normally don't know very much about each other is, of course, no bar to their having strong opinions.

The working-class parents' opinions of teachers are, on the whole, not very flattering. Rarely hostile across the board, they are often sharply critical of particular teachers, and see the teaching force as a pretty thorough mixture of good and bad eggs. Mr Grey's comments, if a little acidly expressed, are absolutely typical as to content:

> The two headmasters I speak of have always said it's the kids. It's never the teachers. Well I'm afraid to say it's only this year that I had the same problem, I've had it for a couple of years, with the younger son. And the headmaster still won't own up. Because the young bloke's picked up something fantastic this year; and it was his previous teacher that was the trouble with Mark as well. It was the teacher he had, that wasn't interested. Was only interested in one thing: money. I just had the same trouble with George: the teacher just never liked George for a start. He had

> it in for George, and that was it. The headmaster, definitely no. He swore black and blue in front of me, and he run this teacher down, in front of me. When I walked out of there, he run down my son, and backed the teacher up . . . As far as I'm concerned, he's no good . . . He's got a teacher that's interested in him this year. Not only is he interested, but he's also a teacher to lift a kid. The one I'm talking about was a young teacher, just come out of – what do you call it? – Advanced Education, he's just taken it on. As far as he's concerned, he's God, and that's it.

Mr Grey, be it noted, praises the teacher who *is* interested in his son and able to 'lift' him. Elsewhere in the interview he praises principals and teachers who will 'go out of their way' for a kid. Mr Poulos, whose son is doing much worse at school than Mark Grey, describes such a teacher in more detail:

> Bill has been going to this school now since he was 13. And I've had one interview with his schoolteacher. And I'd say he's one of the most dedicated . . . He's the one schoolteacher who has bothered to call me in to discuss with him the problems of Bill: what he's got, what he hasn't got, why he's so far behind. And I explained to him why. Actually Bill was 12 months behind the other kids, and he's caught up now . . . Even now Mr Riley is the only teacher who will stay back with students, I've never seen anything like it. To stay back with two or three students and try to help them on their weak subject . . .
>
> *And did that help Bill?*
>
> It helped him a hell of a lot. He's caught up. I was real pleased with that teacher. But, any other teachers in the school, I don't think they could give a hoot. They just put their lessons forward; and if the kids listen, they listen; and if they don't, well, bad luck Charlie, you missed out, and it won't be repeated again.

That's not a fair summary of the attitudes of the teaching force at Rockwell High, but it is obvious how typical survival strategies on the part of teachers could produce that impression on a critical parent. In some cases it comes, literally, closer to home. Mr and Mrs Roberts call a particular kind of teacher 'screamers' because they can hear them screaming at their classes in the school just across the road.

On their side, teachers make quite similar distinctions about homes. They usually see 'good' homes as ones where the parents are interested in the kids, and keep them clean and well-dressed; 'bad' homes as ones where the kids are left to their own devices while mothers have jobs or both parents go boozing at the club, homes which don't support the school's authority and generally are slack and disreputable. The "bad' home is much the clearer image. Some teachers see the whole neighbourhood in which they are working in these terms, as a cultural desert populated by beer-swilling Dads and mindless Mums. Others don't have such negative overall views, but reach for this category to explain the indiscipline, poor academic performance, or sloppiness of particular kids:

> Well, he's untidy, slightly untidy, unkempt hair, not brushed every day, shirt hangs out sometimes. His teeth, I don't know whether it's a fair indicator, but his teeth don't look well looked after, and perhaps at home it's not something that's pursued, or money spent on them to get them fixed. So I think he probably comes from a poor background, his parents haven't spent much time with him, just haven't encouraged him in areas that we would encourage children. (Leo Wilson, Greenway High)

Given their lack of concrete knowledge about the homes, it seems likely that these views are in large measure a response to the problems of school life. In short, they are imaginary, but they have a point – which is, again, survival as a teacher: keeping discipline, and getting the kids to learn. Teachers collectively construct images of families that would either help or hinder these tasks, and load them up with quite a lot of responsibility for what happens in the school. On the parents' side, the images of good and bad teachers are also partly imaginary – as is clear from the absolute contradictions that often occurred in different parents' descriptions of the same teacher. Normally their judgements were based on tiny samples of the teacher's behaviour, sometimes just one incident. We suspect they often have more to do with the way the parents are trying to make sense of schooling generally than with the work of the particular teacher.

It is striking, in fact, how rarely working-class parents think of teachers *as workers* – that is, think of what they are doing in terms of the whole pattern of their job and its strains and opportunities, the character of their workplace, its authority relations, and the teachers' economic and industrial problems. In some ways parents seem to perceive teaching more on the model of being a parent than on being a worker. Hence the indignation that can arise when teachers go by the regulations, and don't seem to care about their particular child.

Ruling-class parents do tend to see teachers as workers – from the perspective of employers, which of course many of them are. They don't hire the teachers personally, but they can, if sufficiently dissatisfied with their performance, sometimes cause them to be fired. Their picture of teachers, then, is much more that of technical specialists who are evaluated according to the results they produce in their area of expertise. They usually have a favourable opinion of their abilities, on the assumption that if they aren't good, they won't last. Parents at Independent schools generally think their teaching force is superior to that of the state schools; this is often a reason they give for choosing a private school.

The respective images of parents and teachers are much less strongly drawn at the Independent schools than at the state schools. The two do see more of each other, and so individual characteristics stand out more than group images. No parent at Greenway High could do what quite a number of Independent-school parents did in our interviews – run through the full list of their child's teachers and comment on the strengths and weaknesses of each one. Their interactions, though sometimes abrasive, usually have more of the flavour of consultations between fellow-professionals than negotiations between sharply distinct groups.

Models of education

Even in the most harmonious school, neither parents nor teachers are agreed on educational philosophies. The kids' schooling goes on in the context of an unresolved debate about its purposes and methods; and it is important to see the relationships between home and school in this larger context.

Eighty years into 'the century of the child', none of the working-class parents we interviewed held recognizably child-centred views of education. Most of them clearly supported firm discipline, teacher-centred pedagogy, and job-oriented curricula.

Why is this? One reason is their lack of sources of information about anything else. They never see books about education. Accounts of schooling in the mass media (for instance, commercial TV and mass-circulation papers) rarely get beyond drugs, sex, and the general awfulness of modern youth. The mass organizations of the working class, the unions and the Labor Party, rarely give a clear lead about it. (It has been NSW Labor Party policy for years to abolish selective schools, a minor but obvious reform; the Labor Premier has promised not to do it.) The parents' own experience of schooling was, for the most part, authoritarian and teacher-centred, if not particularly vocational.

Yet that schooling, as we have seen, failed them. Why aren't they looking for alternatives? By and large they are – but alternatives as *they* see them, not as academics (or even teachers) do. Education is still defined as the transmission of an accepted body of knowledge, in every context they know about. The parent who is bitterly regretful in retrospect about having dropped out of school at 13 is still very likely to blame him or herself, not the school as an institution. 'The alternative', then, is not something different in quality but more of the same – maybe four or five years more – to supply the knowledge that the last generation missed out on. Thus, in a good many families, a strong push from the parents for the kids to stay on regardless of the trouble they run into.

There is another important reason. Education is also 'socialization', in the old, full sense of making the asocial infant a fully social being. This means, among other things, learning to do what you're told, hold yourself in check, accept the necessity to do things you don't want to do. It also means respecting legitimate authority, deferring to those who are older and wiser than you are, keeping in your proper place. All this was well learnt, often at the end of a cane, by the older generation from their elders. It was, in many respects, a survival skill; and it has been particularly important to those of our families who had a long, hard haul to establish themselves in modest comfort and security. They have a name for this kind of learning: 'discipline'.

The 'breakdown of discipline' is not a media invention. It is real, and it is experienced by many of these families as their children move through adolescence. Connected with changes in youth employment and with the growth of 'youth culture', it is also connected with changes in the schools. For progressive educational reforms have had an impact there: the kids are freer, the schools livelier, less orderly and more creative, than they ever were in the past. Many parents approve of this, as meaning more pleasant and humane learning environments than they had. Many also see it (and sometimes these views overlap) as a collapse of discipline. They see kids answering back to teachers, classes in uproar, apparently unplanned curricula, no measurable learning; and they are worried. Some see it reacting back on the family and creating discipline problems there. If this is what new ideas in education mean, they could do with less of them.

So there is a constituency here for the 'New Right' in education, and the demand for more traditional pedagogy is one reason for the shift to private schools – in working-class areas, mainly Catholic schools – in recent statistics. (There are other reasons, such as federal government funding policies.) Yet there are serious obstacles in the path of conservatism. The 'back to basics' movement can't deliver jobs, which are in shorter supply than basic skills – and youth unemployment is the background to a lot of what is going on in high schools now. A shift to heavier-handed discipline is a recipe for more conflict, not stabler authority, in the schools.

On the other hand it is difficult to see a constituency for progressive reforms, at least in the form that educational progressivism has taken in the past. By and large it has done little for working-class parents. Wanting the best for their kids, and supporting the expansion of schooling, they accepted reforms like new primary curricula (the 'new maths'), and comprehensive secondary school organization, largely because the professionals said they were best. The increased turbulence in the schools has increasingly called that expertise into question. There remains a good deal of conditional respect for teacher's knowledge, and a fund of goodwill towards schools in general; but we think educators will only be able to draw on that fund by constructing a new kind of relationship with the parents.

The debate about philosophies in and around Independent schools has had a rather different cast. Here the issues revolve around methods of modernization. Some of these schools have long kept a very traditional pedagogy; and this is subject to criticism from two directions – on grounds of liberalism, and on grounds of efficiency. Because principals in these schools have greater personal authority, and because they can mostly take for granted things for which working-class schools must struggle, (notably the pupils' attachment to academic learning), there is considerably more room for manoeuvre. The variety of educational theory and teaching practice is probably greater among Independent schools than in the very much larger state system.

The defining fact about private schools is that parents who don't like what a principal is doing can walk away from that school and pick another. So the debate about models of education in this context turns into the working of an educational market, in which there is a complex interaction of consumer preferences with marketers' strategies.

At a very general level, a distinction can be drawn between valuing education for what it does *to* you and for what it does *for* you. The latter is the instrumental approach, and in a good deal of the literature is supposed to characterize working-class families' approaches to education. It is true that schooling is instrumentally important to them – as a means of avoiding downward mobility especially – though it is hard to see this is any more marked than the instrumentalism of ruling-class families who use schooling to place children in the right jobs and the right social circles.

What seems to us to be missing from most accounts of the matter is the widespread, non-instrumental, respect for education that is also present among working-class families. The teachers who see working-class suburbs as cultural deserts are entirely wrong in this sense. It is difficult for a regard for learning and knowledge to flower there, given the character of the mass media and the fact that adult education reaches less than one adult in twenty in the population as a whole. But there is a vital possibility and resource nevertheless.

Where do families come from?

The main conclusion of modern research on the family has been that families are not the closed, self-contained units, the 'haven in a heartless world', they are often supposed to be. On the contrary, they are shaped in quite fundamental ways by larger social structures, and some of these ways are highly relevant to education.

Anyone wanting to understand the social context of schooling must try to understand how the students' families come to be the way they are. In this section we will explore three aspects of social structure that clearly have important effects: the organization of work, the organization of cities, and relations between the sexes.

The organization of work

Our sample from Independent schools was evenly divided between families where the father was a manager and those where he was a professional. The kind of work, and the social relationships in which it is done, differ in the two cases.

Consider Mr Walker, the youthful general manager of a company in an expanding high-technology industry, and a high-flyer by anyone's standards. He thinks his son Ian is 'too conservative', and by that he doesn't mean right-wing so much as conformist, inclined to wait at a door until other people have gone through it. In Mr Walker's world, that is a good way to get trampled:

> The world's not going to stand still for traditional ways any more, not in my business anyway. We don't sell any product we sold five years ago, they're all gone. In five years' time we won't sell any product we sell today . . . They're going to be lighter, or faster, or quicker, or cheaper or something. And our people can't think the same way, they can't be doing what they did five years ago.

Certainly Mr Walker is not going to get left behind in the rush. He works like a demon – probably puts in a 90-hour week – and makes sure his second-echelon managers also work their guts out. If they don't shape up, he fires them.

As the executive head of the firm, he rarely deals directly with the workers who actually make his products. The people he has most contact with are those who themselves 'head up' a group – personnel manager, finance manager, product managers, and so on. His very diverse workload still embraces industrial relations – keeping *au fait* with the state of the labour market and the attitudes of workers, reorganizing salaries and bonus schemes to maximize the sales staff's performance, negotiating with unions and devising ways of keeping them out of his industry – as well as a host of other problems such as planning, training staff, dealing with other companies, and keeping up with new technology. He has to be, and is, energetic, ruthless, profit-conscious, and extremely well-informed.

A work situation like that plainly has important consequences for the family. First, it means wealth – big salaries, fringe benefits, and a chance to share in profits through bonuses and share options. That enables the family to live in an affluent suburb and buy a private school education. Second, it means a massive absorption of the husband in his work. Not all managers are as fanatical about work as Mr Walker, but it isn't uncommon. In the life cycle of a successful business family, the middle childhood and adolescence of the kids is likely to coincide with a key phase in the father's career, when he is taking off for the top levels and the demands are particularly strong. This forces a sharp division of labour between the husband and the wife, who in all the business families we met was wholly responsible for running the house (sometimes hiring a cleaning woman to help), had much closer contact with the children, and was responsible for monitoring events at school. Father was usually called in only when there was a big decision to be made or big trouble had arisen.

What is not so easy to understand is the very marked gap between the working lives of men like Mr Walker and the kind of education they buy for their children. The conditions he describes – the constant turnover of products, the pressure for change, the urgency of keeping ahead – are, more or less, the general conditions of existence in capitalist industry when there is any significant competition. And it is a long way indeed from the Queen-and-Country conservatism of schools in which the 'A' form still does Latin, where the Cadet Corps or Divine Service are *de rigueur*, where boys and girls are taught proper pronunciation and Christian responsibility, while their fathers are busy axing sales managers who don't reach their growth targets. The tension here may be one reason why progressive educational ideas can sometimes get a grip in this intensely conservative milieu, as a way of modernizing its schools.

This gap is very much less for families where the fathers are professionals: barrister, surgeon, physician, dentist and professor are among those in our sample. Here the job itself is organized around a body of knowledge, and entry to it is via higher education; it is more closely integrated with schooling from the start. The business of controlling other people that looms so large in managers' working lives is here reduced to small dimensions. Where Mr Walker has a couple of thousand subordinates, a barrister who is a father at the same school, and who in point of wealth and influence would certainly be his equal, employs exactly half a typist.

Professional practice also means greater control over working hours, so there is more scope for a different division of labour in the household. Fathers may become more involved with their kids' schooling and in family life. But the contrast should not be overdrawn. The work demands of setting up a practice can also be heavy (for example honorary work by doctors in hospitals). When professional men are drawn into the organizational side of ruling-class life, holding office in professional associations, being active in Rotary or the Liberal Party, becoming hospital administrators, joining the boards of companies, or taking on a string of consultancies, their schedules too can begin to look like Mr Walker's.

Working-class families are working-class mainly because they stand on the other side of the great divide in class structure, the labour market. Others hire; they are hired. The importance of dependence on a wage can hardly be over-estimated. It immediately bars these families from the suburbs and schools of the rich, for they have no way of accumulating wealth; at best, and after a good many years, they may own the house they live in. In good times, wage-earning families may do nicely, brick will replace fibro and motor-boats and caravans will appear in backyards. They still have no way of foreseeing or preventing a recession that leads to retrenchment, an industrial accident that puts the breadwinner out of commission, a change in technology that obliterates jobs and skills. We have seen the effects of all these events in our interviews.

One wage, especially if it is a labourer's or factory worker's wage, is often not enough. For a family with children to bring up, it is likely to mean marginal poverty. So most of the working-class mothers we interviewed have jobs; indeed some are the main earners for the household. There is nothing new about working-class women having jobs. What is new is large numbers of them having jobs while they also have children at school. They are conscious of this being different from what their mothers did, and some worry a good deal about its possible bad effects on the children, especially when they had to work, for instance to buy a block to build a house on, when the kids were still young.

Nevertheless, having their own source of income has generally strengthened their position within the family. Some working-class families, like the business families, are organized around the father (though not around the father's *career*, since careers hardly exist in their jobs). But a good many are not: they are organized around the wife, or as an alliance of equals. Some have ceased to function much as a unit, and people have withdrawn into separate spheres, staying together mainly for two reasons – to complete the children's education, and because suburbs like Rockwell and Greenway have only one kind of house, the family bungalow, and no couple there can afford to buy or rent two of them.

The workplaces where the working-class parents in our sample earn their keep are very diverse: a boatyard, a railway repair shop, a hospital, a heating plant, a local doctor's surgery (as a cleaner), a local school (as a teacher's aide), new building sites (as a tiler), the windows of city office blocks (as a cleaner), and a considerable number of factories. Most of the jobs are not very skilled, or involve skills that have been learned on the job; one of the greatest assets for workers in the labour market is versatility. Even those men who have a trade ticket have often found themselves doing a quite different job – a butcher who wound up as a window-dresser, a railwayman who found himself in a laundry. Others have started with one trade skill and have diversified by building on it – such as Mr McDonough, an immigrant toolmaker who had gone for a year to Germany to extend his skills on the most modern equipment.

The pride that tradespeople take in their skills, and that less qualified workers also take in being on top of a job they have taught themselves, and that all take in their versatility, creates a basis for a view of knowledge that in some respects competes with the school's. In discussions of work and schooling, the importance of learnt-on-the-job, practical knowledge was often stressed as what was *really* useful. Being 'good with the hands' could be valued as much as being 'good with the head'. It would be going too far to suggest this amounts to a distinct ideology of education; but it is at least a different way of looking at knowledge, firmly rooted in their work experience.

However, workplaces aren't just places where a job of work is done. They are also places where there is authority and control. We saw the top end of this with Mr Walker; at the lower levels are foremen and leading hands. A good many of the working-class fathers in our study, and some of the mothers, have held such positions – or knocked them back.

In the structure of control in the workplace, the foreman is, classically, the meat in the sandwich: exposed to pressure from workers and management, transmitting pressure both ways, able to satisfy neither. Some of our parents who had done it found the demands for higher production and lower costs, and the resentment of their workmates, extremely stressful. Others, who had refused promotion, did so because they knew it would drive a wedge between them and their friends. In thinking about authority structures in working-class schools, it is worth remembering that a lot of the kids are aware of tensions about authority in their parents' working lives. And some of them get a pretty clear message that to climb a hierarchy means to break ties and betray loyalties.

In the absence of an aggressive labour movement, the alternative to climbing the hierarchy at work is to accept subordination. Some people can wriggle sideways, as Mr Arlott has done by becoming a subcontractor in a service industry:

> The subcontract's better, 'cause when you subcontract, you've got no starting time, no finishing time. If you want to sit down for a smoke – or for twenty minutes there's nobody telling you to get up and go back to work.

But that's a very private solution, and in current economic circumstances many people (including his wife) are glad to get any kind of job. Mrs Arlott was sacked a year ago by the American-owned company where she was a machine operator. She has only just found a new job – as a packer, on lower pay, with the same firm. On our screening questionnaire she ticked the answer that said she thought her present job was a good one. Why?

> It's a job.

And that message, too, feeds into the kids' schooling.

The organization of cities

We talked with all the parents in their homes, and perhaps nothing in the study was so immediately striking as the differences between them. Almost all of our working-class families lived in two- or three-bedroom bungalows on quarter-acre suburban blocks. Some houses had worn lino on the floors, sparse and threadbare furnishing, peeling paintwork. Others were modestly affluent, with shag-pile carpets, a bar or a TV den with a wall unit. But all were small and basic by comparison with the homes of our ruling-class parents. Here homes ranged from the discreetly comfortable in the more expensive suburbs, to sumptuous establishments in the foothills, on the harbour, or by the ocean.

The spatial arrangement of the city is itself an important form of social organization. How people organize their domestic life and their leisure partly depends on where they live. And where they live, in turn, depends both on the resources they personally command, and the way the city has been constructed so as to produce class separation.

Some of the working-class families in our study told us how they came to their present suburb:

> We were offered this house and it was the final offer.
> Rockwell: where's Rockwell? No-one's ever heard of it! Back of beyond.
> You are on a Housing Authority list. When Rockwell was offered it sounded like an improvement. But the reality was unbelievable – like the last frontier or the end of the earth.

The second comment expresses the dilemma of people who held to the Australian dream of owning your own home. It was an improvement on landlords; but the reality on offer has often meant severe sacrifices, both economic and social. Isolation and lack of services in new suburbs have particularly affected the women and children. Mrs Grey looks back:

> When we first came here it was terrible. We've been here 12½ years. It was nothing – absolutely nothing. We'd been living with Mum, we had Mark – he was two when we moved here. You get taken out of a house full of people, and you just get stuck here, with nothing: no 'phone, no transport, nothing. And your husband goes off all day and you're just left. It's terrible. Troubles – anyone hurt themselves, you had to sort of ask the milkman and baker, 'would you go for help?' It was shocking.

As this suggests, the arrangement of space organizes gender as well as class. 'Your husband goes off all day and you're just left.' The suburban home is built for a couple and two or three children. It involves the daily separation, not only of generations, but also of men and women, and the women feel it most.

Most of our working-class families lived in suburbs built since the war, and a good many were among the pioneers: as a boy Mr Roberts went rabbit-trapping in the paddocks that are now Rockwell. For many families, these new suburbs represented a real improvement over decaying industrial suburbs in the inner city, and their opinions of their environment are warmer than the ones we have just quoted. But one feature was common – the choices were, and are, painfully limited. Why do they stay here?

It's the only place we can afford.

There were other costs. When the Greys first moved to Rockwell, Mr Grey left home at 5.30 each morning to travel, by bus and train, to work. Mrs Siemens currently spends four hours a day travelling to and from her job in a factory. There is enormous pressure, therefore, to go into debt to buy cars, and two-job families really need to be two-car families. The way the post-war suburbs were built made it almost impossible to live a normal life without cars. At the same time, the fact that people had cars made if possible for developers and governments to build suburbs virtually without facilities or the setting for a communal life. For any kind of social life outside the home and garden – to go to clubs, swimming pools, films, or discos – you have to drive out of Rockwell and Greenway.

The energy and creativity with which working-class families have tackled such bleak conditions is one of the most consistent and notable facts to come out of this study. A good example is provided by the Joneses and their loving construction of their own house, garden, and rockery. They are not in the least exceptional. We are thinking of gardens which were wonders of plumbing, stonework and horticultural science; of backyard workshops which turn out motor boats, go-karts and even racing cars; of a family who built their own theaterette, complete with electrically-operated curtain, theatre organ, dimming lights, and seats salvaged from an old cinema; of a failed attempt to set up a small farm, and successful construction of a family holiday house (ironically called 'the shack' after ten years' steady work on it).

Nor is this effort confined to the adults and their concerns. Bill Poulos likes surfing but he lives nearly 40 miles from the beach. So he has organized a weekend roster with his mates, to wake each other at 4 a.m., walk several miles to the station, catch the fast 'milk train' to the city, change to a bus, and at last put their boards in the surf. These are just a few of the countless ways in which working people have faced the constraints of their situations and conjured up resources to make a cultural world.

Yet it is dangerous to romanticize these responses; we must recognize the real deprivation on which they are based, and the fact that the situation also leads, at the same time, to abrasive neighbourhood relationships, hostility, and even violence. Mrs Grey, again, puts it very clearly:

> It's – I find it's not the area, it's the people. What happened, when we all came here, we were all very lonely, I think, and we all got very involved with each other. Too involved. A lot of children's fights, and parents then got fighting. We all had problems. Today, there's still problems with children. If you correct a child for doing something, you get a mouthful of lip, four-letter words etc. etc. You know damn well it's no use going to the parent, 'cause the parent wouldn't believe you anyway. So you sort of think, 'Well, what's the use of correcting the child. Let him wreck the place!' We've had a lot of trouble with vandals, children and kids, and we had break-and-entries. And we had a steel bar thrown through this window the night of the elections – glass right through here, it came with such force it's a wonder it didn't go through the wall. Could've killed someone sitting on the lounge. It's unbelievable. And this is not the first time. We've had eggs thrown, plants ripped out, money taken. We had a cocky in a cage taken.

Some other mothers sharpen the point. They think it is dangerous to go out on their own streets at night because of the local toughs, have been hassled themselves, and won't let their kids – especially their daughters – go out alone after dark.

That isn't a problem where Valerie Grainger, a pupil at St Helen's College, lives. However, she has others. 'I'd rather live at Vaucluse or Hunter's Hill', she lamented, 'because more people live there'. At least she knows the social facts of life. In Sydney the wealthy and the powerful outlay the lifetime earnings of two or three of our working-class families to cluster around the glittering harbour and on the green ridges along the North Shore Line. In Adelaide prosperity has taken up the Hills slopes, and fills pockets around the parklands and along the shore.

The relationship between ruling-class families and the city isn't just a matter of where they cluster, it is also a matter of their ability to *choose* where to go. Unlike the couples who land in Rockwell or Greenway because that literally is all they can afford, these families can take into account proximity to work; kin, friends and leisure interests; trees and gardens; quiet, pollution-free surroundings; and the choice of schools available for their children. The balance between these considerations may change from time to time. The Balfours, to take just one example, had moved three times in the past five years – from a large suburban home near Mr Balfour's professional practice, to a very large establishment (with sauna and tiled pool) in Sydney's eastern suburbs, to a smaller but exquisite apartment overlooking the harbour. Whatever the current preference, the Balfours (and families like them) plainly have a very different relationship to the city from the Joneses, the Pouloses, and the Greys.

When cities segregate people in their 'private' lives, they also segregate their schooling. While the comprehensive school was proposed as a means of social integration through common schooling, it ran up against the fact of cities segregated on class lines through the operation of the private housing market. Almost all state schools have a 'catchment' drawn from a relatively narrow band of the social spectrum; and this has ensured a large degree of class segregation in schooling, even before we take account of the Independent schools.

When the Siemens or the Greys moved to Rockwell, they moved into an Education Department zone and were automatically assigned to a particular school. What is a zone to the Department is an educational life sentence to a working-class child. That school is immovable, intractable, and unavoidable. On their side, teachers routinely talk of 'good' and 'bad' areas in which to teach. Each morning around eight, they set out in thousands in their cars for the working-class suburbs where they and the students work, and then recede like the tide around four.

The Independent schools tend to be concentrated in the more

affluent suburbs, though because a good many of them go back 50 or a 100 years their location may reflect earlier social maps of the city. (Some are embarrassingly located on what is now prime commercial land, or in decayed districts.) But access to them isn't constrained by anything like the zones of the state system. A good number of the Independent school students we interviewed travel five miles or more to school. Again we see the much greater degree of control ruling-class families have over the organization of their lives. Families like the Graingers and the Walkers can move house, if they wish, to give access to the schools – state or private – of their choice. And from any given suburb, they can decide which of a range of private schools they will employ.

Urban space, then, both reflects the degrees of power that different families have, and determines what the families can be and do. It is not often discussed in this light, but is plainly a very important element in the way families are shaped and connected with larger social structures. The same is true of the schools.

Relations between the sexes

At a number of points already we have seen the importance of relations between the sexes: the division of labour in child care, the pattern of employment, the organization of households, the reform of school organization. These points are related, and it will be useful to make them a bit more systematic. Accordingly, we will speak of them as aspects of a system of social relations structured by gender – for short, 'gender relations'.

Three points about this are vital. First, this is a *system*. It is not a question of one gender pattern in a school, and another in a family, and another in a workplace, all independent of each other. They are related: they mesh with each other to make an overall pattern, one of the most general and powerful structures in our society.

Secondly, the 'system' is one of male power and female subordination. The dimensions of this are as varied as gender relations themselves: male control of governments and companies, the traditional pattern of marriage, the double standard in sexual morality, discrimination in employment, the way media present women as sex objects and men as the people who matter. It is important to recognize that this persists as an overall pattern despite being reversed in particular instances. There are families in our sample, as we have mentioned, where a working mother is the main economic provider and makes the main decisions; yet girls in these households still generally learn the conventional definitions of femininity and boys are likely to learn that they really ought to rule the roost. Nevertheless in such households a tension between local reality and the larger structure is set up, which may be a force for change.

For the structure can change; that is the third point. These relationships are social, not biologically-given. What is socially constructed is subject to historical change. And it does change. Many conventional modern notions – such as the idea that men are breadwinners and women housewives, that motherhood is a vocation for women, that children are a distinct kind of people in need of special protection, and that the family is a realm of privacy shut off from the public world – are actually quite recent, products of the last three centuries or so of western history.

We are living in a period when these patterns are changing, faster perhaps than ever before. The arrival of reliable contraception, the emergence of the new feminism, and the changing pattern of women's employment, are perhaps the most obvious but far from the only signs. This is registered inside many of the families in this study – changing notions about the rights of marriage partners, about the future employment of girls, and so on.

This change is extremely uneven. There are households (though few in this study) where feminism is more-or-less common sense, and where attempts are being made to share power and redivide labour. There are others (a good many in this study) where conventional definitions of contented motherhood and fathers' right to rule are unchallenged, and where feminism is regarded as a kind of temporary insanity. We did some interviews in households where the position of men and women actually has changed but their ideas about what is proper haven't; and in households which are split, for instance with husbands trying to reclaim an authority their wives or daughters will not concede. In others, perhaps the majority, a vague acceptance that women's place in the world is changing went along with practices that mainly reinforced the status quo.

In thinking about gender relations, then, we must be alert to tensions and contradictions within them as clues to what is presently changing or is likely to. We must also be alert to the ways they interact with other patterns of social relations – most notably class.

This interaction, we are convinced, is extremely important in understanding schooling and will be of continuing concern.

For instance, the puzzle raised earlier about the apparent contradiction between business work lives and the content of elite schooling is partly to be answered this way. What is needed for success in Mr Walker's world of high-powered business competition is a particular kind of *masculinity*: motivated to compete, strong in the sense of one's own abilities, able to dominate others and to face down opponents in situations of conflict. The school Mr Walker's son goes to is very effectively organized to produce that kind of character structure, even though it doesn't teach the specific techniques of modern business.

At the start of this section we suggested that families are not closed universes but places where larger structures meet and interact; and we hope to have shown at least some of the ways this is so. We do not mean to suggest that families are simply the pawns of outside forces any more than schools are. In both cases, class and gender relations create dilemmas (some insoluble), provide resources (or deny them), and suggest solutions (some of which don't work), to which the family or school must respond in its collective practice. Conversely, the practice we encounter in discussions with family members must be seen as their creative response to situations that larger forces have presented them with. 'Practice' means an active response. And 'collective' is significant too. A family may not be a sealed unit; but it is usually a closely-knit group which has an intense inner life and a reasonably stable organization. Let us now turn to the impact of this inner life on the children's upbringing and schooling.

How families produce people

In our society, the close kin in the immediate household are central in that still rather astonishing process by which, in only 20 years, innocent infants are transformed into estate agents, football fanatics, Liberal voters, and the unemployed. We do not pretend to offer a theory of the whole process, but our evidence does suggest some points about the ways social structures impinge on the formation of the person.

One of the main organizing principles of the 'nuclear family' is, quite simply, age. Its social relations constitute each member as either adult or child. In recent history this neat little structure has been complicated by the emergence of a third category, 'adolescent', and this is a fruitful source of trouble. For the state of being an adolescent (or a 'teenager') is a constantly dissolving one.

Consider, for instance, Ellen Oldcastle, a 14-year-old at Rockwell High, the middle child of immigrant parents who are comfortable in the neighbourhood though a bit socially isolated. She gets on badly with her father whom she regards as an old-fashioned stick-in-the-mud, while he thinks she is cheeky and ignorant; but gets along better with her mother, a rather quiet person who has given up her job to be home for the kids. They don't allow Ellen to go out unchaperoned. However, a year ago they gave her permission to bring boyfriends home, thinking this might encourage her to mix a bit more widely.

She surprised them by finding one and sticking with him. She now sees Roy, who is an apprentice still living with his parents and a couple of years older than her, several times a week. Mr and Mrs Oldcastle think he is 'a good little worker', can't fault the family, and can't take their permission back. It's all very awkward – she's a bit young for this. Mrs Oldcastle wishes to control Ellen's sexuality and is plainly uneasy that the 'dating' rules she has laid down aren't enough. Ellen stokes the fires by publicly declaring that she doesn't believe in marriage – 'just a piece of paper' – and that people should be able just to live together if they love each other; though she keeps to the letter of her parents' laws. Her parents tend to blame Roy for putting these ideas in her head; to Ellen herself, she has changed simply because she has grown older.

This classic teenager/parent contretemps – which has developed without the intervention of a peer group or 'youth culture' – very clearly illustrates the importance, and the ambiguity, of age relationships as a social force. Ellen is not claiming the right to be a *teenager* but the right to be, in some respects, *adult*; and she neatly, almost wittily, seizes upon the opportunity her parents have given her to press this point. They, for their part, are insisting that she is still a *child*; though also, by the force of their anxiety, covertly acknowledging that she is adult, at least to the extent that she could get pregnant.

It further illustrates the amount of work that goes into negotiating age transitions, especially where they interact with gender. In many homes there is a very carefully planned relaxation of parental control over the kid's sexual life, by finely-graded steps over a number of years. Secondary schools officially treat their charges as being sexually children, though of course other students and teachers know that many of them are not. The tensions set up by covert sexuality are a fruitful source of turbulence at school.

Growing up also means going to work; and here there are complexities where age relations intersect with class. For working-class kids, with a few exceptions, the path to adulthood lies out of the school and into the workforce. Once there, the kids have a new standing in their homes, and attempts to control their sexuality rapidly taper off. For ruling-class kids, the path to adulthood lies through advanced training. Parents will tell them that it would be 'childish' to leave school at 15, and indeed few think seriously of doing so.

We often talk of the nuclear family unit as mother, father and child, but in fact the more common situation is child*ren*. Our interviews have convinced us of the systematic importance of sibling relationships in understanding the upbringing and schooling of the kids. Brothers and sisters face their parents' regime as an interacting group, and are often treated as a unit at school.

Teachers often think about a second or third child in terms of what the older one was like to teach. Parents are well aware of this and may either worry or rejoice about the consequences. Within the family the kids define themselves, and get defined, against each other: this one is the humorist, that one has brains but can't see a joke, the other is the family idiot, etc. Older children may pioneer a relationship with education for younger ones. Thus Joanne Carpenter got taken from her friends and sent to a private school because her brother, who was proving a behaviour problem, had already been sent to a private school for the discipline, and her parents thought they could do no less for her. This happened in the Owens family, where Ruth's change of plan was affecting the relationship with schooling for all the younger kids.

For all this, it is still the relationship between husband and wife that is the basis of the family's organization. We have already spoken of some of the main forms taken by this relationship, and of course there are as many detailed variations as there are marriages.

What is common to all of them is that they are in principle an exclusive sexual and domestic relationship between one man and one woman. And they still by and large convey to kids growing up, that model of domestic and emotional life as the natural and proper order of things.

Arguably, this pattern has deeper significance again. For it is the lynch-pin of one of the major arguments about the fundamental question of how social structures affect human motives, and how social forces thus get 'inside' the person. It is easy, on the one hand, to fall into the habit of seeing children as blank sheets on which social pressures stamp their mark; or on the other, to see children, as many parents do, as having their ultimate character virtually from the day they were born.

The account of human growth coming from the work of Freud avoids this dilemma by seizing both its horns. This approach sees social structure, in particular the organization of the family, as giving form and direction to inchoate native impulses which continue to supply the motive power. On this view the course of children's emotional life reflects the crises inevitably produced by the clash between emotional impulse and social control. A person is formed by the way those crises are resolved; and the family form 'reproduces' itself to the extent it succeeds in this lion-tamer act.

It was no part of our research plan to psychoanalyse anybody; but even at the level we were working, that kind of theory does help to make sense of somc situations we encountered. One is the business families we have discussed a couple of times already, where there is a powerful, somewhat remote and strongly masculine father, and a mother entrusted with the house and child care, who functions as the emotional centre of the household. This seems tailor made to produce classic examples of what Freud called the 'oedipal' crisis, where love for the mother, jealousy and fear of the father, and repression of the forbidden impulses, result in the little boy's identification with the father and the beginnings of a masculinity similar to his.

We weren't observing early childhood directly, but the emotional patterns in a number of these families during the boys' adolescence looked very much like that. It is not surprising, for instance, to find that John Walker's son is strongly identified with his father; chose to go to his present school because it was where his father had gone; shares his father's affectionate but patronizing approach to women, notably his mother; reproduces most of his father's opinions, his pattern of skills at school (strong on maths and sciences) and his career plans. And it is clear that this is not just simple modelling: there are strong emotions and anxieties involved. Among other things, Ian is acutely aware of the imperfect masculinity of his body resulting from a late onset of puberty, and partly in response to that has become a fiercely-determined footballer.

The idea of a formative clash between native impulse and the demands of social structure is also strongly suggested by the lives of some kids who are openly resisting school. Yet there is something missing from this general formula. Why should Ian, for all his father-identification, be slacking in the traces, not competitive enough? Why do some kids come out in open rebellion when others from apparently similar family constellations knuckle under? Especially girls, whom psychoanalytic theory notoriously has difficulty explaining.

Sartre proposed a radical solution: people *choose*, commit themselves to certain paths. Indeed we cannot help it, we are 'condemned to be free'. Formative choices in early life may be inarticulate and ill-understood but they are made nonetheless – and that making is what constructs us as individual persons. Ian is, at some very basic level, choosing not to become quite like John. We can never 'explain' those choices in the sense of predicting them; but we can sometimes understand them and sympathize with them, and we can certainly follow their consequences.

In this research we have tried to see people's lives as projects rather than as predetermined fates and to see people as active constructors of what they have become and are becoming. There is no inconsistency in recognizing that the project may be launched, and the choices made, under terrible constraints. And we have tried to spell some of these out in our discussions of class and gender.

Yet there is a danger in *this* sort of formula that social structures will seem to be inhuman and external forces contrasted with a really human realm of individual choice. Our image of person and society becomes that of a flea freely hopping around inside a cage and, though that may produce fine dramas about fleas, it isn't very helpful if our concern is to do something about the cage. A resolution of the problem, as Sartre among others came to see, can only lie in the direction of a theory of practice: for the 'cage' is composed of what people do. The situations that people like the Joneses and the Greys find themselves in are powerfully affected by the existence of people like the Walkers and the Graingers, and the way they conduct their lives. It is only by examining personal choice and motive in the context of social relations which enter into them at the most basic level, which are constitutive of individual lives, that we will get any kind of grip on the processes at work.

This has been a somewhat abstract discussion, but we thought it useful to set down these points, as we have run up against the issues repeatedly in getting to grips with what a hundred families told us. Our understanding of them has (it is very clear to us) partly depended on the progress or lack of progress we made with theoretical issues, in developing a framework for understanding the relationship between personal life and social structures.

Among other things, it has helped us to get beyond the assumption – which as we have suggested is often in people's interests to make – that family and school are separate spheres containing separate processes. 'The family' does not form a child's character and then deliver it ready-packaged to the doorstep of 'the school'. The family is what its members do, a constantly continuing and changing practice, and, as children go to and through school, that practice is reorganized around their schooling. For its part the organization of the school varies with the kinds of families in its catchment and the nature of their collective practices. It is time to look more closely at those schools.

Attainment, Environment and Education

Eric Batten

Although our appreciation of the complex relationships between environment, heredity and attainment has grown steadily through the last decade, and the universal and consistent variations by social class in the distribution of life chances in general and educational opportunities and attainments in particular are now documented beyond peradventure, there is little to suggest that there has been any significant attempt to come to grips with the implications for education of our increased knowledge.

My objectives in this chapter are twofold: first, to develop at some length those considerations which I see as attaching to the form of interpretation associated with environment–attainment analysis in the United Kingdom. Especially I want to discuss the practice of categorizing survey data as evidence of attitudes or material and socioeconomic circumstance. In the course of this I shall refer particularly to the evidence drawn from the Plowden follow-up research conducted at Manchester (Ainsworth and Batten, 1974). My second objective is to discuss, somewhat more briefly, some difficulties attaching to the well-meaning practical proposals which resulted from such studies – difficulties which need to be considered when assessing the likely outcomes of the piecemeal proposals so far made. Especially I shall be concerned to outline some of the difficulties attaching to the closer development of home–school relations and the practical implementation of the community school concept at the secondary level of education (Plowden, 1967; Halsey, 1972; Midwinter, 1973).

Before dealing in detail with a specific review of the problems of categorizing environmental data in terms of attitude and circumstance variables, it may be of value if I state my general view of the consequence of such forms of analysis. In essence I take the view that the 'attitudinal' interpretations in the analysis of the association of environment with variations in educational attainment have led to the assumption that what is required is parental socialization into the educational milieu; the creation of what Jean Floud once described as teacher missionaries, individuals who will proselytize for education until every family will qualify for the description of 'la famille éducogène' (1961). Such an assumption ignores the growing body of knowledge which consistently demonstrates the incapacity of education to compensate for the effects of the wider society (Jencks *et al.*, 1972), and which validates a similar assumption, made perhaps more instinctively by a large part of the population, that compulsory education has little relevance as a determinant of the future opportunities available for their children.

If this view is accepted, then strategies designed to motivate the closer attachment of parents and their children to an educational system which can *per se* only ever determine the advantage of a tiny minority seems to me to divert attention from what is, I believe, a more central educational consideration, which is: whether it is possible (the moral and political questions are avoided) to motivate the majority of parents and their children to involvement in educational attainment in an educational system which, whatever the official intention, rather than demonstrating respect for the individual and the fulfilment of his potential as its ideal, operates to demonstrate and confirm inequality. Stated thus abstractly, this alternative consideration requires elaboration. In the course of discussing the two objectives with which I opened this chapter the necessary elaboration will be made.

To turn, then, to my first objective. In this country a powerful stimulus to the furtherance of our understanding of the relationships of environment to attainment was the setting up of the Plowden researches and, more recently, the follow-up studies. Using the findings of the Manchester follow-up study to Plowden in particular I propose to discuss some aspects of the 'traditional wisdom' of environmental researches in this country.

Of the 'findings' from Plowden researches into environment–attainment relationships perhaps the two most generally quoted are:

1 Home environment is considerably more influential as a determinant of attainment than school.
2 Of home environmental variables those denoting family

> attitudes to education, ambition and literacy are a great deal more important than those denoting material circumstances and social class. (Wiseman, 1970)

The first finding is, of course, what any thoughtful teacher might have suspected. In essence it is supported by the major analysis carried out in America by Jencks (1972). One response to this finding has been to argue the case for greater involvement of parents in the education of their children. What this might mean in practice could, of course, vary considerably. One suspects that the advocacy of such involvement by individuals and agencies representing quite contrasting ideologies indicates not a common anticipation of the outcome but the likelihood that both elitists and egalitarians see the potential for the furtherance of their own educational and social objectives in the closing of the gap between home and school.[1]

Jencks (1972) takes the argument for parental involvement possibly further than either of the major groups of proponents in the United Kingdom, and bearing in mind his general ideological stance it is perhaps surprising that he does not realize the potential his proposals have for the imposition of conservative ideologies and the entrenchment of elitist control.

The reaction of teachers to proposals for greater parent–teacher involvement, as expressed through their professional bodies, has been highly defensive. To be fair, such relationships do raise

---

[1] At the time of the previous Conservative government, for instance, the then Education Minister, Mrs Margaret Thatcher, in her concern for the preservation of all kinds of school and parental choice as well as of traditional educational methods and 'standards', became a strong advocate of greater parental involvement in what goes on at school. More recently Dr Rhodes Boyson, an MP of similar political persuasion and educational inclination, with characteristic sobriety has in the face of an official administrative conspiracy of silence alerted us all to the violence in secondary schools, the flight of demoralized teachers from our urban areas, the Trotskyite cells of teachers and the professional malcontents seeking, as he sees it, only to destroy our civilization. The right kind of parents could, of course, become a powerful bulwark against such degenerate influences. (NAS conference, January 1975.) It seems at least likely that those who hold such views will have intentions for parent–teacher contact which differ from those who in a humane and idealistic manner envisage that parents have a right to be closely involved in the formal education of their children and may as a consequence considerably influence the attainments of their children. See for instance McGeeney (1968).

difficult questions for the teachers' professional status as widely conceived, and should they ever seriously consider greater parental involvement in schools they would be able to make out a plausible – though not, to my mind, an overwhelming – case for the maintenance of the generally powerful boundaries between themselves and their clients. Such a defence can be made even at a time when research findings have seriously undermined any anticipation that the pursuit of education within the framework of traditional parent–teacher relationships will lead at the primary level to any significant advances in the attainment of educational objectives; and when, as we are currently witnessing, the traditional rationale of secondary education is fast being eroded and the morale of urban secondary teachers is rapidly dwindling.

Before, however, elaborating my discussion of the problems of closer parent–teacher involvement I should like to consider some points arising from the two research findings which, I suggested, were characteristic of environment–attainment analyses at the beginning of this chapter. A series of points arise from the frequently made claim that home attitudinal variables are of greater impact upon attainment than those indicating material and socioeconomic circumstances. First, and fundamentally, I would like to suggest that there are ideological, empirical and common sense difficulties in categorizing variables in terms of attitudes and material circumstances.

I suggest that within the context of environment–attainment studies as traditionally conducted there can be no empirical justification for categorizing some variables as 'attitude variables' and others as 'circumstance variables'. The transposing of a term such as 'attitude', which in some research contexts has a relatively precise though not very useful meaning, to the field of education, where the methods of 'attitude' study are less rigorous and where meanings are less precise, is unjustified empirically and, I would argue, socially irresponsible. In an educational setting such terminology inevitably becomes involved with popular moral and social connotations.

The separation of variables into such categories can be of considerable consequence for the ideological aspects of interpretation and for the determination of policy response. If, for instance, attitudes are regarded as separable from circumstances and, as we have consistently seen (Burt, 1937; Wiseman, 1964, 1970; Peaker,

1971; Bynner, 1972), according to such categorization are regarded as of more importance for attainment, then certain outcomes become more likely. First, failure to attain is more likely to be attributed to individual waywardness. Secondly, as a likely consequence, the problem of the possible educational threshold effects of variations in the distribution of resources receives less consideration than it should (Byrne and Williamson, 1972).

We cannot justify the separation of environmental variables into 'attitude' and 'circumstance' groupings as though attitudes are formed in the minds of individuals without reference to their circumstances. We know that statements of attitudes may be, and often are, relatively abstracted and idealized; the behavioural outcomes of these statements – which are what really matters so far as the relationship between environment and attainment is concerned – are likely to be significantly mediated by the circumstances in which the process is taking place.

In his researches for the Manchester School of Education and for Plowden the late Stephen Wiseman, who was a major figure in the analysis of the association of environment with attainment in this country, consistently argued the salience of attitudes over circumstance. Acland (1973), commenting on Wiseman's interpretation of his Manchester-based Plowden data writes:

> Wiseman's conclusion properly emphasizes the literacy of the home as the most important attitudinal comment. This turns out to be the most consistent predictor of achievement, but . . . one cannot assume that it represents parents' dispositions. It may equally be a measure of socioeconomic status.

In his Plowden follow-up study Peaker tacitly acknowledges the validity of such criticism when he refers to the critics who argued that 'literacy of the home' (1971) was a circumstance rather than an attitude and subsequently transferred the literacy variables in his regression analysis from the attitude composite to that of the parental circumstance composite. The shift is of profound consequence for the traditional view about the relative impact of variable groupings upon attainment. It is clear from Peaker's follow-up analysis that once literacy variables are transferred to material circumstances, then the remaining 'attitudinal' variables are of little consequence for attainment.

In a reanalysis of Peaker's data Acland concludes that 'literacy variables are the most consistent predictor variables . . . The single most important variable is the "whether or not the child is read to"' (1973).

So far I have made two points relating to the interpretation of attitudes. First, I suggested that to talk of attitudes on the basis of inferences drawn from the data collected in the course of environmental analyses of the Plowden type is unsatisfactory. Such inferences are unsatisfactory because they require an unjustifiable degree of ideologically influenced interpretation, which may well in its turn stimulate policies more likely to compound inequalities than to stimulate attempts at their amelioration. Secondly, talk of separating variables into categories of attitudinal and material circumstance encourages the fallacy that they are significantly separable.

I recognize that the first point raises two separate, though to my mind not easily separable, issues. The first relates to the question of objectivity in social science research. The psychometrists who have traditionally dominated environmental research in this country have not seen objectivity as highly problematic. Perhaps because of the abstractions of their mental measurement backgrounds they felt secure in the view that their interpretations of data were highly objective. This is a naïve view because essentially their conceptualization derives from models of men which in themselves have implications for world views or what Gouldner has called domain assumptions. In other words the models chosen and the interpretations made are determined within the framework of what the individual researcher judges to be plausible on the basis of the fundamental elements which influence his own ideology. The difficulty in the human sciences is that there is never, in the last resort, enough evidence to force us from the global preconceptions which condition our determination of a research problem, the methods by which it may be analysed and the interpretations that we make. If we fail to perceive that even the most abstract models and advanced statistical models when applied to the human situation secrete values, then we may have the illusion of objectivity. If, however, we recognize the illusion, then we may be less complacent, less certain, and the consequence will be that the rigour of our method will demand value awareness rather than a claim to value freedom.

It is precisely because of this need for a shift from a claim of objectivity to an attempt at value awareness that I argue my second point, that is, the essential involvement of the social scientist with a concern for the policy outcomes of his interpretations. In the past it has often been argued – partly, I suspect, as a basis of support for the argument of his objectivity – that the social scientist is not concerned with policy stemming from his findings. It seems perfectly clear to me that given the inevitable subjective element in the social scientist's interpretation, then both as a scientist and as a moral human being he must emphasize the qualifications to be placed on his findings and the value basis of his judgements, and that, bearing in mind the relative nature of values, he must insist that his findings are not used to justify, or further, prejudice and inequality. I hope it can be appreciated that I do not regard the points just made as a digression but see them as fundamental to my whole argument about the dangers of describing some data as adequate for the inference of attitudes as separable from circumstances.

In the Manchester follow-up of Plowden which Marjorie Ainsworth and I (1974) conducted, the association of some indicators of family literacy often described as attitudinal variables with material circumstances has been consistently evidenced. The clearest example lies in the association of lack of provision of reading matter with evidence of poor material circumstances. Another variable, to do with the provision of book storage space for the child, relates more clearly to spatial considerations, of the child having his own room and of family size, than to 'attitudes' to literacy.

The intimate association of imputed attitudes with domestic circumstance is again highlighted by the finding that some aspects of the parents' knowledge of the child's progress – again, variables described elsewhere in terms of attitudes – are associated with the mother's occupational circumstance. It was certainly the case for the Manchester sample that an absence of knowledge about the child's progress and a lack of educational aspiration were associated with the mother not working and with poor environmental circumstances.

It seems appropriate here to emphasize that those environmental characteristics which have traditionally been described in terms of attitudes to education are also to be seen in the context of the circumstances in which the child is being educated, and that the effect upon attitudes is interactive between the home, the child and the school. Certainly the findings of Bynner (1972) in his Plowden follow-up study seem to support such an interpretation.

If we wish to infer parental educational attitudes from the extent of parental knowledge about school we must have regard to the fact that schools vary greatly in the amount and nature of their communication with the home. It is likely that those schools with the least to offer their charges will communicate least. Since these are the very schools which the most socially disadvantaged and least able children are most likely to attend, research which taps parental knowledge of the child's progress is likely to find that low attainment and low parental knowledge correlate, and may miss the important intervening variables.

Cloward and Jones (1963) suggest that there is unlikely to be a single causal relationship between parents' educational participation and expressed attitudes, and that the more reasonable assumption is that a complicated process of reinforcement and reciprocal causation takes place between 'attitudinal' and circumstance aspects of the environment.

We have not the means of attributing causal priority to one category of variable rather than another, and it has been suggested that parental attitudes to the child's education may be regarded as a consequence of the child's performance in school as well as a cause. I entirely share Acland's view (1973) that 'Since the distinction between attitudes and circumstances is suspect, the statistical analyses which compare their relative effects must be treated with caution'.

Two considerations follow from this discussion of the ways in which environmental variables are categorized for purposes of statistical analysis. First, the fact that we are enabled to make such categorizations is a consequence of the crude analytic process involved; it does not reflect an existing environmental framework. That is, an environment in experience is a total structure, an integrated process of individual meanings made from a complex of gross and subtle interacting influences. Secondly, it is now clear that the terms used to denote variable categories affect the practical and ideological contexts in which interpretations are made.

Thus, for instance, it has sometimes been implied that those who emphasize the role of environment as opposed to the influence of heredity are egalitarians; alternatively those who argue in favour of inherited determinates of ability are sometimes described as elitists. Certainly in the present discussion of attitudes and circumstances it has tended to be the sociologists who have argued against separation into such categories, and neither Burt (1955) nor Wiseman (1964) was reticent in the view that sociologists are motivated by egalitarian, if not more sinister, ideologies.

So far as practical contexts are concerned it becomes somewhat more likely that if literacy variables become interpreted as circumstances, then they may be regarded as somehow being more the consequence of social influences and more potentially amenable to social action. If, on the other hand, literacy variables are seen as attitudes, they may be seen as representing in those with 'poor' attitudes (i.e. low scores), recalcitrance, indifference and sometimes even inability. Clearly there are striking differences to be anticipated in the response to be made, according to the categorization involved.

There are two further matters relating to problems of environmental analysis which are evidenced by the findings of the Manchester Plowden follow-up. These relate to the tendency to assume that the effect of an environmental influence is constant across social classes and through time.

The Manchester survey provides some evidence to suggest that there may be some differentiation in the impact of maternally rooted variables through time. It appears likely that the influence of the father as an educational strategist, as an occupational role model and as a determinant of material circumstances, becomes increasingly influential as the child grows older. The mother's more diffuse supportive role becomes relatively less important.

For the highest levels of attainment, of course, the child's own aspirations come into close association with those of the parents, although here again it must be emphasized that analysis also indicates the considerable importance of school setting in association with high levels of aspiration.

At an early stage of this discussion it was suggested that the relative unimportance of material circumstance compared with attitudes was a fairly consistent finding of environmental analysts. In the Manchester survey it is clear that as education proceeds so material circumstance variables gain in importance, having their major impact upon attainment at 16-plus (Batten, 1974). Staying on for one extra year and 16-plus attainment are associated overwhelmingly with favourable environmental circumstances, and staying on seems to be a better predictor of secondary performance at this level than attainment at ten-plus.

Sixteen-plus attainment and 17-plus attainment are relatively independent of ability measured at ten-plus. For the child who leaves at 15 correlations with both attainment and environmental variables are consistently negative from seven-plus onwards. Poor environmental conditions are clearly associated with statutory leavers.

The sixth-form entrant is environmentally distinguished from the 16-plus leaver by better housing circumstances and by a mother who is not working. In this case 'mother not working' is an indication of a favourable environment, whereas for the statutory leaver 'mother not working' has unfavourable environmental associations. Other environmental variables also indicate the middle-classness of sixth-form entrants and, of course, the importance of school context.

We cannot suggest that if statutory leavers stayed on at secondary school they would attain well; the primary school attainments of statutory leavers in our survey were generally poor. What is clear, however, is that the motivation to stay on is strongly associated with good material circumstances and a favourable school environment. It appears from the Manchester survey that those aspects of the environment determining the decision to leave school at the earliest possible moment are already apparent by the time of entry to secondary school. The will to attain, as evidenced by staying on at school, is seen as having quite an important effect in an educatively supportive environment. Whilst recognizing the relative incapacity of schools to affect significantly either the home environment or the pattern of opportunities in the wider society for the majority of pupils, it seems legitimate to speculate upon whether the education system could not, if it were so desired, become more internally supportive, and more effective in nourishing the desire to attain.

The importance of school setting requires emphasis. It seems at least doubtful whether an educational system which has the effect of systematically selecting the most advantaged members of the school population for further advantage can effectively motivate those not so selected to want education.

It is suggested, then, that parental influence and material circumstances may vary in their impact upon attainment through time and that school setting may be highly influential in its impact. Material circumstances, though traditionally regarded as of little consequence, appear to be highly influential in their effect upon the leaving decision.

Undoubtedly the clearest predictor of attainment at secondary school, even after controlling for ability at entry, is a place in a selective setting. The analysis of school environments in the Plowden follow-up for Manchester provided clear evidence of the superior educational facilities as well as the environmental advantages of the selective intake. Perhaps it is the selective schools which most value and support those aspects of the home environment associated with attainment, literacy and ambition. For such schools ambition is appropriate. They can confirm future social and economic advantage to a significant proportion of their population. For those who value literacy ambition need not be a highly conscious process; the educational system is such that those in selective schools can, if they wish – especially on the arts side – keep their options open and drift upwards through the educational system without very precise occupational goals in view. Although in the selective setting with a high chance of future success it is possible to emphasize the pursuit of education for its intrinsic worth and deny instrumental involvement, there is no doubt that the pursuit of literacy is closely associated with future opportunity through the traditional external examination system. This happy coincidence is denied to the non-selected and lower-stream child, for whom both the intrinsic satisfactions and extrinsic rewards of education are extremely limited.

However, before developing a discussion of the various proposals which have been made for the amelioration of the educational circumstances and attainments of the disadvantaged I want to discuss a related question that we asked ourselves when interpreting the data of the Manchester follow-up. We were concerned to uncover those aspects of environmental influence which might be regarded as most amenable to external influence.

When the average secondary attainment–environment correlations were partialled for the effects of parental ability, indicated by parents' claimed 11-plus success, and for the effects of child's ability on the basis of ability as indicated at seven-plus it was evident that the parents' ability has a lesser impact upon attainment–environment correlations than that of the child. It is suggested, however, that in practice it is parents who have the major capacity for influencing many aspects of the home environment, especially in areas usually described as attitudinal and in the area of material circumstance.

The Manchester survey indicated that several variables characterized as indicative of attitudes to education and literacy are relatively independent of parental ability, and it is argued that they are in principle those aspects of environment most amenable to the influence of external agencies, such as libraries and schools.

The parents of secondary school children have seldom been the subjects of systematic attempts to enroll their support in the pursuit of better attainment by their children. The analysis of the schools side of the Manchester follow-up survey provides strong support for this view.

The home environment analysis powerfully suggests the extent to which schools control the information made available to parents; are influential in the development of the child's and the parents' ambition; can influence supportiveness with homework; and play an influential role in an elaborate process of interaction between parents, child and school.

It has traditionally been suggested that parental attitudes to education may be the more important environmental influences upon the attainments of the child. At the secondary stage the child's attitudes to education are undoubtedly important too, and it may well be that future environmental researches could usefully concern themselves with the gross and subtle institutional and organizational influences which impinge upon the child's attitudinal development.

Until we are a great deal more knowledgeable about how people learn, how to teach them effectively, and the nature of the influence of environmental characteristics upon their motivation we cannot hope to assess the limits of individual potential. Nor indeed can we accept the present indications as providing strong evidence that we have so far measured the impact of the school upon attainment.

It appears that within the limitations of current modes of analysis we find that individual school environmental variables are of little or inconsistent consequence for attainment. We also find evidence for the view that there are considerable disparities in the provision of educational resources within and between schools, the commonest characteristic of this disparity being that those pupils least well endowed environmentally and intellectually get the poorest school resources.

If this state of affairs were the consequence of a conscious educational policy it would be seen as paradoxical in the extreme. Certainly it would be a consequence without parallel if it really was the case that to deny the pupil the stimulation of adequate resources and conditions is the most effective way of promoting educational attainment, the development of a healthy self-image and high ambition. The more equitable distribution of resources might well be of consequence for the development of school environments in which educationally helpful orientations could develop and in which educational attainments might improve.

Nevertheless, to return to the level of home environmental influence, it is suggested from the Manchester research that parents' involvement with the education of their children is relatively independent of parental ability. Even in that area of environmental analysis where parental ability seems to have the greatest consequence the variables involved frequently relate to parents' educational knowledge or factual information. These are in principle amenable to attempts not previously made to influence or inform the parents.

Perhaps the underlying problem in terms of schools developing more effective means of communication and systematic methods of influencing attitudes is one which cannot be dealt with simply. It is suggested that with their occupational orientation secondary schools have no plausible case which they could employ to involve the majority of parents to motivate their offspring to higher levels of attainment.

In some educational settings educational ambitions are unrealistic, and it is in the context of the educational setting that educational attitudes may be most objectively interpreted. It may be that some parents hold attitudes to school and education (and these are not always synonymous) which are not useful; but then, if education is not, for them or their offspring, functional, it is not easy to appreciate why we should expect them to value it. It is unsatisfactory to interpret their attitudes as existing in a vacuum, as if to imply that those attitudes would necessarily be the same if their objective circumstances changed.

It appears that what we infer as attitudes from statements of hopes, intentions and expectations are to some extent separable from both parental and child abilities. To that extent it may be possible for the school and other agencies to guide parents in their highly influential role of affecting the child's educational attainment.

Parents' ignorance of the child's attainments is not always associated with indifference to the child and his performance but must be seen in the context of the school's having considerable freedom in determining the information which it provides for parents and the amount of contact they have with it.

Similarly, attitudes to literacy are not entirely determined by the ability level of parents or child. The *amount* of parents' reading is less dependent than the *level* of parents' reading upon their ability and more associated with the child's school attainment. If literacy is important for attainment it is easy to see that library provision is likely to be an important agency in its furtherance. The implementation of a useful attitude to literacy seems often associated with material circumstances, and the provision of free reading material through a convenient local source may help in situations where economic circumstances are unfavourable.

Perhaps arising from the previous considerations we might suggest that not only are educational attitudes formed on the basis of interaction between parent, child, school and teachers but also with reference to material aspects of the environment. Just as parents' ambition and expectation develop through their interpretation of the capacities, ambitions and expectations of the child and his teachers in the light of their previous experiences, so their planning and educational strategies, their discussions and their detailed considerations are conducted with reference to the realities indicated to them by their present circumstances. Thus we find, for instance, that detailed knowledge of the child's progress in individual subjects is associated not only with variables suggesting a selective school setting but also with variables related to the size of the family and adequate space in the home.

The educational attitudes developed by parents are for the most part realistic; useful educational attitudes associate more with a selective setting, good school support and good material circumstances. A low valuation of education is more associated with non-selective settings, poor school support and poor material circumstances. It is not clear how we might effectively change the 'attitudes' of those who are thus disadvantaged.

The education system has minimal scope for advantageously influencing the social and economic experiences of the considerable majority of the school population, yet at the same time schools cling to structures and practices which reflect the traditional functionalist viewpoint of the role of education. The functionalist view leads not simply to the creation of educational structures for the selection of a minority for economic and social promotion; it involves, for the majority, a process of negative selection, a confirmation of the disadvantages that the child brings with him to school.

It may, of course, be argued that parents, teachers and pupils do not view education from a sociologically sceptical standpoint, that the assumptions of the role of education are not questioned. I suggest that teachers (themselves streamed) in non-selective schools and in the lower streams of comprehensive schools are likely to have a very clear idea of the motivational inadequacy of the claim that working hard at school will bring future advantage. They will have gained these perceptions through their own professional socialization; through their observation of the disparity in the distribution of educational resources and through their knowledge of where education leads for the majority of their charges.

In the Manchester sub-sample study the analysis revealed a strong association between a selective setting and attainment in all subjects. It seems likely that the attitudes of parents and schools to literacy and attainment usually match, and that as far as the progress of the child at school is concerned we are witnessing a reciprocal and reinforcing process.

Secondary education, with its highly instrumental associations, is likely, through the way in which it structures the pattern of future opportunity, to create appropriately depressed school settings as well as appropriately ambitious school settings. In socially and educationally depressed settings neither appeals to ambition nor appeals to intrinsic educational satisfactions can be expected to motivate good attainment.

The fact that many families already opt out of anything but a minimal involvement in education, combined with the accumulating academic evidence of the great distance between education's objectives and its practical outcome, must create increasing pressure for a more widely-based discussion of the assumptions upon which our education system is based. If teachers and educationists are to bring about such a dialectic through closer relations between home and school, then the dilemma which is facing them is clear: the activities in which parents and teachers become involved might well be more political than educational. It is particularly with this problem that I come to the final section of this chapter.

If inequality of opportunity for education began at home and was separable from the wider inequalities of our society, then it might be reasonable to anticipate that ameliorative policies within schools and communities could change the patterns of motivation for educational attainment. The fact is, however, that in a society in which equality of opportunity is a widely acknowledged social and educational objective, inequality is an entrenched and inherent part of our social organization. The concepts of equality and of average ability – both of considerable currency within education – carry with them an implicit denial of the uniqueness of individuals, and by a process of intellectual elision make it likely that those who are less than equal in their access to social resources and less than average in terms of performance on educational test scores or their placement in the educational system come to be regarded as less than average or less than equal people (Newsom, 1963). The disvaluing mechanisms of social and educational selection deriving from our willingness to categorize individuals according to arbitrarily defined and, in the case of education, irrelevant criteria are the key to the mechanisms both gross and subtle which result in the inequitable distribution of resources. There is an apparent irony in the fact that the very arbitrary, conditional and abstracted categories employed for the definition of problems by social scientists become reified by governments as a basis for action, and in becoming so are further instruments for discrimination and prejudice.

Our society offers highly predictable sets of life chances. Clearly some individuals are motivated to beat the predictions, and do so. Most do not, otherwise actuarial assessments would not hold up. Most have a pretty clear understanding of what their social expectations are. The same is true in education. The considerable array of information (of varying degrees of subtlety) that parents and their children receive combine to encourage a fairly unambiguous set of predictions concerning a child's educational and social future. Within education itself the evidence of inter- and intra-regional variations in educational support (Byrne and Williamson, 1972) and organization (Taylor and Ayres, 1969) is quite clear and generally in accord with the relationship that those who start life with the highest indices of disadvantage receive the resources offering the narrowest range of opportunity.

The call for positive discrimination is one response to this phenomenon, and represents a recognition of the concept of equity rather than of equality as being the more relevant in the ordering of human affairs, and particularly of education. Even so, administrative expediency requires that in the first instance such discrimination should be group-based rather than individually oriented. At the secondary level the major response, so far, to combat the inequitable effects of selection and categorization procedures has been to encourage the development of comprehensive education. Whilst I am unequivocally in favour of comprehensive education, on educational grounds, there is no reason to assume that its introduction will in the short or even medium term significantly ameliorate the inequity of the wider society. Further, comprehensive developments so far have overwhelmingly maintained the selection and grouping devices of the old tripartite system. The barriers which existed before have been subsumed under the roof of a single institution: there are still the significant sorting points within compulsory education (Benn and Simon, 1970); there are still the clearest indications in the organizational characteristics of the overwhelming majority of schools of their anticipation of the child's educational performance and of his future social destination. Further, of course, there remain many schools which continue to service a privileged minority and which by their apparent success in securing the future advantage of their pupils exercise an undue influence on the characteristics of secondary schools in the state system. The comprehensive school is very likely to become the area school, attracting resources according to the educational status of its staff and the social class background of its area.

One response to a growing awareness of this likelihood has been the development of a call for community schools. It is not immediately apparent how such developments can change the general position which has already been elaborated. To be fair, this has already been argued by Halsey (1972), and the moral point is accepted, that the raising of educational standards – especially of the most disadvantaged – should be undertaken for its own sake. Whatever our researches have shown concerning the lack of consistent association of school environmental variables with attainment, it certainly seems unlikely that we might expect that those with the least material resources and indicating the least measured abilities will improve in their attainments if we give them the least satisfactory educational support, which is, on the whole, what happens now.

It has been repeatedly suggested that parents' attitudes to education are more important than their material circumstances. It has seemed to follow, therefore, that by changing the nature of their involvement with parents schools might harness parental influence for the purpose of improving the child's attainments. I have previously argued that the separation of variables into those of circumstance and attitude represents a serious over-simplification, and that family dispositions to education do not develop in a vacuum but are the consequence of a total interactive process. I would like to suggest that not only are the parents' ambitions for their children usually rooted in their objective situation and some sense of their child's capacities, but that so also are the attitudes of teachers which have led to the present patterns of association between home and school. In other words, certainly by the secondary stage it is difficult to see just what schools can communicate to parents which could change their perceptions in the face of their wider experience and accumulated judgements concerning the role of education in affecting their child's future opportunity. This is, of course, true for the majority of the school population. Clearly the intervention of teachers in individual situations can be highly influential. Advantage is by definition limited and relative, and it is not possible to anticipate that the implementation of a general programme of close parent–teacher contact could significantly affect overall patterns of motivation to attain within the context of an instrumentally oriented education system. Teachers probably recognize also that within the confines of polite professional conversation they have little more to communicate to parents than the oracular comments, sometimes constructive, that appear on report forms once or twice a year.

The closer association of parents and teachers, even supposing it can be brought about, must be regarded as a very dubious enterprise if the role of the teacher in these circumstances is seen as that of a troubleshooter for the inadequacies of the educational system and the inequalities of the wider society – if he is encouraged to act in such a way as to persuade parents that the highly bureaucratized system of occupational selection which now passes for secondary education in our society is something they should cheerfully accept, and that they should conspire in the maintenance of an educational system which serves principally to confirm the social disadvantages with which they have endowed their offspring.

Alternatively teachers might become involved with parents, dare I say it, politically. There is an irony here. Is it any less political for teachers to continue to conceal from parents their function of educating for the confirmation of incompetence (Turner, 1965) and disadvantage or to seek to reconcile them to the maldistribution of educational resources than it is to attempt to indicate to them their power as agents with influence, if they wish to exert it, over the ways in which educational and social resources are distributed? I believe not (indeed, I believe that we delude ourselves if we do not appreciate that in many respects education is a political activity), though I do not for a moment anticipate that anything like a majority of teachers would agree with me.

It seems clear that there are, then, considerable difficulties relating to a definition of professional integrity involved in closer teacher–parent relationships. Quite apart from such professional difficulties, however, the growing evidence of the lack of impact of education upon the distribution of life chances; the absence of certainty concerning the effectiveness of pedagogical skills; the implausibility of the defence of education for its own sake; and last, though possibly not least, the lack of popular respectability of teachers' academic knowledge, especially sociology; all serve to make me doubtful whether the teaching profession will indulge in any significant extension of its relationship with the outside world, especially at the secondary level. It is too insecure in itself to undertake any major involvement in an exercise in its own demystification. It has a vested interest in the examinations industry and the status hierarchies which go with it. The existing system is that in which teachers have mostly been socialized, it has played an important part in helping the teacher to gain his professional identity and has quite likely been the basis on his own upward social mobility.

Quite apart from being reasons why I doubt whether any significant increase in parent–teacher contact will take place, they also amount to a basis for doubting whether community schools, with their essentially unbureaucratic approach to education, local teacher–parent-defined goals, community-based curricula, and local involvement, with a high political potential and locally designed organizational characteristics, will find extensive professional support from teachers – or, indeed, administrative and political support – once the full implications are recognized. Proposals for community schools contain within them too great a potential for quite basic questions to be asked about educational and social objectives.

A central difficulty with community schools at the secondary level is determining where they might fit into the existing educational system. If they are to become in effect a category of schools for the disadvantaged, then although they may be better and happier social institutions for those involved in them, and they may lead to higher levels of attainment than might otherwise have been attained, they cannot anticipate that by substituting an ecological curriculum for the traditional academic one they will do more than intensify a sense of educational *apartheid* and seriously exacerbate the question of the political involvement of teachers. For such schools to become the standard they would need espousing by the middle class, who have, at least up to now, exercised the greatest power and influence in the distribution of social resources, largely to their own advantage. Within the present educational ethos, community schools are unlikely to appeal to more than an eccentric fringe of the middle class whose educational idealism has served to blind it to the risk that by accepting such schools it may be missing a chance to provide its children with the smoothest possible path to the confirmation of their future social status.

If community schools accept the characteristics of the wider system and at the secondary level attempt to integrate through their involvement in external examinations, it is again not easy to see how they can avoid contamination by those educational values which have served within the existing educational framework to demotivate the disadvantaged for attainment. Essentially these are the values which emphasize the unequalness of individuals rather than their uniqueness. They invoke selection and competition; they emphasize ascribed status relationships and hierarchy; they define attainment narrowly in terms of academic excellence rather than in terms of excellence, academic excellence being assessed by external examinations which seldom, if ever, may be regarded as indicating academic attainment or a level of excellence in any educational sense.

What, then, are the solutions to the dilemmas which I have tried to outline? It would be to ignore the evidence which informs my judgement, against the spirit of what I have tried to say here and of what I believe in, to proffer the dogmas of simple solutions. One thing is, however, clear. The present state of our knowledge no longer allows the comfortable assumption that education is a significant agent in reducing social inequity.

If we wish to preserve the characteristics of the existing system, which, historically, developed piecemeal and has only subsequently had a supposedly coherent 'explanation' of its role imposed upon it, then we are bound to discover a new rationale for continuing with an educational system the organizational characteristics of which are, as we may observe, educationally dysfunctional for the majority and socially and economically irrelevant overall – at least in terms of the acceptable objectives of an educational system in a democratic society. This appears to me to be an impossible task, and yet I suppose it fair to suggest that an education which has the capacity to absorb considerable resources, most of which are provided by those who receive least (Glennerster, 1972), should have a rationale – a series of coherently stated objectives which provide the basis for a critical assessment of procedures.

My own view is that the evidence now to hand provides the basis of a powerful argument for freeing education from the bureaucratic entanglement which has occurred in the cause of equality of opportunity and the assumption of its social and economic expedience; that we should perhaps seek the more personal, local and relevant forms of education during the compulsory stages, which is what, I take it, community-based education implies. We should do this through following up in practical terms the implications of the concepts of equity and individuality in education and through the assumption of a client-centred consumption ethos rather than the current system-centred investment models of education. The difficulties have not been underestimated, and without the application of the community concept as a national policy there can be little hope of success. We need, however, to emphasize that, whilst community-based education may have as its intention the better attainments of individuals through their initial stimulation by a sense of education's relevance, we are seeking also to develop the capacity for universality. An education which aids the rejection of 'community' boundaries, boundaries which in the long run can be maintained only by prejudice. This is important, because the local community organization has at least as high a potential for tyrannizing individuals and denying their individuality as any central government agency. So far as education is concerned, the individual may be as much threatened by the parochialism of a curriculum as by a depersonalized educational system in which organization becomes an end in itself.

The advantage – the overwhelming advantage – of a community school system is that it could operate a form of education completely divorced from considerations of selection and the instrumental connotations of the existing system. It would have the potential at least for emphasizing through an individualistic approach the affective satisfactions of education. Through the shared involvement in a local and socially oriented curriculum the teacher may evince a level of concern, interest and acknowledgement of the validity of the community experience which can influence parent–pupil acceptance of his affective valuation of education. None of these outcomes is inevitable, but unless they are intended there appears to be no significant educational reason to argue for a change to the community school concept.

Nevertheless if the analysis that I have made is accepted, then it is difficult to see how the informed teacher can feel confident in asserting the validity of the present system or hopeful of any substantial change for the better in the educational outcome as a result of minor modifications.

References

ACLAND, H. (1973). Social determinants of educational achievement: an evaluation and criticism of research. PhD thesis. Oxford University.

AINSWORTH, M. E. and BATTEN, E. J. (1974). *The Effects of Environmental Factors on Secondary School Attainment in Manchester: a Plowden Follow-Up*. Schools Council Research Studies. London: Macmillan.

BATTEN, E. J. (1974). A study of the relationship between some home variables and secondary school achievement. PhD thesis. Manchester University.

BENN, C. and SIMON, B. (1970). *Half Way There*. London: Penguin.

BURT, C. (1937). *The Backward Child*. London: University of London Press.

BURT, C. (1955). 'The evidence for the concept of intelligence', *British Journal of Educational Psychology*, XXV, 158–77.

BYNNER, J. M. (1972). *Parents' Attitudes to Education*. London: HMSO.

BYRNE, D. S. and WILLIAMSON, L. (1972). 'Intra-regional variations in educational provision and their bearing upon educational attainment', *Sociology* , VI.

CLOWARD, R. A. and JONES, J. A. (1963). 'Social class, educational attitudes and participation'. In: PASSOW, A. H. (Ed) *Education in Depressed Areas*. New York: Columbia University Press.

FLOUD, J. (1961). 'Social class factors in educational achievement'. In: HALSEY, A. H. (Ed) *Ability and Educational Opportunity*. Paris: OECD.

GLENNERSTER, H. (1972). 'Education and inequality'. In: TOWNSEND, M. and BOSANQUET, R. (Eds) *Labour and Inequality*. London: Fabian Society.

HALSEY, A. H. (1972). *Educational Priority. Vols. I–IV*. London: HMSO.

JENCKS, C. *et al*. (1972). *Inequality*. London: Allen Lane.

McGEENEY, P. (1968). *Parents are Welcome*. London: Routledge and Kegan Paul.

MIDWINTER, E. (1973). *Priority Education*. Harmondsworth: Penguin Books.

NEWSOM, J. (1963). *Half Our Future*. CACE. London: HMSO.

PEAKER, G. F. (1971). 'The regression analysis'. The Plowden Report. Vol. 2. Appendix 4. London: HMSO.

PLOWDEN REPORT. GREAT BRITAIN. DEPARTMENT OF EDUCATION AND SCIENCE. CENTRAL ADVISORY COUNCIL FOR EDUCATION (ENGLAND) (1967). *Children and Their Primary Schools*. London: HMSO.

TAYLOR, G. and AYRES, N. (1969). *Born and Bred Unequal*. London: Longman.

TURNER, R. H. (1965). 'Modes of social ascent through education: sponsored and contest mobility'. In: HALSEY, A. H., FLOUD, J. and ANDERSON, G. (Eds) *Education, Economy and Society*. London: Collier Macmillan/Free Press.

WISEMAN, S. (1964). *Education and Environment*. Manchester: Manchester University Press.

WISEMAN, S. (1970). The Plowden Report. Vol. 2. London: HMSO.

Reasserting Parental Rights to Achieve Economic Efficiency

Miriam David

The early 1970s in Britain witnessed an economic crisis of unprecedented proportions since the 1930s. This crisis, which led into a deepening economic recession, continued throughout the 1970s. Its effects have, therefore, been manifold. On the one hand, the deliberate attempts both by private capital and industry and by the state to deal with economic problems have included a restructuring of the education industry. Indeed, in this respect education has frequently been used as a scapegoat for the economic ills that have befallen Britain. Silver argued in *New Society* (1978): 'Education was brought into the discussion of every conceivable problem.' Even when education has not been thus stigmatized, it has, almost inevitably, been affected by economic remedies. On the other hand, the effects of the recession have been such as to stimulate groups and classes to action in pursuit of changes in their situation. Thus, the 1970s have been characterized by much educational rhetoric and activity. Whether this has resulted in a fundamental restructuring of the whole system is a much more open question. The core of the discussion has been the relationship between the family and the education system. In particular, the emphasis towards the end of the decade was on establishing and redefining *parental rights* rather than further imposing parental duties, by applying the state's standards. In this chapter, I examine the ways in which, first, the state and, second, struggles by different groups have attempted to change the characteristics of parental involvement in the education system. In particular, it is important to look at the redefinition, through action and edict, of the division of responsibility between parents for their children's schooling and the attempts to change parental relationships within the education system.

As shown earlier, changes in the organization of the education system usually followed from major economic events. In the 1970s, it was certainly the case that both the Tory and Labour administrations tried to revamp the education system. The most important concern has been with the purposes of the education system and how to restructure education to make it both more efficient and more readily serve economic ends. This latter objective emerged only slowly out of the economic depression and became explicit in Labour proposals in the second half of the decade. Hall (1979) has referred to the Labour period of office as 'the great moving right show'. Labour did not any longer even pay lip-service to its traditional ideology and the principle of equality of educational opportunity.

The Tories' treatment of education and economy

Initial Tory concerns, when they were in office from July 1970, were with the fabric of education and the links with broader social policy. Firstly, they laid an emphasis on strengthening and improving school buildings and sought to abolish all primary schools built before 1903, before the passing of the 1902 Education Act. This drive for improvement did not last long: in actual fact few of the primary school buildings were replaced and, more important, the Tories launched a number of initiatives which were concerned with reducing the costs of the education system. One such policy was that of withdrawing free school milk from all children over the age of seven. This action was deliberately taken because of the financial strains the government was beginning to experience.

The second, and most important, educational initiative of the Tory administration was its White Paper, produced at the end of 1972, which attempted to set out a thorough reorientation of the education system. Entitled *Education: a Framework for Expansion* (DES, 1972), it was, in fact, a recipe for retrenchment. Byrne (1978) has stated that it was 'oddly named . . . (since when we have seen the worst planned, and unplanned, recession and cuts since the 1922 Geddes axe)'. The main impetus for the White Paper was the introduction of new techniques of government which affected the ways in which each policy department of central government operated. The techniques were drawn from both American government and private industry and have been variously named as 'managerialism' or 'corporatism' (Smith, 1972; Cockburn, 1977;

Glennerster, 1975). The Tory government adopted a variety of methods in an effort to improve the decision-making process. The particular method that underlay the White Paper was called programme analysis review (PAR) and was first explained in an earlier White Paper (1970) on the machinery of government in late 1970. Essentially a simple method, it has often been argued that it was technically very complex. It merely required the setting out of the programmes financed by each government spending department and the cost implications of their development (Glennerster, 1975).

The Education White Paper, therefore, was in one sense a very comprehensive document, for it covered all aspects of the education system from nursery schools to universities. However, it did not set out the ways in which all sectors would expand and indeed was only slightly concerned with compulsory education by making brief mention of improving the pupil–teacher ratio. Almost inevitably, the main areas of expansion anticipated were non-compulsory – nursery and higher education. There was no suggestion of extending compulsory schooling. Detailed plans to 1981–2 were presented, and shortly afterwards explanatory and explicit circulars were produced. But the focus was on resource allocation. For instance, circular 2/73 on nursery education, published only weeks after the White Paper, was a very expansionist document in financial terms. It argued for the achievement of the Plowden Committee's proposals (1967) for numbers in nursery education (75 per cent of three-year-olds and 90 per cent of four-year-olds) by 1981. This was, though, not to be. The recession began to bite and although for two successive years the DES announced possible programmes for nursery building, few LEAs took up the offers. Then, in a series of public expenditure revisions, the expansion of nursery provision was reduced. Equally the proposed developments in higher education did not take place.

The only other initiative embarked upon by the Tory administration was concerned with maintaining educational standards. In response to alarm expressed by both academics and right-wing pressure groups about standards in school, and especially reading ability (Hopkins, 1978, p. 89), the Secretary of State set up a committee of inquiry in 1972 (chaired by Sir Alan Bullock) to investigate language standards in school. The Committee acted with due speed and the results were published as *A Language for*

Life in 1975 (DES Committee of Inquiry, 1975). The Tory administration was unable to act upon the recommendations since they appeared after the Tories had been voted out of office.

In sum, Tory proposals for a reorganization of education concentrated on non-compulsory education, for apparent expansionism with little financial commitment or inducement. The overriding concern was not with improvements to education but with the adequacy of spending on it. So the Tory attitude was one of fitting education, along with other public services, into a new system of economic management. Underlying this, however, was an ethic of individualism, as evinced by the approach to comprehensive education. One of the first actions of the Tory government in 1970 was to change, by what appeared to be minor amendments, the pattern of comprehensive education. This dramatically altered the relationship between parents and the state. The government rescinded circular 10/65 and replaced it with circular 10/70, which set out the new procedures for the approval of plans for the reorganization of secondary education. The basic change was that plans would not be considered LEA by LEA but school by school (Saran, 1973). Objections to a plan previously were only considered if they focused on the balance between schools. By circular 10/70, objections could be raised about changes to one school which would in effect allow for objections to the reorganization of grammar schools. The main objectors probably would be parents, if the legal evidence of the previous five years were an indication. There had been three major court cases over these issues (Fowler *et al.*, 1973). This Tory change of procedure, therefore, allowed for parents to compete with each other over the system of local schooling. A grammar school parents' association, or PTA, could effectively put an end to plans for a fully, that is, LEA-wide, comprehensive system of secondary education. Thus some parents – those with children currently in grammar schools – would have a greater role in educational decision-making. The status quo of a tri- or bipartite system of education was deemed to carry more weight than an educational change. And, indeed, this proved to be the case. A section of the 1944 Act was invoked to prevent Surrey County Council from disallowing pupils in one comprehensive school catchment area from taking the 11-plus examination. Section 68 allowed the Minister to prevent the 'unreasonable' exercise of powers by LEAs. Thus the parents of some pupils were allowed to opt for selective education. Indeed, the whole thrust of this Tory administration was to support a selective group of parents and only allow LEAs to act against parental wishes (section 76) if unreasonable public expense would be incurred.

Indirectly, in another sense, too, some parents were afforded more responsibilities and influence in the early 1970s. This was because the Tory administration allowed for the raising of the school-leaving age to 16 in 1972–3; a measure promised almost 30 years earlier and postponed several times in the 1960s. Extending the years of schooling inevitably extended the time that children would be dependent upon their parents and, therefore, the amount of influence that parents could exert over them. With this raising of the school-leaving age, there was a good deal less consensus of opinion about its obvious benefits than the previous compulsory extensions of education. In particular, the schoolchildren affected did not appreciate the purpose of such a measure and were unable to accommodate themselves to the notion of long-term benefits. Nor did they, as a whole, appear to appreciate the short-run gains (White and Brockington, 1978).

Equality of educational opportunity: the early Labour approach

On the whole, educational policy was not of great moment to the Tory government. Initially, the first Labour government of 1974 was far more concerned with pursuing specific educational objectives. However, these were very soon followed by a period of severe economic retrenchment out of which a policy of educational curtailment and reduction appeared. Labour's ideological stance, as a result, was completely modified, to one of supporting parental rights rather than achieving equity between parents. In the first two years of Labour being in office attention reverted to the restructuring of secondary education, with the avowed aim of using education to achieve equality in adult life. Three different policy instruments were used with this object. First, circular 10/70 concerning approval of comprehensive schemes was replaced by circular 4/74, which merely reverted to the status quo ante (i.e. circular 10/65). This was seen to be a holding measure pending more drastic statutory action. Legislation did not occur until 1976. In the interim, steps were taken to extend the scope of the comprehensive principle from the maintained sector of schooling to the wider reaches of the public sector. The second policy change was that the government took up some of the recommendations of the two Public School Commissions that its Labour predecessor had appointed. Its policy initiatives were but a pale reflection of the Commissions' far-reaching proposals. The only schools that the government took action over were the direct-grant schools (176 in total). Together, the Commissions had been concerned with all public and independent schools (over 2000 in all) (Public Schools Commission, 1968). The reasons for Labour's caution were its slender parliamentary majority, the obvious Tory opposition, and the fact that this policy did not require any legislative change which might have provoked political controversy. All that the Labour government did was to withdraw, on a staggered basis, aid to those schools receiving grants both for individual pupils and for buildings direct from central rather than local government. The purpose of this action was to clarify the status of the public and private sectors in education and to ensure local (rather than diffuse central) control over public sector secondary education. The stated aim was to reduce privilege and ensure more equality in state education. In fact, the 1976 schools were given a choice over their future position in the educational structure – without a grant, either to enter the LEA system or to become independent of direct state aid. The latter still implied some measure of indirect state subsidy, in the fact that the schools all had charitable status and were exempt from certain taxes (a point which both Commissions had made much of) and that they had to be registered with the DES. The majority of the schools chose independence; only the Roman Catholic schools, which constituted slightly less than one-third of all the schools (Glennerster and Wilson, 1971), chose to come under LEA administration. Indeed, many of the other schools could not have come under LEA control had they wished to do so, for often the LEAs in whose areas they were located found their buildings inadequate and decrepit and their secondary school places superfluous to need. This was a portent for the future.

The effect of the measure was limited. It had been intended to stop LEAs selecting pupils for such schools. Nevertheless, some LEAs, particularly Tory-dominated ones, continued to use their powers under the Local Government Act (Hopkins, 1978) and the London Government Act 1963 (Sofer, 1978) to pay to send some able pupils to independent schools. The aim of the measure, to reduce distinctions between schools and pupils on the basis of academic ability, was not very effective.

In 1975 the government took a further step in this direction of reducing parental choice and privilege by drafting a Bill to legislate for comprehensive education and the banning of academic selection for secondary schools. The Bill itself was extremely brief but was one of the most contentious pieces of legislation in a highly controversial year. It was a year in which the House of Lords took the unprecedented step of trying to hold up six items of legislation, using this Bill as the scapegoat. They did not succeed, but three amendments allowing some measure of selection – for the artistically gifted, for the 'handicapped' and to ensure academic balance by means of banding – were included. So the notion of equal education on social grounds was once again watered down and confused with the notion of 'comprehensive' as a spread across ability ranges. The issue of what constituted comprehensive education clearly was not resolved through the Act, and, although progress towards comprehensive education throughout the 1970s has been inexorable, if terminology only is any guide it is not on any one common basis. Moreover, the Education Act of 1976 was mainly concerned with the maintained sector and not with the independent and private sector of education. It did, however, include clauses to prevent LEAs selecting pupils and paying for their attendance at Independent schools, without permission from the Secretary of State for Education. Although the latter do not touch on the lives of the vast majority of children (95 per cent of all schoolchildren are in maintained schools), those children in private schools will thereby have access to the privileged jobs and become part of the ruling classes.

In its early years of office the Labour government's concentration in education was on secondary schooling. It did little for nursery, primary or higher education. If anything, LEA programmes for nursery education were reduced. The only change in higher education was in terms not of structure but access. Amendments, which did not require legislative endorsement, were made to the rules governing the distribution of maintenance allowances to students in higher education. Previously, only grants to students in higher education, not to those on advanced further education courses, had been mandatory. Grants for students in polytechnics and colleges of higher education now became mandatory, no longer discretionary.

However, most grants to students in further education remained discretionary (a point to which I return). The other development was in terms of the procedures for handling educational disadvantage: the government expanded and reorganized the administrative units in the DES to deal with this problem, partly as a response to the Bullock Report. Here, it concerned itself rather more with the question of the status of immigrants as disadvantaged and sought to devise methods to detect underachievement. The thrust of the Tory concern had been with educational standards. Labour took this forward and, in the context of the increasingly sophisticated managerial techniques being used in government, tried to develop a network of agencies concerned with ensuring the adequacy of all school performance, not only that of immigrant groups.

Labour's concern with education and efficiency

Indeed, as the decade wore on, official concern with the effectiveness of the education system became more and more strident. The Tories had made the first step in the direction of mounting systems of administration that would ensure the adequacy of education. Labour carried this forward, at first tentatively and then, as the economic recession began to bite, more vigorously. Concern with educational standards and the nature of education became paramount. Pressure had been mounting from extra-Parliamentary groups, especially those loosely affiliated with the Tories, for example, those grouped around the Black Papers (Hopkins, 1978). Hall (1979) has argued that the Tories here 'gained territory if not power'. By 1976, the concern of the Labour government to use education as a panacca for social and economic ills began to dominate the political agenda. Initially, a team of HMIs was commissioned to review educational standards in schools. Before their report was ready for publication it was leaked to the press and later became known, infamously, as the 'Yellow Paper'. Since this documented considerable school difficulties, the need for an official public statement on the state of schools became vital. Less than a month later, in early October 1976, the Prime Minister, James Callaghan, in a speech at Ruskin College, Oxford, launched what he called The Great Debate on Education. This was to be a public (never well-defined) discussion of the purposes of education and the relationship between education and the economy. In particular, there was to be debate over the ways in which education prepared children for the labour market and for jobs. The debate, however, was not only to concern itself with the aims but also to consider the nature of educational control. In stating the contours of the debate Callaghan promised:

> There will be a discussion . . . I repeat that parents, teachers, learned and professional bodies, representatives of higher education, on both sides of industry, together with the government, have an important part to play . . .

In this proposal (see David, 1978b) the control of education was modified. Until this point neither parents nor teachers had been included separately in the traditional educational discourse. More important, perhaps, was the inclusion of industrialists. This pointed up the concern to make the links between education and industry much more explicit. This became more obvious as the wheels of the debate were set in motion. First, the debate was never really what it purported to be. It eventually consisted of six regional, invited-audience discussions of a rigidly defined, prepared agenda. DES officials were common to all six debates; so, too, were some of the invited audiences. All categories of participant mentioned by Callaghan contributed but only by invitation. Secondly, and at this juncture more important, the discussions were limited to the issue of the relationship between education and industry. Published agenda were the basis.

The Great Debate was mainly concerned with aspects of compulsory schooling. There was little thought given to nursery or higher education, save in so far as they were implicated by the issue of compulsion. For instance, the whole question of the nature of teacher training was raised in connection with improvements in the curriculum. Mainly the focus was on what children should be taught and to what end. The five areas spelt out were: curriculum and teaching method, school and work, assessment of standards, education and training of teachers. The formal debate lasted for about six months, after which the government undertook to prepare policy proposals. The object of the proposals was to reorient the direction of education and create a new constituency of control. This, of course, was alongside the normal running of the schools. The regional discussions did not resolve all the issues and a number of circulars and discussion documents were prepared for LEAs early in 1977. For instance, the question of what information schools should prepare for parents was the subject of one exploratory circular. The HMIs were also requested to spell out good school practices and did so in a pamphlet entitled *Ten Good Schools* (DES, 1977b). This detailed school organization and systems of control as well as curricula.

By mid-1977 the government felt able to put out a Green Paper for further discussion, summarizing the points made in the Great Debate and pointing towards a reconstruction of education (DES, 1977a). Indeed, there was little new in *Education in Schools: A Consultative Document*. It was essentially a restatement and extension of the Great Debate, but focused partly on parental involvement and educational efficiency. It pointed to Labour's concern with both the need to ensure the accountability and efficacy of the education system and the satisfaction of parents. Parents were mentioned in the introduction, where it was argued that 'parents should be given much more information about schools and should be consulted more widely' but discussion was deferred until the publication of the Taylor Committee's findings. But, in the body of the Green Paper, special attention was given to parents. It was stated (ibid., p. 28) that:

> The group most deeply involved with the school must always be the parents . . . *Parents* – and the pupils themselves – *have a right to know* how well the pupils are doing in different parts of their school work, and to have information on their conduct, attendance and application. Parents for their part *should have the opportunity to comment* on how their children are developing and to make any observations they wish about the school . . . There is also a *place* in the system for *parents collectively* [my emphasis].

In fact, Labour never acted upon two of these three principles. The 'right to know' was embodied in a circular, and subsequently in the ill-fated Bill; 'the opportunity to comment' was not elaborated; 'a place . . . collectively' was put into the Bill, if by that was meant parent representation on governing bodies, but this was never clarified.

Much of this was left in abeyance pending the publication of the Committee of Inquiry report on governors and managers (Taylor Report, 1977). Several discussion papers and circulars later and over a year after the Green Paper, in the autumn of 1978, the government finally drafted a Bill which would give some substance to the debate and to the Committee of Inquiry's proposals. By now the country was definitely in a period of severe economic retrenchment, and the Bill did not envisage any extensions to education. Moreover, the debate over control had been something of a 'charade' – parents were vouchsafed little more than a nominal say, and only as individuals. No new mechanisms were devised to allow for the collective representation of parents. The Bill never reached the statute books.

Involving parents in the control of education

The Committee of Inquiry, chaired by Taylor, which dealt with the question of how individual schools should be governed, was formed before the Great Debate was set in motion: in the spring of 1975. In one sense it had a narrow remit – to consider the management and government of maintained primary and secondary schools. The pressure for such a consideration had been steadily mounting from the 1960s onwards, when participation had been a key political slogan for the left, especially for those who felt excluded from traditional political discourse (David, 1975, 1978a and b). The main pressure – to ensure more adequate representation in the running of schools – was somewhat divided between the demand for more parental involvement and that of making schools more relevant to the needs of the community and the labour force in particular. Among the specific grievances to be considered was the fact that local government reorganization had distanced schools from their main locus of control, the LEA. In that process both teachers and educational professionals had been given less say, along with the community of which the school was a part. Middle-class parents, and mothers in particular, wanted to express their concern for the direction of school policy as well as for their individual rights over their children. The economic crisis had exacerbated parental concern for individual children's success, especially in a rapidly shrinking labour market, and non-working middle-class mothers were more available to articulate their worries.

The Taylor Committee had been set up to solve the conflicting problems of lay, parental and professional control over aspects of education. By 1975, the demands for some new organization of school management could not easily be ignored. The terms of reference of the Taylor Committee were therefore not as narrow as they appeared to be, for it had to consider the relationship between the community, the LEA, teachers and parents. Nevertheless, it was not given any power to consider a changed form of LEA control. Moreover, the selection of the 24 members of the Committee demonstrated that the government expected a report which balanced the demands for involvement of a number of competing and conflicting groups and interests. Three mothers were appointed as the parent members, all of them professional, middle-class women. (It is significant that no fathers were chosen to represent parents *per se*.) Five teachers were appointed, three of whom were headteachers and one a deputy. Only one was a classroom teacher.

The report which ensued from the Committee's two years of deliberation was balanced (Taylor Report, 1977). It covered specifically the composition and functions of governing bodies. The majority of the Committee wished to stick closely to its remit and *reform* rather than retain (or, more dramatically, replace or rescind) the existing system of managing and governing bodies. One member of the Committee opposed the proposals and wrote a separate, brief, minority report. Other members added what they termed 'a note of extension' in which they argued for a clearer definition of parental rights.

The main theme was that there should be 'a clear line of delegated power running from the LEA through the governing body to the head and staff of the school'. Every school required a body to manage its own affairs. Because of past confusion over titles and types of organization, the Committee proposed one kind of body, with one distinctive name – governing body. The composition and functions of the body were also clearly designated.

The Committee was faithful to its terms of reference on composition. The four sets of people mentioned in the terms of reference were to make up the governing body. These were representatives of LEAs, the local community, *parents* and teachers. In defining how these groups should compose the governing body, the Committee relied on the practice of one LEA whose chief education officer happened to be a member of the Committee. The novel proposal was that there should be equal proportions of each group on the governing body. This is what Taylor himself subsequently called 'power sharing'. The Committee did not consider the different proportions or balances of each group within the educational process. It assumed that each group should be given equal weight in decision-making.

The Committee did, however, consider that each group was not homogeneous and was difficult to define. First, it believed that parents were to be represented on the governing body as proxies for their own children, who were the actual consumers of education. The age at which children could make their own judgements about their educational fare exercised the Committee. The DES tried to block the idea that children should participate in the governing body by arguing, in its evidence, that the question was not valid: children were not entitled to hold public office until they reached eighteen years, the legal age of majority. Schoolchildren would have to be excluded from the governing body. The Committee was not content with this advice and proposed that pupils over the age of 16 should either be able to serve as governors, if the law could easily be changed, or, failing that, be observers. If children over 16 became governors, they would replace some parental representatives.

The Committee suggested ways in which the representatives of the four groups might be selected for the governing body. Two sets were to be elected on a regular basis from, respectively, the current body of parents and teaching staff in the school. Pupils and ancillary staff, where needed, would be chosen in the same way, but only in large schools. The LEA and community representatives would be appointed. The method for appointing LEA representatives was not to be changed from existing practice.

In the process of clarifying the work of governing bodies, the Committee tried to modify the existing power relationships. In particular, it sought to delegate from LEAs to governing bodies some of the responsibility for teacher appointments, admissions policy, pupil treatment and some financial control, especially over buildings. The change in power here was to be slight. The Committee wanted the governing body to be consulted but not to have the power of ultimate decision. What Fulton, the dissenter, regarded as the essential object of existing policy, 'a restoration of confidence in our schools by parents and the community', could be achieved only if the following aims were fulfilled:

> Firstly, that there is a good return on the massive investment in education. Secondly, that the people in the education service are competent to identify and provide for the needs of children to fit them for life after school. Thirdly, that the schools can be made more accountable.

None of these goals, according to Fulton, would be achieved by the insertion of this tier of government. He therefore did not want any change in power relationships. Parents' interests were, for him, not about control but 'very much more immediate and personal and it all boils down to how the school affects their child'.

The seven members who wrote a note of extension would concur with this last point. Their aim was to give individual parents more information about each school. To this end, they asked that there be a further change in the law to give 'each individual parent the right in law to the information relevant to the performance of his legal duty'. They added that this access to information should not be construed as 'access to classrooms, teachers or written material except in accordance with the arrangements made by the school and approved by the governors'. They also did not want a further change in power relationships but merely that the schools be more explicitly accountable, especially to parents.

In fact, the Taylor Committee did not establish the case for parental involvement in the control of schools. It argued that the 'consumer' had a right to have a say but this did not necessarily mean that the 'consumer' should work alongside the 'producer' – the LEA and its teachers – in the running of schools. The Committee did not consider that it might be inappropriate to combine these groups into a single body to run the schools. It might be more appropriate to create two bodies to give advice to the LEAs, who are ultimately legally responsible, one composed of teachers (an academic board) and one of consumers, who would be able to act merely as a sounding-board of parental feeling. It was another Taylor (1972) who originally sounded the first warning note on joint bodies. In addition, the case was not made convincingly that parents were the legitimate consumers. Indeed, the Committee did argue, confusingly, that so too were pupils and the local community, composed variously of employers, industrialists and trade unionists. The Committee did not establish the relative claims of parents and the community over the lives of the pupils in schools. If anything, it confused the previous, relatively clear view that children in the state sector of education were, for educational purposes, more the property of the state than of their parents.

However, the Taylor Committee's deliberations were rather overtaken by the pace of events: and yet more strident public pressure for a clear parental role in education, linked with the demands for a clearer system of educational public accountability. Thus, whilst the government was formulating legislative action on both the Taylor Committee's recommendations and the Great Debate, it issued new regulations concerning schools' relationships with parents. Two circulars were published in late 1977. One formalized the information that schools were expected to give to both prospective and participating parents: what might be termed a prospectus. It was explicit in its concern to satisfy parents, although the draft circular of July 1977 listed items which should '*normally* be made available to parents' (my emphasis). The actual circular repeated that phrase and asked LEAs to draw up 20 items of *written* information about its individual schools for public consumption. The other (circular 14/77) retreated on the likely commitment to parental participation in schools, arguing that:

> the proper functioning of the educational system in England and Wales depends on the effective co-operation of the schools, their teachers and their governors and managers; the local education authorities; and the Secretaries of State with their departments and HM Inspectorate. The Secretaries of State have no intention of changing this position which reflects the provisions of the Education Acts. At the same time they recognise the legitimate interests of others – *parents*, industry and commerce, for example – in the work of schools [my emphasis].

However, it required LEAs to provide

> systematic information about curricular arrangements in local authority areas throughout England and Wales. This will enable the Secretaries of State to assess how far the practice of local education authorities meets national needs and will assist in the

> preparation of future educational plans, particularly for the training, recruitment and employment of teachers. The information collected will also be of value to their partners in the education system and to the Schools Council.

Legislative action on the policy debates and discussions was a long time in the making because of internal Cabinet disagreement over the extent of parental control and choice in secondary schooling. This was also confounded by the political objective of using education as a panacea for youth employment problems.

Labour's approach to education and the economy

As has already been argued, the Great Debate attempted to clarify and develop the relationship between education and the economy. However, the discussion here was in terms of a long-term strategy. At the same time, concern was expressed for a much more immediate problem – that of dealing with youth unemployment, in particular, the growing army of unemployed school-leavers. Initial solutions to the problem of unemployment had been based within the Department of Employment and schemes such as the Job Creation Programme had been devised. Although in some instances new jobs or created jobs might rely on the LEAs, as with other departments of the local authority, LEAs were not directly implicated in solutions. As the problem did not abate but became increasingly large, further consideration was given to it. In the first instance, the Manpower Services Commission (MSC) set up a review body to consider the parameters of the issue. The DES and representatives of the LEAs were involved in this review. The Holland Committee (Manpower Services Commission, 1977) considered the various ramifications of the problem and suggested several additions to the existing solutions of 'on-the-job' training. First, it proposed to separate two groups of young people – the 16- to 19-year-olds and those 20 and older – for whom two different programmes were to be developed. One package for the 16- to 19-year-olds would involve special job-training schemes, which could and might be conducted under the auspices of the education service, especially in colleges of further education. Those attending such courses would be entitled to a flat-rate maintenance grant from the MSC. This would also apply to the jobs created under the Youth Opportunities Programme and to those in the STEP schemes.

This proposal raised problems of equity with provisions within the education system. Different grant schemes existed for children who remained at school past the statutory school-leaving age and for those attending courses in the further education sector. However, neither the Educational Maintenance Allowance (EMA) scheme for school pupils nor the grants for further education were either automatic or at the level of subsistence. EMAs were discretionary awards and subject to a test of parental means. The intention was very explicitly and well expressed by the parliamentary Expenditure Committee (1974) which investigated EMAs in 1974:

> 16- to 18-year olds today make many more decisions about their ways of life than they once did . . . but we do not regard them as having the right of independent choice where their education is concerned any more than they enjoy, as minors, independence in the eyes of the law; nor should they look upon the EMA as a substitute for wages.
>
> We are equally sure that nothing we recommend should tend to undermine the responsibility of parents for bringing up their children . . . We endorse the words of the 1944 Act: the purpose of EMAs is 'to enable pupils to take advantage without hardship to themselves or their parents of any educational facilities available to them'.

In fact, the level of allowance, even without regard to parental means, varied enormously throughout the country. The same was true of awards to study in further education: both the level and the granting of the award itself varied throughout the country. Again, this award was based upon a system of partial help to enable a student to continue in education, regardless of parental means or circumstances. It was not intended that the grant would be equivalent to a living (if minimum) wage. This differed enormously from the objectives of the MSC grant, which was, in any case, never aimed at the same target group of 16- to 18-year-olds.

The DES and LEAs were willing to co-operate with the MSC and its plans to solve the youth unemployment problem, but at the same time they began to consider ways of incorporating job training into the education system and, moreover, of allowing for automatic entitlement to both courses and grant aid. Thus, the educational politicians tried to get onto the agenda a scheme of EMAs for *all* 16- to 19-year-olds who chose to stay within the education system. However, the proposed level of EMA was to be lower than the award offered by the MSC and was to be subject to a test of parental means. In other words, the scheme was a plan to increase the years of dependency on both education and parents, rather than to provide a system of early help with work. So far, the scheme has founded on bureaucratic grounds – the conflict between the DES and the Department of Employment (DE) for resources to finance the scheme. The implications of the EMA scheme are that it would extend the powers of education, and commensurably reduce the powers of the DE. At the same time it would also increase parental influence and parental responsibilities.

Labour's attempt at educational legislation

The 1978 Education Bill, which never reached the statute books because of the general election in May 1979, was the culmination of Labour's educational initiatives. It brought together the twin concerns of the four years of Labour administration – parental involvement in education and the links between education and the economy. The emphasis, however, was on the former rather than the latter. It did not even consider the question of equality but focused on how to achieve economic efficiency. The Bill related to three issues of parental involvement: school government, school admissions and school attendance. As regards education and the economy it only sought to legislate for EMAs for 16- to 19-year-olds and, initially, only on the basis of a pilot scheme. The details of the proposed legislation were as follows. The clauses on school government took up the Taylor Committee's proposals in a modified fashion. They only related to the composition and type of governors. They did not concern the functions or the workings of governing bodies. In respect of composition, the Bill proposed that each governing body (and this was to become the generic term for such bodies for primary and secondary schools) would include representatives of the LEA, teachers and parents. The LEA representatives were to be appointed by the LEA (in the traditional manner), the teacher representatives to be elected by the teachers in the school and the parents to be elected by the parents of children currently in the school. Four other *types* of governor were also mentioned: representatives of the voluntary foundation if that were the kind of school; representatives of the minor authority for a primary school if it existed in such a situation; for secondary schools only, appointed members of the community; and the fourth type was a major official concession – the possibility of pupil governors, but only of those pupils aged 16 or over. The Bill stressed that the future usual practice would be for *every* school to have its own governing body but LEAs could apply to the Secretary of State for Education for special dispensation to group governing bodies. The clauses on school government therefore showed a major shift in Labour principles towards the sharing of school control with teachers and parents. The most important change was the incorporation of parent representatives into school government. This was at least an indication of how Labour had reneged on the principle of equality of educational opportunity, in that they now allowed some parental voice in decisions about education. However, traditional governors have had few real controlling powers and have acted rather as a system of support for the school and a mediator between school and LEA. Since the functions of governors were not to change it may be that the Labour government regarded the inclusion of parents as a concession to the growing parental lobby and more as a symbol than a real sharing of power.

The other main parental issue included in this proposed piece of legislation was over the admission of pupils to particular schools. As regards secondary schools, the Tories have always made much political capital out of whether sufficient parental 'choice' is provided, especially in a system of comprehensive schooling. Under the existing legislation (the 1944 Education Act), schools – either primary or secondary – were to be provided in accordance with parental 'wishes', and yet with regard to the principle of 'the avoidance of unreasonable public expenditure'. It was this latter, more general issue that the Labour government sought to clarify in the proposed legislation, rather than the more specific question of the distribution of particular kinds of secondary school. The Bill suggested new terminology – parental 'wishes' were to be replaced by parental 'preferences' and 'unreasonable expenditure' became 'efficient use of financial resources' or simply 'efficient education'. To elaborate, the Bill required each school to be clearer about the numbers of pupils to be admitted each year and, crucially, how that complement should be chosen. The main new criterion of admission was to be *parental preference*, the clause expressing it as follows:

> Every LEA shall make arrangements for enabling the *parent* of a child to *express a preference* as to the school at which *he* wishes education to be provided for his child in the exercise of the authority's functions and to give reasons for his preference [my emphasis].

In essence, this clause merely restated the existing legal principle, except that, instead of parental wishes *en masse* being regarded, *each individual parent* was now to be vouchsafed a *say* in *his* child's schooling. So a new right was to be created. But, unfortunately, the rest of the legislative draft detracted from that principle. The LEAs' responsibilities to comply were hedged around with modifying conditions, which again, in essence, were the same as hitherto, namely 'the avoidance of unreasonable public expenditure'. There were to be four conditions for non-compliance:

(i) if the LEA believed the preference to be contrary to the interests of the child;
(ii) if the preference *either* prejudiced the provision of *efficient education* in the preferred school,
or prejudiced the provisions of *efficient education* in the area of the LEA,
or the preference prejudiced the *efficient use of financial* resources available to the LEA [my emphasis];
(iii) if the child was from outside the LEA and prejudiced one inside the LEA;
(iv) if the school operated selection of pupils according to the principles of the 1976 Education Act and the child was incompatible with them.

In other words, the LEA was afforded *discretion* to evaluate parental preferences either according to the criterion of efficiency (financial or educational) or according to the status or needs of the child. Point (ii) might be as vague as the old principle had been, but points (i), (iii) and (iv) allowed the LEA even more 'let-outs' than hitherto. However, under another sub-clause, parents were given the *right of appeal* (my emphasis) against an adverse decision on the part of the school governors or LEA, first to the LEA and ultimately to the Secretary of State for Education. And LEAs were required to ensure that parents did not express their preferences in ignorance of the schools available. LEAs were to be required to publish annual information about their own maintained schools and those schools they used which were either maintained by another LEA or were voluntary schools. This information was to be extensive – on the size limits of the school, the admissions policy and role of the governors and LEA and the circumstances under which out-county pupils would be admitted. In addition, the terms under which school attendance orders were to be issued were to be modified according to parental preference. Again, this set of clauses appeared to be creating new individual parental rights, but they were to be severely limited and restricted and in all probability would not alter the real situation drastically. The main change would be that all parents would be given a *say* over the school to which they would send their children!

The third set of clauses bearing on parental rights were somewhat more indirect, relating to financial awards and grants. The Labour government proposed, first, to introduce a *pilot scheme* to provide educational maintenance allowances (EMAs) to all 16- to 18-year-olds continuing in, or resuming, full-time education and, second, to extend the list of courses in higher education. Although no date was set for the commencement of the schemes and no details of the level of award set, both impinged upon parental rights. In particular, the introduction of EMAs purportedly allowed pupils to remain in, or resume, schooling or further education regardless of parental financial conditions. But EMAs did not provide pupils with the right to a 'wage'. They allowed each parent the right not to prevent his child from benefiting from the education system – by providing a small grant which would be varied according to parental financial means. In other words, financial hardship should no longer dissuade pupils from extending their education. Again, this parental right was neither absolute nor generous. According to the discussions prior to the drafting of the Bill, the grant would only allow parents to avoid dire pecuniary stress : it would not be large, or near subsistence level. For example, it would not compare with either the level of supplementary benefit for that age group or the awards provided through the Manpower Services Commission for young people undergoing courses of basic skills while technically unemployed.

The Bill was also used in an attempt to tidy up other aspects of educational legislation and here, too, it indicated a changed direction of educational aims. First, it allowed for nursery school teachers to work in nurseries provided through the DHSS and yet remain in the education service. This enabling clause was important for the new direction of preschool provisions. Secondly, provision was made for advanced further education to be under central direction, through the establishment of a Council for England and one for Wales. Indeed, Welsh education was to be enhanced by yet another provision, the payment of grants for courses taught in the Welsh language. This would allow for the separate development of Wales and Welsh education. Finally, the Bill reiterated the fact that the Sex Discrimination and Race Relations Acts applied to the education service, including the provisions of the Bill.

Parental rights in education: the Tory view

Thus, by 1979 the issues of concern to both Tory and Labour administrations had been brought together, if briefly, in one major Education Bill. Although the Tories, in opposition, voiced objections to specific aspects of the Bill, its concerns were in general those that the Tories had put into the political agenda. They certainly were not traditional Labour objectives. In fact, the Tories, on regaining power in the general election of 1979, acted very swiftly to develop their own educational legislation, claiming it to be a reversal of all that Labour had stood for. The 1979 Education Act, passed into law in July 1979, was, as the new Secretary of State for Education, Mark Carlisle, himself argued in Parliament, 'simple in scope . . . its sole purpose is to remove the compulsion placed on local authorities and governors of voluntary schools to reorganize their schools on comprehensive lines.' It aimed to rescind the Labour government's 1976 Education Act, which required LEAs to reorganize their secondary schools on comprehensive lines.

The arguments in the Act's favour were neither simple nor lacking in contradiction. The reason for repealing Labour measures was that they were 'solely about compulsion . . . not about the quality of education or standards . . . Parents – not politicians – should be given the opportunity to choose schools best suited to their children.' He then added:

> Above all, those areas which have fought hard to retain their grammar schools should be allowed to do so. We are not prepared to stand by and allow the destruction of schools which have proved their worth against the wishes of local people.

He was thus making it clear that the Act was not a charter for *all* parents but for those parents whose children proved academically able to attend grammar schools – traditionally, 20 per cent at most of the relevant age group. Moreover, those LEAs who chose to 'go comprehensive' would not be afforded the same 'freedom of choice' as those reintroducing selection at 11: curiously (given the principle of parental choice), their plans would have to be vetted both by politicians *and* at central government level, i.e. by the Secretary of State for Education. In addition, however, he said that he would introduce another Bill, 'in which choice of parents and the needs of their children will be a central feature'. The contents of this Bill were to be revealed at the end of October 1979, and were likely, save for the question of comprehensive schools, to mirror those of the Labour Bill. For a new government the issue of parental rights in education had at least a prompt preliminary resolution.

Although the Tories here appear to be *the* advocates of parental rights, this was not the complete picture. The Labour government, while in office from 1974 to 1979, also did much to legislate for parental rights in education. It, too, was sectarian in its choice of which parents to favour, while, like the Tories in political rhetoric appearing to favour *all* parents. Labour's policies were a good deal more extensive although ultimately not so legally effective. At least five policy prescriptions, at different levels of legislative effect, had had a bearing on the issue.

The context for educational revision

What was the context in which these new policy objectives developed?

At the beginning of the 1970s, public discussion, as expressed in the media, was focused upon the question of educational direction and educational standards. These topics were raised not by politicians of either political party but by intellectuals and academics outside the traditional political arena. In a series of pamphlets, of which the first two appeared in 1969, they argued that standards in school were falling: there was increased violence, truancy and indiscipline and progressive methods were the root cause of the problems. Why the pamphlets, called Black Papers, should have received so much media attention is a question that is still being asked and still requires an adequate answer. One set of explanations is to be found in Adam Hopkins' *The School Debate* (1978). He argued, that, first, according to Cox, one of the main pamphleteers, many teachers 'secretly, almost guiltily . . . knew that informal methods were not working' (ibid., p. 85). The implication was that they supported the fears about educational decline expressed in the pamphlets. Secondly, the articles in the pamphlets were written by entertaining writers. Thirdly, their alarmist facts and figures attracted much attention and enabled people's positions to be polarized into traditional or progressive. The fourth, and most important, reason was that the then Secretary of State for Education, Edward Short, a former headmaster, allowed the first Black Paper to become 'an educational bestseller' by stating to the NUT that its publication day was 'one of the blackest days for education in the past one hundred years' and that the backlash against progressive education had created 'the crisis of the century'. Nigel Wright in *Progress in Education*, although reviewing the evidence of the Black Papers, did not attempt to explain why that evidence, which he claimed 'reveals a staggering number of errors, inaccuracies and misrepresentations' (1977) became the talking point of the decade.

Other explanations for the popularity of the ideas and their later political acceptance may be found in the changing economic climate. From the Second World War on, there had been a steady improvement in living standards and changes in the composition of the labour force. In particular, the service sector of the economy began to expand and jobs became increasingly available. Women, and especially married women, began to be employed in the organized labour force in increasing numbers. By the early 1970s, however, this trend to improvement was slowing down and an economic crisis was beginning to be felt: jobs were scarcer and the unemployment rate rose dramatically throughout the 1970s. A concomitant of the rising standards of living in the 1950s and 1960s was rising expectations and aspirations, generated through increased educational opportunities. By the end of the 1960s it was clear that not everyone's aspirations would be fulfilled. Many of the aspirations were for parents to provide equivalent educational opportunities for their children. The frustrations of potentially blocked aspirations began to find political expression in the field of education – and this may go some way to explaining the popularity of the Black Paper critique, confused though it was.

The discussion of declining standards and the consequences of progressivism in education was certainly not an isolated incident in the early 1970s. The Black Papers sparked off a considerable backlash of criticism of the educational status quo. Two other major events illustrate the impact that such ideas were beginning to have in educational politics. One was the fight, with the Inner London Education Authority (ILEA), at the William Tyndale Junior School. The other was the controversy over comprehensive schooling in the Tameside LEA. Both events were about standards, direction and also control in education, and both took as a basic assumption parental involvement in schooling. Indeed, both events and the Black Paper controversies illustrated the increasing parental lobby in educational politics: but this lobby was not one of all parents, merely some middle-class parents. The events at the William Tyndale Junior School have been well researched elsewhere (Auld, 1976; Ellis *et al.*, 1976; Gretton and Jackson, 1976). The remarkable point, which has not been very well documented elsewhere, was that the fight over standards, progressivism and indiscipline was initiated not by officials or school managers but by *parents* and most especially mothers, concerned solely about their own children's schooling. I have discussed this issue at length (see David, 1978a). It signalled a new, and what was now considered legitimate, involvement of mothers in the running of schools. Hitherto, as Baron and Howell showed (1974), parents were not even regularly given a say on governing or managing bodies. The parents of some children at the William Tyndale school not only were able, without the traditional political means or channels, to raise the issue to hysterical proportions but got a public inquiry and, far more important, had the teachers sacked for indiscipline. (Of course, the mothers were initially fighting about pupil rather than teacher indiscipline.) The dispute brought together two of the three major concerns of the 1970s – standards and control. It also, as Roger Dale (1979) has argued, 'was not the cause but merely the occasion of the major changes in the English education system – the current restructuring and redirection'. Indeed, it was around the time of the setting up of the public inquiry into the William Tyndale dispute (Auld, 1976) that the Taylor Committee was established. The 'Yellow Paper' on standards was leaked to the press at the same time as the Auld Report was published. Both government initiatives were justified in terms of wishing to respond to the educational crisis provoked and to prevent further Tyndale-like problems. Taylor himself claimed that, with his proposals, 'another Tyndale situation could not arise.'

The first Tameside incident was also an escalation of the issues raised in the Black Papers. This event, too, has been discussed fully in other literature (Griffith, 1976). The Tory councillors' reversal in 1976 of local Labour policies to achieve comprehensive education in the Tameside LEA was both a reaction to the restructuring of education and a reinforcement of the increasingly overt Tory policy of supporting parental involvement in education. The opposition to comprehensive education was justified on the grounds that parents would be denied freedom of choice in education. In this incident, as in all similar anti-comprehensive schooling cases and as Nigel Wright has so eloquently argued, the concern was never with all parents, or, for that matter, all children. It was to preserve parental choice for, at most, 20 per cent of parents of 11-year-olds in the LEA. Wright has stated (1977) that 'the paradox of this [Tameside] exercise in freedom of parental choice was that 560 families had their choice rejected, while 240 were accepted'. He added in criticism of the general Tory position about problems created by comprehensive schools 'to disappoint 5 per cent is better than to disappoint 70 per cent, but have we the right to disappoint any parent?' In fact, he argued that the figures of disappointment in Tameside were an underestimate since, first, only 800 parents applied for grammar school places and, secondly, 'all the researches indicated that a majority of parents would have liked their child to go to a grammar school – not surprisingly'. In a footnote, he cited a *New Society* survey of 1967, which 'found that only 10 per cent of parents would choose a secondary modern school for their child'. So, presumably, even those parents in Tameside who did not apply for a grammar school place were to some extent disappointed: hardly an indication of parental choice and satisfaction with a bipartite system of education. Nevertheless, the issue raised in the media was Labour's dogmatism and Tory fairness with regard to educational provision. Comprehensive schools were attacked, of course, not only because they prohibited parental choice but also because they perpetrated a decline in standards and indiscipline. The comparison was always between grammar schools and comprehensives and not between comprehensives and secondary modern schools. In fact, as Wright has convincingly demonstrated, comprehensive schools, for all their faults, have not contributed to a decline in standards; nor, of course, have they been any more than marginally the reason for the improvement in standards (measured by examination results) that has occurred in the last two decades.

The resolution of the Tameside dispute in the courts in August 1976, in favour of the Tories, provided an occasion for Labour response. Indeed, the Secretary of State for Education was replaced in the summer of 1976, perhaps as a result of the government's defeat, and the 'Yellow Paper' was leaked to the press shortly after the House of Lords pronounced on the Tameside appeal.

The other underlying contextual factor throughout the 1970s was the rapidly escalating economic crisis which created rising unemployment. As the decade wore on, unemployment became more and more concentrated amongst one sector of the population – school-leavers, especially (but not only) those leaving at the statutory age of 16. This required a government response! The first sets of responses were in terms of cutbacks in public expenditure, particularly spending on education. These cuts inevitably provoked a massive and angry response especially in terms of local campaigns but no reduction in impact was planned by the government. It was only later in the decade that the response was positive and in terms of a restructuring and redirection of educational provision (discussed above).

Although the decade was characterized by unemployment, women's employment prospects did not fare as badly as men's, mainly because of the rigid sexual division of labour in the economy. In other words, women's jobs did not suffer the same vagaries of the economy. The main beneficiaries were mothers of school age, but also of preschool children. This change had an important impact on maternal or parental exercise of responsibilities, but there was no government initiative to modify maternal responsibilities. Indeed, working mothers were accused by the right-wing protesters of being responsible for the indiscipline in schools, because of their neglect of their children (see, for example, a circular sent to all parents in Avon in 1977 (County of Avon, 1977)).

Working mothers began to organize, demanding changes in the daily organization of schooling and in the nature of preschool provision. The impact of this movement was manifold: between 1976 and 1978 there was a flood of official documents suggesting changes in preschool provision and the hours of schooling. However, most of the discussion went on outside the formal system of education. The DHSS was, in fact, the first body to respond officially to the demands for day-care and government involvement in preschool provision. Its response was tempered – a preliminary survey (Office of Population Censuses and Surveys, 1977) and a conference to discuss 'low-cost day-care' in 1975. Out of this conference came some minimal DHSS and DES co-operation and a joint circular to local authorities recommending local co-operation between education and social services and with voluntary organizations. No money was proffered to make co-operation viable: the emphasis was placed on involvement of the voluntary sector. This initiative prompted more official proposals for extending preschool provision, but all these official reports were from only quasi-governmental organizations and as yet (1979) have had little impact on policy change. The TUC set up a working party to consider provision for the under-fives from the point of view of working mothers. It came up with some imaginative and important suggestions, such as work-based, government-sponsored facilities and local authority-employed child-minders. There has been no public debate about the proposals. The government's think-tank – the Central Policy Review Staff (CPRS) – also considered the question of day-care for the children of working mothers. It recommended, above all, greater co-ordination and information exchange between government departments, especially the DHSS and DES. The Equal Opportunities Commission (EOC), established in 1976 as a result of the Sex Discrimination Act of 1975, also considered the issue of day-care. First, it set up an investigation into the running of ten existing nurseries with a variety of controls. The report showed the feasibility of several different types of scheme. Second, the EOC published in autumn 1978 a small, vibrant pamphlet entitled, *I Want to Work, but What about the Kids?* (EOC, 1978). These recommendations went further than the others in linking preschool provision with after-school and holiday facilities. The report recognized the necessity of continuity in child-care responsibilities from preschool to school days. It highlighted the problems that ensue from school activities which affect mothers' involvement in the labour force, especially full-time work.

Although there has been a slow but steady build-up of recognition of the lacunae in day-care facilities, there has been little official development or response. The only minor step, from the point of view of the education service, was the legal recognition of the relationship between nurseries and nursery schools. A brief clause was inserted in the 1978 Education Bill to ensure that nursery-school teachers working in LA social services nurseries would not suffer any loss of status and would remain employees of LEAs (and therefore on teaching salary scales, which were higher than those for nursery nurses).

The traditional arrangements for schooling – hours of the day and school holidays – were not considered for amendment by the government despite demands to alter the nature of maternal responsibilities for schooling. On the contrary, as the economic crisis deepened, mothers' daily responsibilities for ensuring their children's schooling increased in a variety of ways. For example, working mothers were under attack for some of the problems of the educational system. Some LEAs actually formalized this attack. For instance, Avon LEA developed a 'contract' with parents to ensure that school problems would be reduced. There was an implicit assumption of constant maternal availability. Secondly, during strike action by low-paid workers such as school caretakers, which closed schools for days and weeks, mothers were forced to take as their first priority looking after their children. They were therefore unable to continue their employment satisfactorily.

Thirdly, some official responses to the problems of schooling have been to increase daily maternal responsibility rather than to modify the education system around the needs of working mothers. For example, the original schemes for the extension of nursery education in the early 1970s, embodied in circular 2/73, recommended parental participation as a key to the success of preschool education. This was based on the research findings that the 'home' was a more important influence on learning than the school. It was also assumed that mothers could be taught, through helping with their children at school, better standards of childcare. This direct involvement of mothers in the classroom has also begun to occur increasingly in primary schools, too.

As the 1970s began to draw to a close, educational debate moved into a further mood of pessimism. This was occasioned by the accumulation of startling demographic evidence of a rapid decline in the future numbers of schoolchildren, with the effects already being felt in some regions and some schools in the country (Mack, 1979). Instead of this being an occasion for the introduction of new educational schemes such as the extension of preschool facilities in the emptying primary schools, the development of community facilities in school buildings or a move towards recurrent rather than rigid education, it has been characterized by a traditionalist mood. This was summed up in February 1979 by the head of one comprehensive school arguing informally about 'how to save our curriculum, how to save our teachers and how to save our headteachers'. In sum, the 1970s have been notable for moves to reinforce the notion that children are the private property of their parents and yet of utilitarian value to the wider society.

It is still necessary to ask why Labour acceded to the right-wing pressures and went so far as to modify legislation to create new, individualistic parental rights. It must be pointed out that Labour, whatever its political rhetoric, has never been unequivocally the party of the working class or one espousing the principle of equality. Indeed, as was most cogently pointed out by Finn *et al.* (1977), there has been since the 1920s a duality in Labour ideology between efficiency and equality. For this reason Labour has always had an uneasy relationship with the working class and, in the field of education, with teachers. In previous decades, but especially in the 1960s, the path steered between these two poles has always been uneven. In the 1960s the party veered towards the goal of efficiency rather than that of equality. Labour educational policies in the 1970s may be seen as an extension, and reassertion, of the efficiency principle. Parents have been given the semblance of rights in the 1970s, not for their own sakes but because it was felt that they would then, in their own interests, encourage the development of improved educational standards and would help to lift the economy out of the recession. In other words, parents were to help reform the education system by pressing for better school standards. This, Labour believed, would contribute to stemming the economic recession. Attempting to legislate for parental rights in education was not without reason and was not blind reassertion of right-wing political ideas. It was because Labour believed that the involvement of parents in their own children's schooling would provide the solution to the economic crises of the past decade. In effect, parents were to be made individually responsible for the future of both their children and the economy. The state would be absolved from the full responsibility of the fiscal crises. So, by the end of the 1970s, ensuring the efficiency of the education system and the economy became both a parental right and a maternal duty.

References

AULD, R. (1976). *Report of the Inquiry into the William Tyndale Junior and Infants Schools*. London: ILEA.

BARON, J. and HOWELL, D. E. (1974). *The Government and Management of Schools*. London: Athlone Press.

BULLOCK REPORT. GREAT BRITAIN. DEPARTMENT OF EDUCATION AND SCIENCE (ENGLAND) (1975). *A Language for Life*. London: HMSO.

BYRNE, E. (1978). *Women and Education*. London: Tavistock.

COCKBURN, C. (1977). *The Local State: Management of Cities and People*. London: Pluto Press.

COUNTY OF AVON EDUCATION SERVICE (1977). External Influences and Pressures on Schools. Unpublished mimeo.

DALE, R. (1979). The Politicization of School Deviance: Reactions to William Tyndale. Unpublished paper. Milton Keynes: Open University.

DAVID, M. E. (1975). *School Rule in the USA. Professionalism and Participation in School Budgeting*. Cambridge, Mass.: Ballinger.

DAVID, M. E. (1978a). 'The family-education couple: towards the analysis of the William Tyndale dispute'. In: LITTLEJOHN, G. *et al.* (Eds) *Power and the State*. London: Croom Helm.

DAVID, M. E. (1978b). 'Parents and educational politics in 1977'. In: BROWN, M. and BALDWIN, S. (Eds) *Year Book of Social Policy in Britain*. London: Routledge and Kegan Paul.

DEPARTMENT OF EDUCATION AND SCIENCE (1972). *Education: A Framework for Expansion*. Cmnd 5174. London: HMSO.

DEPARTMENT OF EDUCATION AND SCIENCE (1977a). *Education in Schools: A Consultative Document*. Cmnd 6869. London: HMSO.

DEPARTMENT OF EDUCATION AND SCIENCE (1977b). *Ten Good Schools: A Secondary School Inquiry*. HMI Series No. 1. London: HMSO.

ELLIS, T. *et al.* (1976). *William Tyndale: The Teachers' Story*. London: Writers and Readers Publishing Co-operative.

EOC (1978). *I Want to Work but What about the Kids?* Manchester: Equal Opportunities Commission.

EXPENDITURE COMMITTEE (HOUSE OF COMMONS), EDUCATION AND ARTS SUB-COMMITTEE (1974). *Educational Maintenance Allowances in the 16–18 Years Age Group*. (Third Report). London: HMSO.

FINN, D. *et al.* (1977). 'Social democracy, education and the crisis'. In: *On Ideology*. Cultural Studies No. 10. Birmingham: Centre for Contemporary Cultural Studies.

FOWLER, G. *et al.* (Eds) (1973). *Decision-Making in Education*. London: Methuen.

GLENNERSTER, H. (1975). *Social Service Budgets and Social Policy*. London: Allen and Unwin.

GLENNERSTER, H. and WILSON, G. (1971). *Paying For Private Schools*. London: Allen Lane.

GRETTON, J. and JACKSON, M. (1976). *Collapse of a School or a System?* London: Allen and Unwin.

GRIFFITH, J. A. G. (1976). 'The Tameside opinion', *New Statesman*, 29 October.

HALL, S. (1979). 'The great moving right show', *Marxism Today*, 23, 1.

HOPKINS, A. (1978). *The School Debate*. London: Penguin.

MACK, J. (1979). 'Quality, not just quantity, for London's schools?', *New Society*, 47, 857, 8 March.

MANPOWER SERVICES COMMISSION (1977). *Young People and Work* (Holland Report). London: MSC.

New Society (1978). 'The World of Childhood', 46, 846–7, 21–8, December.

OPCS (1977). *Pre-School Children and the Need for Day-Care*. London: HMSO.

PLOWDEN REPORT. GREAT BRITAIN. DEPARTMENT OF EDUCATION AND SCIENCE. CENTRAL ADVISORY COUNCIL FOR EDUCATION (ENGLAND) (1967). *Children and their Primary Schools*. London: HMSO.

SARAN, R. (1973). *Policy-Making in Secondary Education: a Case Study*. Oxford: Clarendon Press.

SILVER, H. (1978). 'Education and public opinion', *New Society*, 46, 844, 7 December.

SMITH, T. (1972). *Anti-Politics*. London: Charles Knight.

SOFER, A. (1978). 'Educational arguments in 1977'. In: BROWN, M. and

BALDWIN, S. (Eds) *Year Book of Social Policy in Britain*. London: Routledge and Kegan Paul.

TAYLOR REPORT. GREAT BRITAIN. DEPARTMENT OF EDUCATION AND SCIENCE. WELSH OFFICE (1977). *A New Partnership for Our Schools*. London: HMSO.

TAYLOR, W. (1972). 'Family, school and society'. In: CRAFT, M. *et al.* (Eds) *Linking Home and School*. 2nd edition. London: Longman.

WHITE, R. and BROCKINGTON (1978). *In and Out of School: the ROSLA Community Education Project*. London: Routledge and Kegan Paul.

WRIGHT, N. (1977). *Progress in Education*. London: Croom Helm.

Part Two

Relations Between Parents and Teachers

From Compensation . . . to Participation? A Brief Analysis of Changing Attitudes in the Study and Practice of Home–School Relations

John Bastiani

Until a few years ago, it would have seemed quite reasonable to portray the field of home–school relationships as three very different, self-contained areas, each with its own characteristic approaches and outcomes.

First, there was an extensive *research* tradition, which grew in conjunction with the development of health, education and welfare services in post-war Britain. This tradition, firmly rooted in the context of an ideology of equal opportunity, can more recently be seen in the formulation of policies to meet special educational needs.

The second of three approaches within the home–school field was a sub-literature which grew not so much out of educational practice itself, as out of its *rhetoric*. This material reflected a growing public interest in education and a belief in its value (especially during the 1960s). It was accompanied by the steady expansion of the teaching profession with its premium upon good advice and positive experience, together with the beginnings of a new kind of professionalism amongst teachers. Written largely by 'elevated' practitioners, its style was uplifting, if somewhat idealistic, playing down both actual and perceived problems.

The third, very different, element consisted of the *actual practice* of schools, teachers, parents and pupils itself. Such accounts as there were stressed the primacy of teachers' and parents' views of each other. There is almost no direct evidence of the actual communication, contact and involvement involving families and schools. In many ways this serves as a reminder of the rather shadowy and ambiguous place of home–school relationships and activities in the professional lives of teachers and in the expectations of parents at that time.

In recent years, however, a number of important and far-reaching changes have taken place in the field of home–school relations (described elsewhere in this reader), which have made it possible to re-examine the recent past in a more searching way. From such a viewpoint, the development of the study and practice of home–school relations, at different times, appears to be characterized by widespread and deeply held *beliefs and values*, rather than differences of form and approach.

The present account is an attempt to develop a framework that will make it possible to examine, in a critical way, the main beliefs and values that characterize the field and the way in which they have influenced policy and practice. Such an account, rooted in the concept of ideology, goes beyond the conventional bibliographic 'overview'. It suggests, in outline, the kind of analysis that might be used to uncover some of the dominant ways of organizing thought and belief about a set of topical, related issues, and their implications for policy and action.

It will be required, either directly or by implication, to give attention to:

- characteristic ways of conceptualizing the field and its main territories (within a model of social behaviour);
- ideological assumptions and beliefs;
- key questions and perspectives;
- salient issues, preoccupations and areas of concern and interest;
- notions of what constitutes important and convincing evidence, and, from this, characteristic ways of obtaining it;
- widely-accepted approaches to the analysis and interpretation of data;
- central forms of presentation of its work to identifiable audiences.

Sometimes the dominant ideology and its related forms appears to be the result of a gradual adaptation to slowly changing social contexts and evolving attitudes, at other times a more radical departure from cherished beliefs and practices; sometimes the field seems characterized by a general consensus, at others characterized by disagreement and conflict; sometimes the study and practice of home–school relations seems purposeful and progressive, at others a form

Home and school ideologies

	Central values/ political ethos	Characteristic methods of study and research	Typical examples	Key policies and strategies
Compensation	Environmentalism and social engineering Ideology of equal opportunity	'Political arithmetic' studies Epidemiological/distribution studies Correlation analysis	WISEMAN (1964). *Education and Environment* PLOWDEN (1967). *Children and Their Primary Schools* MARJORIBANKS (1974). *Environments for Learning*	Compensatory and positive discriminatory measures Family intervention
Communication	Consensus politics Rationality as the basis of social behaviour	Surveys Organizational case studies Education shops	PLOWDEN (1967) FINLAYSON (1971) CYSTER *et al.* (1980). *Parental Involvement in the Primary School* (NFER Survey).	Enhanced professionalism (through improved communication and relationships) The 'good practice' model of educational change
Accountability	Consumerism: Interests, rights and responsibilities Monetarist economic and social policies	Market research methodologies – surveys and structured interviews – preference studies Network studies	EAST SUSSEX LEA/UNIV. OF SUSSEX (1979). *'Accountability in the Middle Years of Schooling' Project* ELLIOTT *et al.* (1981). *Cambridge Accountability Project* WELSH CONSUMER COUNCIL (1984). *Parents and Schools*	Identifying and meeting customer needs and wishes Working with external audiences, e.g. parents, employers, etc.
Participation	Participatory democracy and the 'Open Society' – devolved power and shared responsibility – partnership between equals – pluralism and diversity	Action research Small-scale developments Co-operative developments Parent-led initiatives	NEWSON, J. and NEWSON, E. (1977). *Perspectives on School at Seven Years Old* TIZARD *et al.* (1981). *Involving Parents in Nursery and Infant Schools* NOTTINGHAM UNIVERSITY SCHOOL OF EDUCATION (1981). *'The Development of Effective Home–School Programmes' Project*	Parental involvement at home and at school Parents as educators Community education and development

of political opportunism or the product of teacher morale. Finally, such an analysis recognizes home–school relations as both problematic and changing, for all parents, teachers and pupils, in different ways, at different stages of their schooling.

(i) Compensation

Compensatory ideologies have dominated theory, research, policy and practice in the home–school field for a long time in post-war Britain. Indeed, they continue to exert an important influence to this day, particularly where the relationships between schools and working-class communities are concerned.

Compensatory approaches have their roots in post-war reconstruction and the monitoring of the formation of the Welfare State, being particularly strong in relation to the health, education and welfare of children and young people. The large-scale studies of the 1960s (Douglas, 1964; Plowden, 1967; Robbins, 1963), in their concern to chart educational access and performance, became increasingly concerned to unravel something of the differential effects of home, school and neighbourhood in ways that were to influence both policy and practice. Within such a perspective, a powerful 'environmental correlates' tradition developed which has been updated and consolidated in recent years (e.g. Marjoribanks, 1974, 1979), through the use of more sophisticated techniques of statistical analysis.

There is probably no better way of coming to terms with compensatory beliefs, and their influence, than through a careful examination of the Plowden Report. For it remains the biggest single influence upon the study and practice of home–school relations in Britain. Close examination of the Report – both of its researches and its recommendations – contributes to the analysis of many key questions concerning the development of the field. Such an examination also exposes both the strengths and weaknesses of compensatory beliefs and attitudes, amplified through the Plowden legacy, and suggests different values and alternative perspectives.

The 1964 National Survey, commissioned by the Plowden Committee, began where Wiseman had left off:

> . . . home/family factors are most significant in shaping the educational achievement of pupils, [and] that . . . the most important finding, perhaps, is the demonstration that the major forces associated with educational attainment are to be found within the home circumstances of the children. (Wiseman, 1964)

From this starting point, Plowden developed the view, which became widely accepted and deeply entrenched, that the *attitudes* of parents and the interest they show in their children's educational progress, far outweighs the material features of the home, such as income, family size etc.

The report ends with the much-quoted declaration that:

> Before the inquiry it was plain . . . that parental encouragement and support would take the child some way. What the inquiry has shown is that 'some way' can be interpreted as 'a long way', and the variation in parental encouragement and support has much greater effect than either the variation in home circumstances or the variation in schools . . . if the least co-operative parents rose to the level of the most co-operative, the effect would be much larger than if the worst schools rose to the level of the best or the least prosperous parents to the level of the most prosperous . . .
>
> It has long been recognized that education is concerned with the whole man: henceforth it must be concerned with the whole family. (Plowden, 1967)

From such conclusions, a number of things follow:

- Inequality in education might be overcome without deep structural changes, through changing people's attitudes (apart from gross material deprivation, which requires discriminatory measures including the re-allocation of important resources).
- If parental interest and support are crucial for achievement then it follows that the school should do what it can to increase this interest and support.
- Parental interest and involvement, which has educational pay-offs for their children, can be stimulated by the efforts of teachers, through better relationships and improved communications.
- Above all, the major task becomes that of making the least 'successful' families more like the most 'successful', opening the

door for the extensive application of deficit models of family life, and the implementation of the interventionist, compensatory and positive discriminatory strategies of the late 1960s and early 1970s.

Although there are now recognized to be serious limitations in the ways in which Plowden conceptualized and studied relationships between families and schools, it is also necessary to acknowledge its enduring contribution to the debate about social background and educational achievement and in putting home–school matters 'on the educational map'.

The Plowden Report has been taken as a model or prototype for subsequent research and follow-up surveys; its thinking and recommendations were endorsed through a number of policy and resource decisions, the best known of which was the introduction of educational priority areas and other measures; it is probably the study in the field best known to practising teachers and could be said to embody a consensus view about home–school relations which was, for a long time and to some extent still is, the conventional wisdom; finally, it provided the framework, which stood for many years, for an informal basic code of practice, which was slowly but steadily taken up by schools and teachers in the decade following its publication (q.v. Cyster *et al.*, 1980).

So the Plowden Report gave official and effective sponsorship to the belief that the reform of home–school relationships and practices was important, and that this would lead to a significant improvement in the school performance of many children, particularly of many of those who were then regarded as 'underachieving' because of an unsupportive home background. More than this, however, the Report implies that such action should form part of a school's responsibility towards its parents and that it is teachers who, by virtue of their professional knowledge and authority, should take the initiative.

The limitations of Plowden's thinking, embodied in its research designs have also become more noticeable with the passage of time. This is largely attributable to subsequent shifts of attitude and perspective amongst those involved with both the study and practice of education. But it has been reinforced by the way in which much of the post-Plowden legacy accepted the report uncritically, building its findings into subsequent work, thus amplifying its weaknesses and exposing them more clearly. Nowhere is this more widespread than in the proliferation of teacher-dominated, practical accounts, characteristic of the late 1960s and early 1970s.

At its most extreme this legacy serves to perpetuate the parent stereotypes of staffroom mythology and folklore with parents (particularly working-class parents) seen as a largely passive, ignorant and undifferentiated body, with a limited interest in their children's schooling, needing the enlightenment from initiatives taken by knowledgeable professionals (although such a view has always been challenged by the work of Jackson, Young, ACE, Midwinter and others).

The 'environmental' tradition, represented here by Plowden, can now be seen as a perspective which has important limitations and areas of myopia. The idea of social engineering, however well intentioned, now seems to embody a rather mechanistic view of social behaviour and its capacity for change. It ignores the ways in which home–school relations are *made* (rather than predetermined by global factors) through the interaction of teachers, parents and pupils.

Plowden, in particular, has been taken to task for making false distinctions between attitudes and material circumstances, ignoring the ways in which these are inextricably related. Above all, such studies ignore the social, geographical and political *contexts* in which schools, families and neighbourhoods operate, a point made forcefully by Halsey (1978):

> The association of social class (and ethnicity) with educational achievement will not therefore be explained by a theory or eliminated by a policy which falls short of including changes in public support for learning in the family and neighbourhood, the training of teachers, the production of relevant curricula, the fostering of parental participation, the raising of standards of housing and employment prospects, and, above all, the allocation of educational resources.

So compensation ideologies have occupied a dominant position in the field of home–school relations in Britain and continue to exert an influence, particularly in areas where conventional educational arrangements are clearly ineffective. Their strengths and weaknesses can be seen more clearly through the examination of competing and contradictory beliefs and attitudes, some of which will now be outlined.

(ii) Communications

Despite a tendency to overstate the case, there can be no doubt that the development of home–school practice really took off during the 1960s. Equally, it is clear that much of the credit for this is due to the acceptance of beliefs endorsed by the Plowden Report and the recommendations for practice found in its 'Basic Programme'.

The inheritance of such a legacy can also explain the need, articulated a decade later, to see how much progress has been made and to chart the latest patterns of concern and behaviour. The studies that emerged in this way (e.g. Daynes, 1977; Webb, 1979; Cyster *et al.*, 1980), whilst often limited in conception and scope, are useful in contributing to a clearer picture of the surface features of the landscape. They are strong at revealing the spread of attitudes and practices through our schooling system, together with their distribution and frequency. They are not so strong in revealing significant variations or in their capacity to *explain* what they describe. Above all, however, such a perspective is concerned with the processes of communication and contact:

> Few other social institutions have changed their attitudes and techniques as quickly and as fundamentally as the primary school. Sometimes there has been little short of a revolution, since the parents were at school themselves. They may hear about these changes in a garbled way from other parents, or perhaps from the mass media, before they learn about them from the school. The school should explain to them so that parents can take an informed interest in what their children are doing. Parents will not understand unless they are told . . . (Plowden, 1967)

From such a viewpoint, problems of relationship between families and schools can be largely attributable to failures of communication. If parents do not know, it is because they are not adequately informed. If they do not understand it is because they lack appropriate opportunities to see, to discuss and to become involved.

Within this perspective, knowledge and information are treated as non-problematic. Parents will act rationally and responsibly in accordance with the picture of the life and work of the school that they are given. Finlayson (1971), for example, drawing upon data from both the Plowden research and the NFER comprehensive school surveys, undertakes a critical analysis of the relationship between parental aspiration and school achievement. Such a relationship, he claims, is explained in terms of:

> the parents' acquiring information about their child's progress in the primary school; only after they have obtained such evidence do they begin to get realistic aspirations for their child . . . Informational components directed at parents can provide a rational and empirical basis for parental attitudes. (Finlayson, 1971)

Within such an ideology, there is a premium on the provision of appropriate *opportunities* for communication, contact and involvement and the development of their most effective *forms*.

Just as a two-way flow of information between home and school is seen as being largely neutral, rational and non-problematic, so too is 'good practice'. Indeed, a feature of the relatively small number of in-service opportunities in the area, at this time, follows a model whose main purpose is to disseminate established good practice, more or less intact, by experienced practitioners noted for their commitment to 'better home–school relations'. It is through the development of extended and enhanced professionalism (incorporating the concomitant attitudes and skills) that progress becomes possible. The spirit of this development is captured by a primary headteacher, in reporting a piece of action research in his own school:

> It is the responsibility of teachers to help parents voice their feelings and wishes, to articulate more effectively, to know their way around the educational system as most middle-class people do, and to use it actively instead of just accepting it. We teachers can do this by drawing parents into the process of education, showing them how we teach and what they can do at home to reinforce this. (Green, 1968)

For a long time (and to a lesser extent it still survives) the ideology of rational and open communications, rooted deeply in consensus politics, has been a feature of governmental policy and action. This certainly applies to relationships between families and the health, education and welfare services. A range of illustrations can be found in:

- a succession of reports from government departments (Plowden, 1967; Court, 1976; Taylor, 1977; Warnock, 1978);
- government-sponsored studies and policy documents (e.g. the Primary and Secondary Surveys, produced by HMI, 1977, 1979);
- recent legislation, e.g. the 1980 and 1981 Education Acts.

From these examples, perhaps the clearest expressions of the ideology are found in the Court and Taylor Reports, dealing with child health and the management of schools respectively:

> We have found no better way to raise a child than to reinforce the abilities of his parents to do so . . . families could be better at bringing up their children if they were given the right information, support and relationships with the caring professions, when it was needed and in a more acceptable way. (Court Report, 1976)

> Every parent has a right to expect a school's teachers to recognize his status in the education of his child, by the practical arrangements they make to communicate with him and the spirit in which they accept his interest. (Taylor Report, 1977)

In the most obvious sense developed in this brief account, a 'communications' ideology represents one of a possible range of models of interpersonal and institutional behaviour. In a different sense, it is not so much a self-contained view of the world or belief system, as a recurring thread in the study and practice of home–school relations, whose importance and emphasis shift according to differing contexts and changing circumstances.

Within the latter view, its major contribution is to direct attention to the nature, range and quality of the *practical arrangements* that are made for communication and contact between teachers, parents and pupils. It is through an attempt to assess the effectiveness of such arrangements that we can enter the arena of accountability.

(iii) Accountability

It could be argued that the ideological shift of emphasis away from liberal egalitarianism towards educational consumerism was a small shift in time but a fundamental change of values. It represents a movement from an ideology whose central tenets are concerned with various interpretations of social justice, to one whose chief concerns are economic, based upon the doctrines of monetarism and a free market economy. The notion of the accountability of public services took root, and spread, against a background of the politics of recession, attempts to bring about the large-scale reduction of public services and the fact of falling pupil numbers.

With an ideology of accountability, educational consumerism flourishes through the complementary concepts of 'demand' and 'choice'. Its political appeal lies in its value as a tool for planning and evaluating the services that are available, within fixed cash limits, on the basis of the consumer's rights to determine the nature of the provision.

Educational consumerism, intensified through the pressures of a contracting system, can be identified through commonly shared themes and approaches and also through their strong disposition towards market research methodologies, such as the heavy use of survey techniques, questionnaires and structured interviews.

Key studies have been concerned to map out the actual patterns of home–school activity and to sample parental attitudes and preferences. These were linked to a number of areas that had become important items on the agenda of the so-called Great Debate, such as uniform, standards, preparation for work, etc.

Within this perspective, too, parents are seen not only as important in their own right, but as the largest constituency within the broader notion of external 'audiences'. This broader focus opens up, for the first time, a number of study and research possibilities, such as the examination of neighbourhood grapevines or the analysis of media images of the education system.

The values of an accountability ideology are often easily traceable through project titles, the nature of the sponsoring bodies' interests and the strategies used for the collection of data. Illustrations include the Sussex and Cambridge Accountability Projects, NOP survey work for the National Consumer Council, which has itself recently developed a direct interest in the consumption of educational services, in separate studies in Scotland, Wales and England (Bassey, 1978; Cyster *et al.*, 1980; Becher *et al.*, 1981; Elliott *et al.*, 1981; Welsh Consumer Council, 1984).

Within these shared themes, two very different portrayals of external audiences have emerged. The first of these operates within a consensus model in which relationships between families and schools are seen as problematic for *all* families, regardless of educational philosophy or social background. Such an approach is embodied in, for example, the work of pressure groups like the Advisory Centre for Education and operates on the assumption of a shared parental perspective and widely-held values.

This can be contrasted with the more recent emergence of a model which opens up the possibility of 'values pluralism', based not only upon relatively crude structural characteristics such as social class, region and other subcultural variations, but more subtly and in the direction of individualistic explanations, based upon personality, belief and experience. Here the analysis moves beyond the picture provided by tables and percentages, or by generalizations about parents as an undifferentiated group, to utilize qualitative methods. The use of open interviews, in particular, yields a picture which highlights some of the limitations of crude market survey research:

> What the surveys failed to reveal was the extent to which open evenings could be a quite different experience for different parents . . . Parents approached these consultations with different attitudes and expectations, teachers handled parents in different ways, and the child's progress and behaviour in school also influenced the tone of proceedings. This was also true of other forms of teacher–parent contact. Neither the transactions between teacher and parent, nor the criteria by which these transactions were judged to be useful, satisfactory or insufficient, were common for all teachers or for all parents. (East Sussex LEA/ University of Sussex, 1979)

Studies rooted in an ideology of accountability, both through a concern for common parental needs and experience and through a study of important variations, have made a valuable contribution to the field. They have charted additional parts of the landscape, identified new concerns and helped to de-mythologize particularly murky areas, such as the world of parents' evenings and school reports.

Within the context of accountability studies and policies, parents are seen as a major external audience with whom schools, to be effective, need to create and sustain a dynamic and constructive relationship, based upon mutual respect and the full exchange of information:

> But teachers still recognize that they have been placed by society in a position of trust and many now realize that they may have to show considerable initiative to secure the continued renewal of that trust. For politicians and pressure groups, therefore, accountability is about increasing external influence and control; while for teachers it is about securing the renewal of trust within the current framework of delegated responsibility. (Eraut, Barton and Canning, 1979)

Such a renewal of trust, it is implied, takes place through the school's responsibility to keep parents informed about what it is doing and how individual pupils are progressing. Within such a view, the acceptance of educational and social change requires the new elements to be rendered more familiar, predictable and consistent, through increased opportunities for contact and discussion. Despite an increasing sense of obligation to explain and justify both policy and action, home–school relations are still conceived as being professionally led and organized to achieve school goals and purposes.

Finally, accountability values, which are empirically oriented, are often rooted in a consideration of the practice of individual schools. But they are also located against a background of wider issues and public concerns. They embody a view of parent–teacher relations which goes beyond a summation of the dealings of individual schools and their families to portray an important element in the workings of an educational *system* within its wider social and political contexts.

(iv) Participation

In some ways, 'participatory' ideologies can be said to embody beliefs and practices that are an established part of the field of home–school relations alongside others and which, like them, have been fashionable in the past, usually within small-scale projects.

They might also be regarded as a later form of development, higher up the evolutionary ladder, as part of a linear and progressive conception of social and educational development.

For participatory beliefs and strategies draw from, and extend, elements from the others in this typology. They attempt, for example, to identify and compensate for a range of special family needs; they place considerable emphasis upon the process of communication, although this is here seen as a two-way process; they acknowledge the rights and responsibilities of parents and other audiences. But 'participation ideologies' are much more than an aggregation, or reformulation of other values, containing two elements in particular which give them a special place in the current analysis.

In the first place, they represent something of 'the claim of the ideal', as goals to aim for, however difficult to achieve in practice. Even more strikingly, participatory beliefs are often used to fuel a radical critique of the home–school field, generally endorsing alternative goals and strategies. These two possibilities mark them out from the rest of this typology.

The central feature of a participatory ideology is that it recognizes the existence of both shared goals *and* complementary roles for teachers and parents. The only way in which such divergent elements can be reconciled, however, is through the devolution of power and shared responsibility, where teachers and parents work together, depite their differences, through non-hierarchical relationships, in a partnership of equals.

Such a perspective emphasizes co-operative, rather than joint activity, recognizing the value of *both* common efforts and separate, distinctive contributions. It does *not* presuppose either complete harmony or perennial conflict, rather that the inevitable differences should be acknowledged and tackled through practical compromise.

Its characteristic style is small-scale and personal, rather than operating through bureaucratic processes or institutional procedures which require the force of regulation and law. The voluntary principle lies close to its heart and its essence is involvement and action. In an interesting comparison Watt (1977) suggests that there is much that schools can learn from the preschool playgroup movement, suitably modified:

> By its insistence on the rights and competence of parents to take

> at least part responsibility for the education of their own children, and its emphasis on the regenerative power of responsible participation in community life, the playgroup movement at its best has shown its potential for providing a focus for a radical reanalysis of traditional relationships between parent and professional, between family and community, and between parent and child. At its most radical it has challenged traditional concepts of professionalism and accountability in education. (Watt, 1977)

Such a reanalysis involves extensive de-mythologizing of the life and work of schools, together with the mutual recognition by teachers and parents of each other's problems and resources. Above all, it calls for the development of radically different attitudes, relationships and ways of working (Bastiani, 1987). Even so, such changes are most likely to occur as a response to changes in the wider society, involving the fundamental relationship between families and schools. As Acland says of current trends to involve parents more fully in their children's schooling:

> . . . it still seems to me that these programmes do nothing to alter the fundamental relationship between home and school. The potential for the parents to make choices or decisions about their child's education is not increased, nor would the schools be in any way more accountable to those who use them than they are now. The essence of parent participation is that parents come to school, learn about the way the school operates and through doing this become more effective so far as their children's education is concerned. It is clear that parents are there to understand and accept; they are not there to represent their own position if this conflicts with that of the school. There is not room here to discuss the transfer of power from teachers to parents. I merely want to point out that involvement programmes as they are now being run do nothing to expand parents' freedom to make choices, though they may appear to be making schools more responsive to parents. (Acland, 1971)

Having said that, the main obstacle to the development of participatory beliefs and practices is that not everybody shares the ideals! Their cause is advanced by a small but significant number of schools and parents' organizations, often engaged themselves in pioneering and developmental work, or as the result, paradoxically, of inspired or strongminded leadership. In the field as a whole, however, such values are under constant threat and challenge from many directions and from other teachers, parents and politicians alike.

Home and school ideologies: some general issues

Ideological analysis remains a potentially valuable tool in the examination of the beliefs and attitudes that are embodied in educational policy and practice. It is useful in an attempt to unravel some of the changing assumptions that have characterized home–school relations generally, at particular times and in changing circumstances; it can help to identify some of the central values which shape and underpin new laws and regulations and the emergence of guidelines for policy and practice.

At the same time such an analysis, with its emphasis upon beliefs and attitudes, has its own peculiar dangers and limitations. In the first place, it is too easy to see attitudinal change as a linear, rather one-dimensional historical process. As can be seen by a number of contemporary developments in education, nothing could be further from the truth! In the home–school field, for example, pathological and compensatory ideologies, which tend to blame families for their alleged deficiencies, are still both widespread and influential. On the other hand participatory ideologies continue to be attractive to a minority in theory, but highly elusive in practice. Similarly, values which stress the primacy of open communication are not to be consigned to the historical dustbin but need to be developed in appropriate contemporary forms.

Nevertheless there has been what amounts to a steady shift in attitudes in the home–school field which is also reflected in the area of the application of findings, in policy-making and in practice. At the heart of the Plowden legacy there developed, within a rather optimistic view of social change, an uplifting rhetoric about home–school 'partnership', with its emphasis upon warmer social relationships and improved channels of communication. School influences became dominant and it is perhaps possible to view this period as an attempt to *colonize* parenting, with its emphasis on parents borrowing minor teacher skills, upon the extension of schooling into family life and upon parent education generally.

More recently, despite the persistence in some areas of a view of parents as an ignorant, undifferentiated mass, and even of the need to compensate for the 'inadequacies' of working-class family life, a counter-view is emerging. This stresses the complementary nature of teacher and parent roles, the need to recognize important differences between them and to confirm parental strengths, in a spirit of co-operation. Such a view also recognizes the differences of perspective and experience *amongst* parents and a consequent need for the co-ordination of efforts.

Genuine change also requires, in addition to the development of new attitudes, the acquisition of appropriate knowledge and skills. This draws attention to the nature and impact of both initial and post-experience training, and the provision of appropriate opportunities and experiences for teachers, parents and pupils.

Whether such changes are thrown into the melting pot by contemporary events, remains to be seen. For, at the time of writing, heavy and widespread damage to both positive attitudes and progressive practice in the home–school field has been caused by the prolonged, and increasingly bitter, dispute between the government and teachers. This conflict is probably having more effect on teacher–parent relations than any other events of recent decades. Such factors also serve as a warning against seeing attitudinal development and change too much in personal and psychological terms, or as dispensable and optional extras, that people may adopt at leisure.

Above all, however, a contemporary perspective on home–school relations is obliged to recognize its paradoxical nature. On the one hand there is some evidence of more constructive communication taking place between families and schools, involving parents and teachers. Such a view, of educational institutions which are more publicly responsive and parents who are better informed and more involved, supports the idea of a general overall improvement in the field of home–school relations.

Set against this argument, in apparent contradiction, is an increasing awareness that home–school relations play an important part in the management of educational success and failure and their effect upon the future lives of young people. This serves to illustrate a growing recognition that families and schools are very different kinds of institutions between which tensions are inevitable.

The examination of beliefs and attitudes enables us to look at the rise and fall of competing values but it goes beyond this. For it can provide a framework with which to carry out a critical analysis of home–school study and practice in terms which allow for the analysis of the strengths and weaknesses of different strategies and approaches.

For example, compensatory and accountability policies tend to support one-way, top-down strategies which are not very sensitive to the experience of parents and children, or to local circumstances. On the other hand, they do recognize that schools are part of a wider system. This enables political and legal support to be identified, along with the reallocation of resources or the reshaping of training programmes.

The comparative analysis of competing beliefs and attitudes in a major area of social life also enables important links to be made *across* forms of inquiry and development. By concentrating on common ideological components, for instance, the present account can pursue links between both the study and the practice of education, between theory, research, policy and practice.

Such a focus makes it possible to examine the ways in which key notions pass in and out of the professional rhetorics, find expression in government sponsored studies and researches, or are used to support a rationale for areas of practical development. This is particularly valuable in dealing with a number of notions that lie at the heart of current concerns. For such notions as 'parental co-operation', 'home–school partnership' and 'parental choice' have been appropriated and exploited in different ways.

Such slogans often form a cornerstone in the rhetoric of very different campaigns, seductively inviting approval and consensus. But rigorous analysis and the collection of evidence often tell a very different story! For such notions, which characterize the rhetoric of very different ideologies in the home–school field, generally turn out to be extremely elusive and highly problematic. This makes their close examination an essential task for almost all forms of study and inquiry which focus upon the relationships between families and schools.

References

ACLAND, H. (1971). 'Does parent involvement matter?', *New Society*, 16, 9, 71.

BASSEY, M. (1978). *Nine Hundred Primary School Teachers*. Slough: NFER.

BASTIANI, J. (1983). Listening to parents: philosophy, critique and method. PhD thesis. University of Nottingham.

BASTIANI, J. (1987). 'Professional ideology versus lay experience'. In: ALLEN, G., BASTIANI, J., MARTIN, I. and RICHARDS, K. (Eds) *Community Education: An Agenda for Educational Reform*. Milton Keynes: Open University Press (in press).

BECHER, T., ERAUT, M. and KNIGHT, J. (1981). *Policies for Educational Accountability*. London: Heinemann.

COURT REPORT. GREAT BRITAIN. DEPARTMENT OF HEALTH AND SOCIAL SECURITY (ENGLAND) (1976). *Fit for the Future: Report of the Committee on Child Health Services*. London: HMSO.

CYSTER, R., CLIFT, P. S. and BATTLE, S. (1980). *Parental Involvement in Primary Schools*. Slough: NFER.

DAYNES, R. W. (1977). Towards effective parent/teacher contact. MA (Ed) dissertation. University of Southampton.

DOUGLAS, J. W. B. (1964). *The Home and the School*. London: McGibbon and Kee.

EAST SUSSEX LEA/UNIVERSITY OF SUSSEX (1979). *Accountability in the Middle Years of Schooling Project: An Analysis of Policy Options*. Education Development Centre, University of Sussex.

ELLIOTT, J. *et al.* (1981). *School Accountability*. The SSRC Cambridge Accountability Project. London: Grant-McIntyre.

ERAUT, M., BARTON, J. and CANNING, T. (1979). Some Teacher Perspectives on Accountability. Working Paper from the Accountability in the Middle Years of Schooling Project. University of Sussex.

FINLAYSON, D. S. (1971). 'Parental aspirations and the educational achievement of children', *Educational Research*, 14, 1.

GREEN, L. (1968). *Parents and Teachers – Partners or Rivals?* London: Allen and Unwin.

HALSEY, A. H. (1978). 'Education and social mobility in Britain since World War Two'. In: MADDISON, A. (Ed) *Educational Inequality and Life Chances*. Vol. 1. Paris: OECD.

MARJORIBANKS, K. (1974). *Environments for Learning*. Slough: NFER.

MARJORIBANKS, K. (1979). *Families and Their Learning Environments: An Empirical Analysis*. London: Routledge.

NEWSON, J. and NEWSON, E. (1977). *Perspectives on School at Seven Years Old*. London: Allen and Unwin.

NOTTINGHAM UNIVERSITY SCHOOL OF EDUCATION. The Development of Effective Home/School Programmes Project: a programme of research and development. See BASTIANI, J. (1983).

PLOWDEN REPORT. GREAT BRITAIN. DEPARTMENT OF EDUCATION AND SCIENCE. CENTRAL ADVISORY COUNCIL FOR EDUCATION

(ENGLAND) (1967). *Children and Their Primary Schools*. London: HMSO.

ROBBINS REPORT. GREAT BRITAIN. DEPARTMENT OF EDUCATION AND SCIENCE (1963). *Committee on Higher Education*. Cmnd 2154. London: HMSO.

TAYLOR REPORT. GREAT BRITAIN. DEPARTMENT OF EDUCATION AND SCIENCE/WELSH OFFICE (1977). *A New Partnership for Our Schools*. London: HMSO.

TIZARD, B., MORTIMORE, J. and BURCHELL, B. (1981). *Involving Parents in Nursery and Infant Schools*. London: Grant-McIntyre.

WARNOCK REPORT. GREAT BRITAIN. DEPARTMENT OF EDUCATION AND SCIENCE (1978). *Special Educational Needs*. A report of the committee of inquiry into the education of handicapped children and young people. Cmnd 7212. London: HMSO.

WATT, J. S. (1977). *Cooperation in Pre-school Education*. A research report. London: SSRC Publications.

WEBB, D. (1979). 'Home and school: parental views', *Education*, 3-13, 7.2.

WELSH CONSUMER COUNCIL (1984). *Parents and Schools*. Cardiff: Welsh Consumer Council.

WISEMAN, S. (1964). *Education and Environment*. Manchester: Manchester University Press.

Parents as Educators

Jackie Goode

> It is a truth universally acknowledged that a single man in possession of a good fortune must be in want of a wife. (Jane Austen, *Pride and Prejudice*)

Universally acknowledged truths often get obscured, and whilst we may continue to subscribe to them, may warrant close scrutiny and reassessment! The value and nature of the marital relationship as seen by Jane Austen is one example of this. The fact that parents educate their children is another.

A century or so of state education has served to obscure the universally acknowledged truth that a major element of parenting is education. Academic disciplinary boundaries may attempt to consign 'socialization' exclusively to the family, and 'education' exclusively to the school, but parents and teachers know better. They are not always aware of what they know however! Of course education is a partnership between the home and the school, but teachers may be hard pressed to describe the dynamics of how pupils and parents are socialized into the institution of the school. Of course children learn all sorts of things at home, but parents do not describe themselves as 'educators', but rather as overseers and participants in 'family life'.

I should like to examine parents as educators more closely: to put the idea into an historical context with a brief look at how the family has been studied in the past; to listen to parents themselves talking about what they do in educative terms; and finally to relate this to the work of teachers, in an examination of the interface between home and school, and the implications of the impact of the one on the other for the making of home–school relations.

Contemporary educators' interest in the family often derives from a concern with social problems. From Plowden onwards, a central focus has been the family's contribution to the outcomes of schooling. Studies have been dominated by a problem-oriented approach – the decline of the extended family network, the disintegration of the nuclear family, family dynamics requiring therapeutic intervention, the lifecycle of the family in terms of crises. Writings on the family are doom-laden.

If the family is looked at not from the point of view of its contribution to external systems, but in its own terms, a different picture emerges. As far as education is concerned, school outcomes become only one part of a picture which contains opportunities for children to learn in a cognitive, social, developmental, affective and experiential sense, and in ways which may or may not be compatible with school-based learning. As Leichter (1974) comments, such a viewpoint means that private or specialized knowledge, such as information about ethnic customs or languages not used in the school, take on particular importance. This viewpoint would also include attitudes and values which may be deliberately excluded from the school curriculum, whilst in addition, a whole list of skills can become relevant, depending on the interests, traditions and concerns of particular families.

In looking at what parents *do* as opposed to who and what they are, and in extending the examination to the whole range of outcomes of familial education, rather than the negative contributions families may make to other institutions, Leichter evolves a concept of 'educative style'. 'Educative style' includes such components as the manner of criticizing and appraising the mode of integrating experiences over time, the level and rate of activity, the ways of combining and segregating particular tasks, the character of response to cues from others, the mode of scanning and searching for information, and approaches to embarrassment in learning situations. These components of educative style interact in different ways as the individual engages in, moves through and combines diverse educational experiences over a lifetime.

Leichter's approach is one which focuses on processes of interaction. What might be called the 'hidden curriculum' of the home – the processes within the home which lead to the development of educative styles – are also significant for what has been called 'deutero-learning' or learning to learn: learning how to ask questions, how to organize activities, how to appraise external evaluations. They are all important for an understanding of education, even if they are not explicitly seen by participants as educational, and even if they do not necessarily involve 'teaching' and 'learning'.

An interaction approach is also appropriate for an examination of what happens when home and school meet – the process of the making of home–school relations. Whether consciously acknowledged by the participants themselves or not, 'educative styles' and 'deutero-learning' form much of what parents try to communicate to teachers when children enter formal schooling:

> It's not a matter of disobedience. She very often spends more time arguing about why she should do something than it would actually take to do, but this is Yvonne and we accept it. We know that she will do it, but she just has to have her little say.

Parents perhaps find it more acceptable than teachers that they can learn from their children, and that it is not a one-way process. Studies of mother–child interaction have demonstrated that the caretaker's behaviour is shaped by the child, and the concept of lifelong education suggests by implication that parents, although older and more experienced than their children, continue to learn from them as they enter new parental roles. Parents learn about children, about child development and its trends, about teaching and learning, about strategies of schooling, about the variety of behaviour and experience to which their children's associates will expose them. In this sense contact with the life of a child opens up a new vision of the world, and the full range of the child's activities becomes a potential source of education for the parent. The experience of adjustment and readjustment to changes in the child, given the child's comparatively rapid rate of maturation, is another potential source of education for the parent. The fact that interaction with the child inevitably requires continuous shifts on the part of the parent serves as a pressure for continuous learning.

The shared learning which takes place within the family is not of course confined to parents and children, but also takes place between brothers and sisters. Sisters and brothers serve not only as role models for each other, but as sources of evaluation, as challengers and stimulators. Like peers, they may also have direct educational influence on one another via their shared activities, although the ways in which such education proceeds are so much a part of the fabric of daily existence that they are sometimes difficult to discern:

> They came up one morning giggling and we could hear pots rattling upstairs and er . . . giggles as they spilled the tea, that sort of thing, and they brought a tray with two breakfasts on, and David had set to and started it, and we've had continuing reports: the first time Yvonne turned the bacon over . . . the second time she did an egg and er . . . little things like that as he's gradually helped her along . . . or she's poured the tea out, something like that. Oh, it's lovely.

It is perhaps because of the shared nature of learning within the family that parents do not think of themselves as educators. What they do do more consciously is to 'parent'. Unlike teachers, they receive no professional training for this task, and must simply learn 'on the job'. In a similar way to teachers, however, they are subjected to a sometimes confusing mixture of influences, fashions, advice, and admonishments. A parallel trend in both activities has been a gradual move towards 'child-centredness'. Newson and Newson (1974) note an overall shift in the philosophy on the relationship between parents and their children internationally and at every social level, from a largely authoritarian to a largely democratic model. The essence of this democratic ethos is a principle of reciprocity: children are taught to respect the rights and wishes of others, via endless verbal persuasion and reiteration. It is a painfully slow process dependent on the gradual growth of self-awareness and social empathy. The child is also valued as a person whose wishes and desires must be respected, and they are accorded status in their own right:

> We explain why, in *our* opinion, why we don't think they should have it or do it. Now, if they've got a constructive argument why they should, we're quite willing to be persuaded otherwise. It's a discussion format that we use. We discuss virtually everything as a family unit. It's not just mum and dad deciding, and not necessarily the kids deciding . . .

It is in this democratic context that Wells (1978) has described the qualities of 'talk' between parents and children in the home.

Most of the conversations in the home are initiated by the child, arise spontaneously from the activity in hand, and are free from any pressure to teach and learn particular facts and skills. The learning that does take place at home usually occurs via interaction with the adult as participant, it is idiosyncratic and personal, it can be short-burst or obsessively sustained for long periods depending on the child's own interest, and the rhythms of family life. Demands such as shopping can be a temporary break before an activity is lovingly resumed, and the environments for learning range from the house, the garden, the street, to the car-park, shops, waste-ground, neighbours, milkman, shopkeeper.

This forms a sharp contrast with many features of school-based learning, where talk is predominantly initiated by the teacher, who often asks questions to which she already knows the answer, where the context is largely confined to the classroom (Bassey, 1978), and where what is learned is short-burst, fragmented, and compacted into segments of time. A little of something every day seems to be the recipe, regardless of stage of development, particular needs, or patterns of interest or skill at the time. As one bright, lively child commented to her mother at an open evening:

> This is my interest book, Mummy. I hate doing my interest book.

Teachers themselves are aware of some of the problems a child faces in the classroom, but are not always able to overcome them, as this conversation at a parents' evening reveals:

> Mother: He'll say, 'Oh, I haven't finished any writing yet. It's taking me a long time today 'cos I keep queuing up'.
>
> Teacher: Yes . . . we're actually trying to work on this, to reduce the number of children in that area . . . but we're not satisfied.
>
> Mother: No, it's not very good. One day, I said, 'What have you been doing this afternoon?' and he says, 'Nothing', so I says, 'Why?' and he says, 'I've been sitting at the table just waiting for the teacher to come to us.' He said, 'I kept putting me hand up but she was busy'.

One can sympathize here with the bored and frustrated child, the dissatisfied mother, and the hard-pressed teacher. Before turning to what parents themselves have to say about their own roles as educators, I should make it clear that I am not advocating that schools should simply imitate the 'good home' even if that could be defined. Although they both have an educative function, the school complements the informality of the home, by necessarily introducing the child to more formal ways of acquiring and utilizing knowledge, and to a way of life which enables the child to adjust her own needs to those of others. The organization of the school draws, in this task, upon the skills of highly trained professionals, and what I will be suggesting is that these teachers could be used far more effectively if they could find ways of working with parents towards a redefinition of their professional role.

Parents are aware that home and school represent two different worlds for their children, simply from listening to them talk and observing their behaviour:

> When Chris started school, he came home one day and walked out of his coat, and dropped it just where it was, behind him, so I said, 'Chris, pick up your coat for me, will you love, please?' and he just wanders by . . . I asked him again. 'In a minute' – so I got cross then, and I says to him, 'When your teacher asks you to do anything, do you tell her you'll do it in a minute?' He says, 'Noooh!' . . . so I says, 'Well, why can't you be a good boy for me?' and he said, 'Mum, when I come home, all my good's worn out' . . . he'd been so good that he just couldn't last any longer . . . and he'll switch it on again at nine o'clock tomorrow morning!

One of the differences between these two worlds, already illustrated by the 'queuing up' syndrome, is the degree of egocentricity afforded to the child at home, whilst teachers operate a group standard. Parents naturally want 'the best' for their children, and the amount of attention they are able to give leads to an intimate knowledge of their own children which develops in all the different settings of family life, and as the child changes, develops and matures. Parents make comparisons between their children, and between their children and themselves, are able to refer to heredity as a source of information and explanation, to pick out traits and to draw inferences about the implications of these for their children's future.

In the light of their experiences, parents make and adjust their evaluations about their children, and develop a repertoire of skills for handling each of them, learning what 'works' and what doesn't:

> She used to bring books home from school, and we used to lie down on the rug together, and I'd help her with her reading. It got that bad that I was getting annoyed, which is very unusual, and in the end, she just wouldn't do it. She knew it, but she wouldn't do it. And in the end, I threw the book, you know, 'Sod it! I've had enough!' – and virtually straight after, she never looked back. That's the way that's worked with her. The same with swimming. She could do it, but she was giggling and laughing, and wouldn't concentrate, so I said, 'Right, sod off in the little pool with the babies. I don't want to know. I'm not wasting any more time on you'. And she went in the little pool for a while, had a little cry, and then came back, and off she went!

Sharp and Green (1975) showed that teachers operate very shaky theories of learning, consisting of a loose collection of concepts such as 'readiness'. When questioned, they found it very difficult to give a clear account of the theoretical foundations upon which their educational judgements were based. Parents too find it difficult to explain in theoretical terms the concepts they operate when helping their children to learn, but an examination of what they say about their children's learning reveals that they do in fact share a number of operational concepts with teachers. They distinguish between heredity and environment, between innate and learned behaviour, they are aware of modelling, and also of the need to motivate children when increased effort is required in order to achieve a necessary goal:

> 'Chip off the old block' sums it up perfectly.

> You used to take them to see me play football: 'You teach me to play that, Dad! Oh, I hope I can do it. I'm gonna become one of them when I grow up.' You know, like all little boys are.

> Sometimes when you watch them playing, you can see yourself in something they're doing, and you think, 'Oh, do I do that? I don't carry on like that!' and I suppose you do . . .

> I think he's clever enough to do it – if he applies himself – I think he realizes himself that opportunities being what they are, I think he realizes that if you're gonna make something of yourself, it's become more and more essential that you *do* stay on.

Learning is seen then as being promoted by this mixture of innate ability, modelling, motivation and application. The content of the learning can from an early age extend in a very real way beyond the school curriculum as with these five-year-old twins' interest in their father's job as foreman in a lace factory:

> They ask me what I do and how's lace made and what's it made from and how does it make it and why does it come out like that and what happens to it when it does come out . . .

If the family itself does not possess the necessary resources to supply what is needed, extended family and local community may be exploited on a reciprocal basis:

> Mother: If we can't help with schoolwork . . . we find – we go and ask somebody who can, like with erm, fractions I was never any good at them at school and er, the chap next door but one is a woodworker, you know, and he deals with fractions so we nip round to him. We always find someone to help and we've got dictionaries upstairs, er, encyclopaedias and we get them down.
>
> Father: It works both ways, we've had kiddies coming round here asking things . . . we've finished up with three or four encyclopaedias stretched across the settee helping Sharon's friend with her homework . . .

So the curriculum of the home and parents' roles as educators is not carefully thought out, planned, organized but is part of the rhythm of family life. Taking an interest, offering support, validating and confirming children's abilities and interests, becoming involved. I can put it no better than this mother:

> I think a lot of parents do it without realizing that you're doing it. Just the fact that you show interest in what they're doing, and erm, you know, sort of become involved. Not to take over. I think it's important that you don't take over . . . they've been doing a project on Nuthall in Georgian times . . . I've learnt more from Chris, but by Chris asking me . . . he's come home, and he's said, 'Do you know, mum, that there was so many coalminers, so

> many so-and-so's.' Now all really Chris's been doing is involving me – I think by being involved, and being willing to be involved, it's helped him, because then he's been even more interested . . . but just listening, yeah, I think you help. But I think you help almost subconsciously. But I think by being interested, you make them want to find out even more. Not necessarily saying, 'Right, get your books out, we'll have so-and-so done,' you know, I think you've just got to be available . . . but I don't think you ever think, it, it must be educational to a degree . . . I don't think you ever set a time of day aside and think, 'Right, we'll do some clever stuff!'

As Elizabeth Newson (1976) argues, parents are experts on their own children. The information they possess may not be held in any systematic way, but they nevertheless have intimate, unique knowledge no matter how diffuse and fragmented it is. This knowledge must be utilized by professionals, and parents can be helped to develop their skills as good witnesses, to be aware of the nature of evidence, to become good observers, and good analysers of information. If this pattern of observation–diagnosis–intervention is already a feature of the curriculum of the home did parents but realize it, teachers could tap this resource by promoting such skills and by supplying appropriate tasks and materials to enable parents to utilize their skills more effectively.

When the child starts school the curriculum of the home is inevitably influenced by the curriculum of the school. Parents will have certain expectations of the school and of the ways in which it will benefit the child. These expectations will be added to and amended by the child herself as she 'brings the school in to the home' in her accounts and in her observable behaviour and by the contacts and communications the parents begin to have with the school and the teachers directly. It is at this point, the child's entry to the formal schooling system, that the making of home–school relations begins.

Parents' own intervention may become more conscious, as their children become pupils, and they become parents of pupils. As the child enters formal schooling, parents become more aware of activities which might be interpreted as supportive of the kinds of learnings which the child will encounter in school. In making judgements about their child's experience of schooling, they may promote and complement this experience, or they may take action, in a reversal of the traditional concept of compensatory education, to compensate for perceived failing in the school curriculum. The ultimate example of this is to remove the child from the school, whilst some parents at this end of the scale undertake covert teaching themselves, or hire a tutor for extra tuition in problematic areas.

Parents as educators is not a static concept. The family has a life-span, and the roles of parents acting as educators will develop and change as the lives of its members are lived, not the least important influence in this being the child himself as he asserts his individuality and uniqueness, and thereby contributes to the part parents play in his learning, as they follow his leads, and are constrained by his personality.

Chart A represents these overarching influences on parents' educative roles, and in it I offer a typology of those roles in relation to the child's schooling, before turning finally to an examination of how parents are influenced into adopting some of these positions at an early point of contact between home and school – the child's transfer from nursery to infant school.

Because parents have hitherto had primary responsibility for their learning, the point of a child's first entry into school provides valuable insight into the making of home–school relations, and into how teachers and parents are assigned particular roles in the child's learning. Parents are very conscious at this point of the school as an institution, and the learning that takes place there is seen as 'proper' learning. For many parents, nursery is seen as a transitional stage en route to school, and although viewed very positively, its benefits may be seen as largely *social* in nature, rather than as an educational experience in its own right – 'He's been to nursery, and they've sort of knocked him into shape a bit . . .' as one father put it. Parents may be familiar with the concept of 'learning through play' but *what* is learned is rarely articulated, and the nursery curriculum may be contrasted with the 'proper' learning that takes place in the infant school. In describing the difference between the two curricula, parents often contrast *play* with *work*. Proper learning denotes the accomplishment of the skills of reading and writing, and for this to be achieved, the requirements frequently repeated by parents are those of *sitting down* and *concentrating*. The ubiquitous phrase 'sitting and learning' illustrates that the two are seen as going together.

I am not suggesting that this perception is inaccurate, and that learning to write, for example, can be achieved without sitting down!

Chart A Parents as educators – a typology

← The active role of the child in the process →

Confirmatory Actively encouraging, supporting and confirming the work undertaken by the school.	**Complementary** Attitudes, relationships and activities, initiated by parents which by their nature are likely to promote learning. S. Bateson's 'deutero-learning' (i.e. 'learning to learn'), Leichter's 'learning styles', or the 'hidden curriculum of the home'.	**Compensatory** Parent-initiated action to encourage the school to meet a requirement in which it is perceived to be failing, undertaking the task oneself, or supplying alternative personnel to do so.
(a) *Home-based* 'Bringing the school into the home', i.e. school-based learning shared.		Supplying the school with information about the child, alerting the school.
Homework – attitude to – help with	Socialization, preschool experience, preparation for school.	Undertaking home 'teaching'.
Exams – attitude to – help with	Modelling specific skills, attitudes and behaviour.	Hiring a tutor.
(b) *School-based* – Parents in the school – Parents in the classroom	Developing traits conducive to learning, growth, development etc. 'moulding'. Regulating the child's handling of materials in space, or activities in time.	Removing child to another school.
(c) *Linking* (a) and (b) are teacher–parent contacts and communications – how they affect the parent-as-educator roles.	Outings and activities – providing experiences, resources, mediating the world to the child.	
	Having aspirations and expectations.	
	Careers guidance.	

The developmental aspect of how parental roles change

← over time →

What is significant however, is that a sharp distinction becomes apparent between the *kinds* of learning that take place in the nursery and the infant school, and between the *ways* in which children learn in the two places. *What* is learned in the nursery is often not clearly understood. Tizard (1978) has illustrated how some parents explained sand and water play by references to the seaside, for example. Nursery play may be associated exclusively with social as opposed to cognitive learning. The freedom to pursue an activity for as long as one wishes and to abandon it before returning to it is seen as appropriate for the nursery – but at the infants' school it is anticipated that you will have to concentrate for a long period of time on one thing, and move on not when *you* are ready, but when the teacher and the rest of the class is ready:

> She'll have to learn that she's got to sit down a bit and concentrate. She will concentrate for a certain amount of time, and then she'll go on to something else, but . . . she'll probably have to learn to accept that she doesn't go on to something else until the teacher's ready, that the whole class goes on to something else.

In this context, learning becomes a product of being taught. The initiative for learning shifts from the child to the teacher. The results of these changes sometimes seem miraculous to the parents. These parents had tried unsuccessfully to introduce their son to the sitting and learning routine before he started at the infants', and were most impressed not only by how quickly he had adapted to these constraints, but by the fact that he had also learned to write his name as a result:

> Before he started school, he didn't know how to write his name. He wouldn't . . . we'd sit with him and say, 'Come on – let's see if we can learn you how to write your name', and he just wasn't bothered about sitting down learning. He's more bothered about, you know, playing with his cars . . . but he hadn't been at that school a fortnight, and he was coming home, and he'd wrote his name. We really didn't think he'd learn that quick, you know. He came home, he says, 'Look, I've wrote me name!' It were all up and down, but he'd wrote it, you know, and I thought, 'Crike! In a couple of week! He's done it already!'

Robert's mother on the other hand remained anxious despite some teachers' attempts to reassure her:

> I think he's a little less concentrating than all the other children. The nursery teacher mentioned it. And we went to the evening for parents whose children were going up into the link class, and I mentioned this. I said, 'My little boy doesn't seem to be able to concentrate for two seconds on something', and the link class teacher and the head, they said, 'Oh, *all* children are like that', so I thought, 'Oh, thank goodness!', you know, 'he's no different to any other!' but the nursery teacher said that he did seem to concentrate just a little less than all the others. She could get the others to actually concentrate on doing things more than she could Robert.

She remained unconvinced that *all* children are like that (if that were so, why had the nursery teacher alerted her to it?), and despite the best of intentions, she went on to conjure up a pretty unattractive picture of what awaited her son. Learning by 'being taught' begins to sound like torture:

> . . . he does know that it'll be *different*, because I've told him it's going to be different. I said, 'You've got to sit down, and she's going to actually teach you how to read, and how to write,' and I said, 'You've got to sit still while she actually teaches you all this', you see, trying to instil in him that he's got to learn how to sit still . . .

Will Robert learn that such is the nature of learning, or that this is the nature of schooling? The difference is crucial. We spend *15,000 hours* of our lives in school. Learning is a lifelong process which can be embarked upon either as an enjoyable exciting journey with valuable rewards, or as a frightening imposition by external forces, fraught with the dangers of failing to comply. Which of these things a child learns about learning ('deutero-learning') at this early stage in his school career is bound to have a huge impact on the results of that career.

As the child moves from play to work, from learning to being taught, she is also undergoing a process of socialization. Parents do not distinguish this from learning itself. Learning to become a pupil seems to be a prerequisite of learning how to read and write. This failure to make a distinction between learning and institutional socialization has important implications for the roles of teachers and parents as educators and for the relationship between them.

We may ask for whose benefit and to what purpose these parents try to prepare their children for the rigours of the infant classroom. Is it so that they will be better equipped for the learning process or so that they will 'slot in and tick away nicely' as one mother put it, without incurring the teacher's wrath and making her job more difficult? The two may be synonymous in practice, but when parents fail to recognize the institutional component of learning at school, they accord the person of the teacher more credit than she is due, and devalue their own potential contribution.

How far do teachers collude with the building of this picture of themselves? One of the most striking messages parents receive about learning in the infant school, is that there is a right and a wrong way of going about it. Implicit in this idea is that the school knows and is competent in the right way, and that parents frequently demonstrate the wrong way, with disastrous consequences for the child:

> They shown us the way *they* learn em, so I can understand their point of view when you teach em *your* way and then they've got to teach em the *right* way sort of, you know . . . sort of their way of learning.

And what might be called a professionalization of learning was made even more explicit to this parent:

> But Mrs C. his teacher's name is, she said she prefers them to come to school not knowing nothing. She says, because sometimes parents are showing them one way, and it's different to *our* way, and the children are getting confused, thinking, 'Well, me mum showed me how to do it this way, and me teacher's shown me how to do it this', you know, so she says, I prefer children to come like your Stephen, not knowing nothing – and then she can sort of show 'em right from scratch, you know, right from the beginning.

It follows that if this parent accepts this empty vessel theory whereby she hands over her son 'not knowing nothing' to be taught '*their* way' her own contribution to her son's learning is severely limited. Other parents get a similar message but are not so accepting:

> . . . at this particular school, they like you to be involved in the things they do at school, but as far as your child's work and things like that are concerned, I think they like you to leave that to them. They like you to join in with things, you know, erm, anything that's going off at school – sport and all that – you're involved in all that, but the actual work that the child does, I think they just prefer to tell you their bit, and er, you know . . . I try to teach her myself, I'm not bothered what they think, to be honest!

Parents learn from the school that the important business of learning which is now beginning is one which should rightly be left in the hands of the professional, and that to try and help the child yourself at home only serves to confuse her and make the teacher's job that much more difficult.

When parents do ask what they can do to help their children learn, however, the advice they are given can sound suspiciously familiar:

> Teacher: Well, to talk to them a lot, and show interest in what the children want to do, you know, I mean, spend time with them, like looking at books, as far as reading's concerned, playing games with them, answering their questions really. I mean, nowadays, the, the, one of the big problems is television. I mean, er, it's a case of: 'Shut up and be quiet, I'm watching the television.' I think er, if er, if parents give *time* to their children, if they want to know about a particular thing, you know, what they're playing with, or something they're looking at, or, and have time to answer their questions . . . take them about, er, you know, on Saturdays and show them things, this is the best thing the parents can do for their children . . .

Playing games and showing an interest, answering questions, giving time, taking them about, showing them things, explaining things – these are exactly the things described earlier that parents do with their children as part of family life. It may be that like parents themselves teachers know that parents do these things but have not realized the implications. Teachers have not applied this knowledge to their view of home–school relations.

What seems to operate at the point of starting school, is a suspension of the parents' role as educators and substitution of parents as helpers of the educators – the professional teachers who receive children who know nothing, knock them into shape, get them to work the right way, and produce miraculous results.

In this making of home–school relations the parents are ascribed the marginal role of 'co-operating with' the teacher:

> . . . They're co-operative. You don't get many that will not co-operate with you . . . I like them myself . . . very ordinary people, but *nice* people, you know, they're kind people, you know if you ask for anything in the school, they're only too eager to help. If you ask the children to bring things to school, er, they're very good like that, you know . . .

Parents are only too eager to help, but they may readily accept that the school knows the right way of doing things, and that their intervention can damage this essentially professional activity. Some are happy enough to 'leave it to them', and are impressed by the results teachers produce, but those who do have anxieties may not have them allayed by prevarication. Almost as a self-fulfilling prophecy, we saw the mother impress on her son that he'd got to 'sit still and be taught'. That dimension of the making of home–school relations which involves the professionalization of learning therefore, can at the same time assign parents to the marring of the learning process, and take initiative away from the child, who becomes a passive recipient: 'She said she prefers them to come to school not knowing nothing . . . and then she can sort of show 'em right from scratch.' There are alternative models of professionalism for teachers, which also accommodate alternative models for parents as educators.

What I would advocate is a redefinition of the role of the professional teacher which does not change his status as some writers have suggested to that of childminder (as though this were a menial task) but which does not deskill parents. The rationale of this redefinition is threefold: a recognition of parental rights and abilities; a recognition of potential for children's greater educational progress, as highlighted by such initiatives as the Haringey Project; and a more realistic assessment of what we should rightly ask of our teachers. It is a democratizing argument. In many other fields, perhaps most notably medicine, people are demanding greater responsibility for their own lives, their own health, their own experience of childbirth, their own learning. If this is applied to teaching, the role of the professional teacher becomes that of co-educator. We could see a real partnership between teachers and parents in which the teacher complements the parents' unique specialist knowledge of their child with wider knowledge of the current theories on child development, the parents' skills and opportunities in the informal learning environment of the home and the tolerance afforded to the child's egocentricity, with an introduction to the more structured institutionalized setting of the school, which prepares the child for the institutional constraints he will encounter throughout his further life. It becomes part of the professional teacher's role to discover kinds of learning other than the already familiar school-based kinds, and to enable parents to discover and develop the contribution they make to this process. If asked directly what educative roles they play towards their children, many parents will say that they don't. Encouraged further, they can go on to describe practices and approaches that many teachers would admire and applaud. For teachers who wish to work towards a more genuine partnership in home–school relations, recognizing, encouraging, and enabling parents-as-educators can be the beginning of creating different but complementary roles for the professional teacher and the lay parent.

References

BASSEY, M. (1978). *Nine Hundred Primary School Teachers*. Slough: NFER.

LEICHTER, H. J. (1974). 'The family as educator', *Teachers' College Record*, 76.

NEWSON, E. (1976). 'Parents as a resource in diagnosis and assessment'. In: OPPE, T. and WOODFORD, F. (Eds) *The Early Management of Handicapping Disorders*. IRMMH. Amsterdam/Oxford: Elsevier.

NEWSON, J. and NEWSON, E. (1974). 'Cultural aspects of childrearing in the English speaking world'. In: RICHARDS, J. (Ed) *The Integration of the Child into a Social World.* Cambridge: Cambridge University Press.

SHARP, R. and GREEN, A. (1975). *Education and Social Control: A Study in Progressive Primary Education*. London: Routledge and Kegan Paul.

TIZARD, B. (1978). 'Carry on communicating', *Times Educational Supplement*, 3 February.

WELLS, G. (1978). 'Talking with children: the complementary roles of parents and teachers', *English in Education*, 12, 2.

From Normal Baby to Handicapped Child

Timothy Booth

Few sociologists have tried to make sense of mental handicap. For the most part they have been content to study one stage or another in a retarded person's career through life without attempting to step outside the meaning attributed to subnormality by clinical definition.[1]

The limited amount of sociological research that has been undertaken in this field, it is true, has made a practical contribution to our insight into the intimate world of the mentally handicapped and their families and to our awareness of the complexities of the public issues surrounding the support, education and care they receive. As a result we have learnt something of the strains and tensions, as well as the compensations and rewards, which give texture to the relationship between parents and handicapped child;[2] of the burdens and disappointments confronted along with the pleasures and satisfactions that are earned by those who look after them;[3] of the vulnerability which so often mediates the contacts between families with a mentally handicapped child and the wider community;[4] and of the deficiencies and failings, tempered by some achievements, on the part of the public services which process and provide for the mentally handicapped.[5] In this way, by small degrees, a measure of progress has been achieved in humanizing the professional's view of subnormality as a problem of pathology or personal functioning by giving voice to the feelings and credence to the accounts of their clients who experience it as a problem of living.

Yet a common assumption which links most of the sociological literature on mental handicap is that mentally handicapped people form a category of persons who are essentially different from others and that, contingent on this difference, the task of the sociologist is to describe how they are integrated in or excluded from the social arrangements and institutions by which we order and regulate our group life. The fact which differentiates them as a separate class of persons is their diagnosis or ascertainment as subnormal. This criterion of difference is clinically defined in terms of capacity of mind. The assumption then amounts to an acceptance of the view that the same criterion – namely, intellectual capacity or performance – serves not only to identify a clinical condition but also to distinguish a social status. In this way, sociologists have adopted without question and taken for granted a clinical perspective on subnormality.

In this chapter I shall adopt a different frame of reference in order to sketch the beginnings of a sociological perspective on mental handicap. In doing so it is not my purpose to attack the clinical perspective on subnormality; though I do want to suggest that sociologists for their part have been too ready to assume that the way subnormality is represented by clinicians corresponds to how it appears to the families of mentally handicapped children and to others in their wider social circle.[6] I aim to show that becoming a mentally handicapped person is not just a matter of clinical evaluation and diagnosis; that it is a social process which can be understood in terms of the changing meanings given by parents to their child's behaviour and revealed in the way they act and feel towards him. From this point of view mental handicap is forged, by the families of retarded children, from their experience of living together.

Clinical and sociological perspectives

This aim runs contrary to the well-established idea – seldom questioned and rarely articulated – that the way the mentally handicapped are treated and the way they behave can be explained as a social effect of their retardation; or, put another way, that to cite the diagnosis is to satisfactorily account for differences in their behaviour or in the way others behave towards them. If mentally handicapped people are by convention and custom treated differently in society, so the assumption goes, then this is quite simply because they are fundamentally different in nature; and if the balance between personal independence and reliance on others, autonomy and compliance in social relations, or the social esteem and stigma by which they are held in respect differs in scale or degree to that granted to others, then this is because they are naturally different in their intellectual capacities and social capabilities.

This perspective – which I shall call the clinical perspective – views subnormality as a fixed attribute of the person that intrudes uniformly on all aspects of living; a brand, as it were, which a person carries with him as an indelible mark of his singularity. But as a result of the insistence that the social consequences of subnormality are intelligible in terms of the diagnosis, the clinical perspective does not always accord with the practical accounts given by parents of their own experiences of bringing up mentally handicapped children. This is particularly evident in three types of cases where the opinions or decisions of the parents frequently conflict with the attitudes and judgements of the professional.

First, cases in which parents talk about their children in ways which seem not to give credence to the overriding clinical fact of gross disability – 'it might sound funny to someone outside but to us he's as normal as you like' – or who describe their children in terms which do not acknowledge the clinical fact of severe handicap – 'He's just like one of the rest of us'. The only way of making sense of thoughts and feelings such as these within the clinical perspective is through discrediting them by refusing to admit them as true representations of the person's underlying emotions. These parents are said to be 'unable to face reality' and their responses are interpreted in terms of such concepts as psychological defence or denial of the problem, as a way of coping with the painful and threatening feelings of shock, grief, guilt and shame that assault them.[7]

Secondly, in cases where the approach and practices adopted by parents for meeting the challenge of caring for and rearing a mentally handicapped child do not conform to the needs of the child as assessed by the professional onlooker, whether social worker, doctor or whoever. Again the tendency is to disavow the stock of beliefs and skills which parents draw on in handling and bringing up their child by interpreting them as unwholesome signs of a deep-seated maladjustment in the parents' relationship with their child and in their attitudes towards and acceptance of his handicap. Hence, those families which learn to accommodate their child by a routine which shelters and safeguards him from the demands of life risk being branded 'over-protective'; whilst those who underplay his disability, choosing not to make allowances but preferring to include him as an ordinary member of the family, are exposed to the accusation of having failed to come to terms with the situation they face or having rejected the child.[8]

Thirdly, in cases where parents openly and earnestly assert that looking after a handicapped child has not had harmful or damaging consequences for the other members of the family, or on the quality of family life in general, despite the facts of gross personal dependence: 'He's been no harder to bring up than any other normal kiddie' or 'Alvin has not hampered us socially or in any other way' or 'I honestly feel that we haven't had to put any more care and attention into David than we would have to a normal child'. The clinical perspective reflects the adage that 'a handicapped child is a handicapped family'[9] and so repudiates these accounts as misrepresenting the true burden of caring for a handicapped child. Accordingly, it shifts our attention away from the question of how parents vindicate these views and focuses instead on putting forward reasons why they should try to deceive others or delude themselves about the troubles they bear.

In more general terms the clinical perspective, which interprets social artlessness or incompetence as symptomatic of individual pathology, and which accounts for the realities of discrimination and prejudice they encounter in terms of the facts of their disability and their deficiency of skills, is inadequate for explaining the social roles which mentally handicapped people are allocated and the status ascribed to them in the private world of close personal relationships where they figure as individuals rather than cyphers.[10] It prompts us to focus too exclusively on the important but narrow band of characteristics they share as a result of their common membership of that class of people we label 'subnormal' at the expense of appreciating the distinctive qualities and accomplishments that distinguish them as individuals. If we are to try to understand what it means to be subnormal in social as well as in biological terms then we have to show how the difference identified in diagnosis is realized and sustained in the daily lives of mentally handicapped people.

This task entails that we recognize two things. First, that the salience with which the handicap features as an aspect of a person's identity and the degree to which it pervades their performance of social roles does not hinge merely on the gravity of impairment but on the significance that is attached to it by the handicapped person and those with whom he associates. Secondly, that the way in which the handicap is revealed, its conspicuousness and the appearance it assumes may change on different occasions in different places at different times.[11]

Unlike its clinical counterpart, which can be said to exist regardless of whether a person thinks of himself as retarded or whether others treat him as someone who is retarded, subnormality as a social state is created and shaped by human activity. It is framed precisely by the way in which the social behaviour of the mentally handicapped and the treatment they are accorded differentiates them from their peers and contemporaries. From this standpoint, the task of describing subnormality in its social form is equivalent to the task of describing the social meanings that are imputed to the clinical diagnosis.[12]

This sociological perspective is based on two notions which together present another aspect of the reality of mental handicap:

First, it focuses on the origins and unfolding of the social meanings attributed to subnormality. In this sense, the sociologist is interested in the idea of subnormality rather than, as the clinician, in the condition it denotes. The task is to find out how people conceive of subnormality who have no knowledge of its pathology; in other words, how they apprehend what it means to say of someone that he is subnormal.

Secondly, it holds that subnormality is given form as a social state as distinct from a clinical category precisely by the way in which the social behaviour of the mentally handicapped and the way others act towards them breaks the rules and understandings which ordinarily govern our social conduct and isolates them as being in some way odd, aberrant or different. In other words, the sociologist sees subnormality as constituted from just those modes of behaving which the clinician would explain as a symptom or effect of severe retardation.

From this point of view then subnormality is a quality of relationships between people which is disclosed in the way mentally handicapped people fail to live up to the claims and expectations which are made and held of their contemporaries and reaffirmed by the allowances and adjustments which others feel compelled to make in the way they manage their relations with them.[13] It follows that subnormality, as a socially defined role, may assume many forms and take on many guises – irrespective of the severity of an individual's handicap – depending on the sort of concessions and compensations which people feel they have to make, when mixing with mentally handicapped people, in the way they customarily behave towards socially competent others in like situations. In turn these vary and alter, with more far-reaching concessions having to be made in some situations or in some relationships than in others, depending on the stringency with which norms of reciprocity are applied, and the ability of the mentally handicapped person to satisfy the rules of give-and-take and fulfil his obligations to those around him.

Method

In the rest of this chapter I aim to illustrate and give body to this general discussion of the idea of subnormality in order to lay the foundations for a more detailed analysis of the social meaning of mental handicap. Specifically, by describing the sequence of events leading up to children being classified as severely subnormal I hope to indicate how the idea of subnormality is created and shaped by parents in the course of their everyday social experience. My intention is to show that the meaning of the term 'subnormal' is not exhausted by clinical definition but that, on the contrary, the label merely serves to identify a condition the reality of which is, for the families of retarded children, in large measure a social construction.

The material on which this paper is based has been drawn from the case histories of 46 families each of which had at least one severely subnormal child. In half of these families the child was living at home; in the other half the child had been admitted to permanent residential care in a large subnormality hospital. It was collected during the course of a controlled study of the problems experienced by families in accommodating severely mentally handicapped children in the home and of the social factors which contribute to the admission of some children into long-stay hospital.[14] Over a period of five months, 132 interviews were completed with the parents and recorded on tape; each family was seen at least twice and most were visited on three or four occasions.

In this short account I have deliberately sought to condense the experiences of these families into a framework for analysis by omitting or overlooking the idiosyncrasies in their case histories and by drawing together and stressing the similarities. Of course, this approach does not do literal justice to the history of events or to the gradual unfolding of parental apprehension, anxiety, alarm and bewilderment captured in our records. It is not my aim, however, to try to narrate the personal drama acted out in the context of the mundane regularities of family life which typified the period leading up to the final diagnosis; nor to document precisely the different routes taken by families through the maze of health, welfare and educational services – involved at one stage or another in the screening and detection of developmental handicaps – before a conclusive assessment was made. Rather my purpose is to describe how what we call 'severe subnormality' emerges as a social status which can be defined in terms of how a mentally handicapped person is valued by others in the network of relationships which constitutes his social world.

Let me set the scene of this discussion by recounting the relevant fragments of two case histories which reflect a pattern of events common to the experience of a large number of families who participated in the study.

Case 1: When Bruce was eight or nine months old his mother Mrs Gordon[15] noticed that he didn't seem to be sitting up very well. She took him to the family doctor who told her, 'He's a big baby and a bit lazy. He'll be all right'. Not until he was about 21 months old did Mrs Gordon again voice the fear that something might be wrong with Bruce. Then she told her parents that she was worried because she didn't think he was 'keeping up to his stages properly'. They advised her to consult her doctor, but added that in their view there was nothing wrong with him. Mrs Gordon took Bruce to her GP and told him of her concern. He said, 'You can't tell by looking at him' but 'if you're not sure and I'm not certain, I think we'll have him into hospital'. One week later Mrs Gordon took Bruce to see a paediatrician. The child was admitted for 4 days of tests after which Mrs Gordon was told that he was mentally handicapped.

Case 2: Mrs Mallin's suspicions were first raised when Martin was only a few weeks old, after she noticed that he wasn't following stimuli with his eyes. At this time, the district nurse was making the usual post-natal home visits and Mrs Mallin took the opportunity to mention her fears about the baby's health – to which the nurse replied that she was worrying too much. However, the feeling that there was something wrong persisted. Mrs Mallin remained convinced that the baby's reactions were altogether too slow. Eventually, she went to see the family doctor but again he merely assured her that there was nothing wrong and advised her not to worry. Still anxious, she took her worries to the doctor at the local health clinic. He discounted her fears as unfounded. When Martin was just short of a year old, they asked a specialist to examine him. After tests he confirmed that their suspicions were well-grounded and that Martin was in fact badly handicapped.

Each of these case histories chronicles the crucial stages in a drama which prepares the ground for the creation of subnormality as a social state. In what follows, I want to discuss each stage in turn with the aid of short vignettes from the case records.

The arousal of suspicion: lay conceptions of irregularities in child development and behaviour

In most cases it is the parents who take the first initiative and instigate the process that eventually is to bring them into contact with the agencies that arbitrate on the question of what is to pass for normality. Only two children in the study were diagnosed at birth and both of them presented the more obvious physical stigmata of mongolism.[16] For the remainder, their transformation from normal baby into handicapped infant was more prolonged and devious.

The bulk of the clues which first prompted the parents' concern about their child referred to aspects of the child's physical condition or appearance – 'It was the smallness of his head that bothered me';

to the rate of physical or social development – 'He was a bit backward in coming forward'; or to the prominence of certain behavioural quirks and mannerisms – 'His reactions were so slow. He didn't ever seem to smile on cue'.

There was considerable agreement among the families on the nature of the clues which first occasioned their suspicion. Though there was often a wide variation in the age at which these clues were seen to become symptomatic of a more fundamental affliction. One family began to suspect there may be something wrong with their daughter when she showed no sign of attempting to sit up at six or seven months old while another did not refer their son to a doctor until he was two-and-a-half years old and still incapable of sitting unaided and without support. In another case, the parents of an 18-month-old girl consulted their family doctor because she had not yet learnt to walk while another family delayed seeking advice until their son was three and still not walking. This points to a wide-ranging lay consensus on the milestones of growth tempered by a much greater measure of flexibility in timetables of normal development.

The interpretation of these clues as evidence for suspicion about the child's welfare was a crucial factor marking the first phase in the organization of parental doubt about the child. It was the meaning that the parents gave to these clues which determined the age at which the child entered the process from which he would emerge as 'severely subnormal'.

For those parents who immediately read the child's tardiness in keeping up to the timetable by which they charted normal progress as indicative of some underlying malaise, the age at which the child began the passage[17] into subnormality varied with the nature of the symptoms he displayed:

> The Gooches say, 'It was when she wasn't sitting up that we began to get a bit worried'. They compared their daughter to a nephew who was three months younger. He was 'doing so much more and advancing so much more quickly' that they finally went to their doctor.

> Mrs Levy realized that there was something wrong with Guy when he reached the age of five or six months. As compared to his older brother when he was at the same stage, Guy didn't seem

to 'respond' and he had kept his 'foetal face' much longer. Mrs Levy approached the clinic doctor for her opinion.

When Alan was nine months old, Mrs Arnold noticed that he displayed no signs of attempts at speech. By the age of 18 months she knew 'that there was nothing there' and she also noticed that his co-ordination of his hands and feet was bad. She sought her doctor's advice.

Mr and Mrs Gregory thought Kenneth was 'a very good baby' until they compared him with a relative's child when he was eight or nine months old. Whereas his cousin was 'climbing all over the place', Kenneth was 'doing nothing at all'. 'After that, everybody's baby seemed to be doing things and Kenneth not'. So the Gregorys took him along to the welfare clinic.

But many parents, by one device or another, managed to ignore or postpone judgement on the signs of irregular development which for these others had immediately been seen as cause for anxiety.

This was particularly the case among parents of children with manifest physical disabilities. Here, the known infirmity served for a time to avert suspicion about other aspects of the child's condition:

Michael was born with a cleft palate. He was very difficult to feed and very slow to put on weight and grow. When he was two years old he developed cataracts which left him with only partial sight. His parents say that they knew all along that he was backward for he was very slow to sit up, walk, and talk. He was still in nappies at the age of five. But they thought that all these difficulties were the result of his physical problems.

While David was still a baby, Mrs Storthes noticed that he would periodically grimace or shudder. She took him to hospital where he was diagnosed as epileptic. He suffered frequent fits – as often as every 20 minutes – the worst coming when he was nearly two years old. But gradually, medication eased the severity of these fits until they gave no more trouble. Only then did Mrs Storthes realize that there was more wrong than just fits.

For some of these parents the hardships and sorrows of learning how to cope with a physically handicapped baby undoubtedly closed their minds to the prospect that there might be something else wrong. For others, however, the physical handicap was the least threatening explanation for their child's behaviour. Although they were sensitive to the warnings and cues that pointed to a more fundamental malady they nevertheless struggled to reconcile their child's predicament with the most favourable long-term prognosis, even if this meant repressing the truth of their own feelings or colluding in an unspoken pact of mutual self-deception:

> Nigel was born with a cleft palate which caused considerable difficulties with his breathing and feeding. Mr and Mrs Duncan saw the major problem as 'keeping him alive'. 'We deluded ourselves into thinking that once this had been corrected, Nigel would develop and grow better.' However, Mrs Duncan admits that when she was eventually told by a paediatrician of the diagnosis of severe mental handicap, 'I wasn't a bit surprised I just knew, I knew already in my heart'.

Another group of parents, though heedful that their child was not as advanced as other children of the same age, succeeded for a time in interpreting the ambiguous cues they were given in an innocuous or benign way which did not seriously threaten to prejudice or impair his integrity. For some, this was made possible by the conviction that the causes of the trouble were organic in origin and that with proper treatment their child would soon catch up with others – 'I had thought her backwardness was due to some glandular trouble actually. I didn't think for a moment it was something that could never be put right'. Others were fully prepared to accept that their child was dull of understanding and slow to learn – 'We just thought he was ordinarily backward' – or, in less disparaging tones, that their child showed what amounted to an almost wilful reluctance to exert himself – 'He wasn't late enough on anything to really make us worry. We just put it down to being a lazy boy', or 'He was just a sleepyhead' – without seeing these qualities as signifying that anything more serious was amiss.

Some parents confessed that, looking back, they were either predisposed to ignore or quite blind to the evidence before their eyes – 'You don't realize they're not developing normally. He seemed normal. I don't know why because it's obvious now'.

In some cases this resulted from the deliberate decision to avoid falling into the role of worrisome parents. One mother, a former nurse, explained that 'having seen so many sick babies, the tendency is to think that all babies are like that. I was determined not to worry about my own child, not to be an anxious mother'. In order to uphold this attitude, these parents chose to suppress, overlook or play down the signs of wayward behaviour which might have forced them to reconsider their responsibilities. In other cases, parents acknowledged that they simply failed to observe or discern those facets of their child's behaviour which, with hindsight, they could now appreciate had been unusual and irregular. For some of them, this was achieved by resorting to the common expedient of most parents: blocking their minds to the undesirable or unwanted traits that if admitted would tarnish their image of the child they desired – 'I was looking for the things that were good about Leslie and I didn't see the others'. But more explained their omission in terms of their own ignorance or naïvety, stemming in the main from their innocence as young mothers and their unfamiliarity with babies – 'I was slow to recognize her development wasn't quite normal. As a first child I'd nothing to compare her with':

> Mrs Rodgers says that 'not knowing babies' at the time she 'didn't notice anything wrong' with Sidney although she 'knew he was slow'.

> Mrs Selby admits to being slow to recognize the signs of handicap in Christine but puts this down to being 'too young, too green . . . too young to make a fuss. If she'd been my second child, I would have known right away'.

In the light of their latter-day knowledge their past experiences assume a meaning that was not immediately evident to them at the time.[18] Certainly the more experienced mothers, who were swift in picking up the initial cues as warranting concern, confirmed that they had relied on their experience of rearing other children to guide them – 'I don't think I would have noticed if I hadn't have had the other children'. What the reality of the present testifies were the symptoms of handicap appeared to these new parents in their past context in a different less dogmatic guise:

> It didn't hit home that anything was wrong. Now you can look back and think: 'Well, why didn't you question these things?' It just grew on us. As he got older we just accepted the problem. We were in such a problem that we couldn't see it.

Finally, there was a group of parents who though wary of their child's progress nevertheless chose to procrastinate rather than follow up their suspicions. In spite of the fact that most of these parents were conscious of a strong sense of foreboding and feeling of uneasiness about what tomorrow might hold for their child – 'For a few months it had been dripping on my mind that something was wrong' – they nevertheless put their faith in an optimistic outcome to their worries; often backed by the reassurances and encouragement of relatives and friends. They hoped for improvement in the face of their fears; trusting that everything would sort itself out in time. As one family said who chose to defer searching out the truth which they feared they might not want to hear:

> We were both hoping that there was nothing really wrong with the child – always hoping for the improvements to happen next week. And of course the next week never came.

However, for most parents the lee-way for these responses of procrastination, ignorance, circumvention or transference to the initial portents of handicap is limited. Sooner or later, as ad hoc explanations for the child's lack of progress are repeatedly discounted by the evidence of impaired development, and as the incongruity between the child's performance and parents' common-sense readings of the problem mounts, the last shadows of optimism fade into concern about the child's well-being and uncertainty about his future.

At this stage an undefined question mark hangs over the child. On the basis of the clues provided by common-sense timetables of child development, the parents have worked up a *generalized suspicion* about their child's well-being. Their interpretation of these clues at this point amounts to nothing more specific than the fear that there is 'something wrong'. This verdict, that all is not well with the child, provokes the decision to seek professional advice on the cause of the trouble and chronicles the beginning of the change in the status of the child.

The professional's response: prevarication

Only a few of the parents who took their suspicions for professional appraisal and consulted their family doctor or the local health clinic received an immediate diagnosis of retardation. For the remainder, the outcome amounted to the declaration of a moratorium on further change in the child's already fragile and vulnerable status:

> Mrs Gooch's doctor told her that he didn't know if anything was wrong with her daughter because 'children varied so much'. 'He advised us to give it a month and see what progress she made.'

The doctor's responses were of two kinds: one dismissive, the other appreciative of the parents' anxieties.

In some cases, the parents' suspicions were dismissed with no more than a vague reassurance and the advice not to worry. These parents were offered no plausible alternative explanation that would nullify the fears which had brought them to seek the doctor's advice and help them to satisfactorily account for what they saw as oddities in their child's demeanour in a non-menacing way. The doctor restricted his role to the clinical task of finding out if there was any medical justification for what the parents held to be wrong or exceptional with the child and passed over the telling issue of why it was troubling them so much. Having certified that at this stage there was nothing about the child which called for any action on his part, the doctor terminated the case:

> Linda 'didn't speak on time' but when Mrs Maxwell consulted her family doctor she was told only that she expected too much and that nothing was wrong. When she didn't walk, Mrs Maxwell again went to see her doctor to be told only, 'First you're worried about her not talking, now it's not walking'. She comments, 'He seemed a bit annoyed so I didn't go anymore'.

> When Geoff was two years old, Mrs McCloud took him to the doctor on the grounds that he was too quiet for a child his age. The doctor told her that she worried too much and that she should feel lucky to have such a quiet baby. He advised her not to compare Geoff with other children.

The doctor's confident prognostications temporarily mollified the parents but left unanswered the questions that had been kindled in their minds by those features of the child's development which they had decided were out of the ordinary. They had referred to the doctor in the hope that his science would furnish them with a rational account of their child's apparent slowness which their common-sense reckoning had failed to provide. The attempt by the doctor to reassure the parents by fiat merely ensured that when the authority of his voice and his dogmatic tones began to fade with time, the sense of trepidation which had spurred them to call on his advice would occupy their thoughts again.

In other cases, the doctor was sympathetic and responsive to the feelings of agitation and alarm signalled by the parents' suspicions. But on examination he came to the conclusion that for the moment their concern was unfounded. What the parents had taken to be unusual enough to warrant the opinion of an expert, the professional disowned as belonging to the commonplace:

> When Vicky was ten months old, Mrs Castle noticed that she wasn't sitting up properly. She took her to the health clinic where she was told that Vicky was just 'a lazy baby'.
>
> Mrs Rymer realized that Stuart was 'slow' in maturing but when she mentioned this fact at the health clinic on one of her regular visits, they told her 'not to worry, he'll catch up'.
>
> Mr and Mrs Harvey noticed that Eileen wasn't 'pulling herself up in her pram', 'beginning to be active' (or) 'grasping things'. Mrs Harvey commented on some of these points to the doctor at the health clinic who concurred with her judgement – 'Yes, she is slow' – and advised that she consult her GP. When they did raise these worries with their family doctor, he replied, 'Eileen's just a beautiful dumb blonde. She's not interested. She doesn't want to do these things yet'.

Here, the doctor ratifies the parents' lay judgement that their child is behindhand in his development but explains this fact in terms of the natural diversity of talents. The onus is put on the parents to adjust the phasing of the expectations they hold of the child. This signifies the first compromise in a whole series of concessions the parents will eventually have to make in the way they handle their child which plot his emerging status as a subnormal child. Without saying outright that something was wrong with the child the doctor managed to avoid the conclusion that all was well by placing him in an indeterminate position 'behind' others of his age.

But this outcome appealed to the parents' own reasoning and satisfied their immediate wish for a resolution to their troublesome doubts about their child. Unlike those parents whose worries, dismissed by their doctor, returned quickly when they found themselves unable to reconcile his assurances with their own observations, these parents were able to keep faith with this assessment by revising their estimates of their child's potential to fit the facts of his performance. Accordingly, it took longer for the discrepancies between opinion and fact to reach the limit beyond which it became more and more difficult to hold the view that the child was merely backward or slow, and to herald the revival of parental doubt.

The problem for the doctor at this stage is that so many of the symptoms described by the parents do not differentiate their child's development from the normal course of babyhood and infancy: 'Young handicapped children differ from normal children mainly in potential rather than in capacity.'[19] The insecurity which characterizes the parents' feelings about their child is mirrored in the uncertainty which the doctor faces in the clinical setting. He has to devise a strategy which allows him both to cope successfully with his own clinical uncertainty and to appease the parents who are nervously searching and pressing for a diagnosis. This means resisting all demands and pressures to commit himself one way or another to an authentic decision whilst relieving or neutralizing the suspicions which urge the parents to press for a definitive judgement. The tactics of categorical reassurance or normalization,[20] each of which support a wait-and-see policy as we have seen, both succeed for a time in deflecting or deferring parental doubts and by this means gain time for a more positive indication of symptomatology, if any at all, to emerge.

While in retrospect many parents were willing to believe that their family or clinic doctor 'didn't tell me sooner because they weren't sure themselves', others were sceptical about their openness and readiness to confide in them. As one father said, 'I often wonder why he didn't voice what he must have known earlier'. At this point the problem of clinical uncertainty begins to emerge and become confused with the way indeterminacy is invoked and used as a means of managing the parents.[21]

Several reasons were cited for this attitude of distrust. Some parents, like Mrs Masterson, 'wondered if the GP put off telling us because we were doing so well with her'. In cases such as this, the implication is that the doctor knowingly withheld a diagnosis in order not to jeopardize the parents' sense of duty to the child and to permit the growing bonds of tenderness, constancy and love to foment and secure their relationship. Others believed that their doctor may have been 'trying to cushion us from the shock of diagnosis' during a particularly stressful or unsettled period of their lives when other strains and pressures were already falling on the family. For instance, one family who held this view had their eldest son in hospital with leukaemia at the same time as they first consulted their doctor about his younger brother.

Finally, there were parents who maintained simply that their doctor 'didn't want to talk about it' with them; that 'he didn't want to know'. A forceful illustration of this attitude is provided by the case of the Fletchers who only learnt of their daughter's mongolism from a locum GP when she was 16 months old even though, as it turned out later, the diagnosis had been communicated to their regular family doctor immediately after Mrs Fletcher was discharged from maternity hospital. Here the decision not to tell the parents, or to nurture their suspicions by suppressing information, seems to be informed by the idea that parents will be more ready to receive and grasp the diagnosis if they already are convinced themselves that something is wrong with their child. It is implied that until this dawning of awareness any effort to unmask the truth is likely to compound the shock for the parents and provoke resentment against the doctor and a rejection of the diagnosis.

But whether this prevarication was the result of clinical uncertainty or the attempt to programme the diagnosis, the effect was to consolidate the child's ambiguous and transitional status midway between health and sickness; normality and abnormality. He is left straddling two classifications of reality, one of which grants him a weak hold of his personal integrity while the other threatens lifelong dependency. This stage then is characterized by a period of dormancy in the biography of the subnormal child during which events serve only to mark time.

The growth of conviction

Things do not remain static for long however and the passing of time puts strain on the transitional status negotiated for the child by doctors and parents, promising further movement and change in his public identity. Sooner or later it becomes evident to the parents that their child is falling further behind other children rather than holding his own. As one mother commented, 'Things began to get obvious then for other children were standing and Terry was still lying'.

Faced once again with having to find an explanation for their child's retarded development, the parents update their old suspicions. What had before registered as little more than an insinuation now turns into the conviction that the child's 'slowness' is evidence of some sort of deep-seated disorder:

> After being told that Sidney would 'catch up' given time, Mrs Rodgers let things ride until she noticed that his younger brother was 'rapidly catching him up'. Then she 'went to the clinic determined that something was wrong'.

Urged by a new spirit of determination and perseverance, the parents apply themselves to the task of working for a definite diagnosis:[22]

> Mrs Castle rejected the opinion that Vicky was only a 'lazy baby'. She comments, 'I knew myself she wasn't a lazy baby' and adds, 'I started to fight from then onwards to see what was wrong with her'. She saw the family doctor and told him that she 'wanted to know what was really wrong with Vicky'.

> After having been told not to worry about Julie by the health clinic, Mrs Conniston asked to see a specialist. He decided that she was physically handicapped and arranged for her to receive physiotherapy once a fortnight. But Mrs Conniston wasn't satisfied and she asked for a second opinion. Her GP arranged an appointment at Great Ormond Street where they confirmed the diagnosis of physical handicap and offered physiotherapy every week. Mrs Conniston was still unhappy however and when Julie was two and a half she asked that she be given an IQ test.

> When Christine was three years old she was put under the care of a psychiatrist. Mrs Selby kept pressing him to commit himself and tell her what was the matter with her daughter but he warded off her questions. She repeatedly requested him to arrange for Christine to be given an EEG but he declined to do so. Only when the Selbys moved house and Mrs Selby asked her new doctor was Christine referred to hospital for an EEG.

These efforts mark the beginnings of the final negotiations between parents and doctor which are to precipitate the child into subnormality. On the basis of lay standards of normality, the parents have now passed beyond the threshold of tolerance within which they can indulge or excuse further transgressions or minor infringements of the normative criteria and moral rules distinguishing acceptable from deviant behaviour. This point seems to be reached when the child's behaviour, or the pitch and timing of his future development, becomes unpredictable for the parents in terms of their everyday knowledge of the wills and ways of children.[23] In approaching the doctor once again the parents are not, as on earlier occasions, asking for his professional opinion on whether or not there is something wrong with their child. This question has been concluded, outside the surgery or clinic, in the home; the parents are persuaded that their child is 'not right'. Their aim now is to make this judgement, and their child's fate, intelligible in terms of the language of medicine.

The vacuous label

> You know there is something wrong with your child and you're told there is nothing wrong with him at all and, 'We don't know what you're worried about'. Then nine months later your child is mentally handicapped. It's all wrong.

Diagnosis completes the degradation of the child. A last consensus is reached on the reality of the child's condition which establishes his status as severely subnormal. He is finally and irrevocably stripped of all claims to normality, past or prospective. As Garfinkel has put it, 'What he is now is what, after all, he was all along'.[24] Though the efforts made by the doctor to explain 'what sort of child he is' and the clarity and precision with which he communicated the diagnosis to the parents varied widely.

In a few cases, the parents were given a full clinical diagnosis of the origins and causes of their child's retardation; one mother acknowledged that her doctor 'spent a long time with me and really went into it'. More often, when evidence of etiology was lacking, parents were offered a functional diagnosis – such as 'brain damage' – which provides a credible and publicly acceptable reason for the child's limitations without touching on their pathology. Finally, in a number of cases, parents were given what might be called a figurative diagnosis which described their child's condition in euphemistic terms using a vernacular rather than a specialist mode of expression: 'She said he was backward. They've never given it a name' or 'They just said he was just backward. They never said he was mentally handicapped' or 'They'd give you the impression that he was mental but they never spoke outright and said he was'.

In the light of this information given to them on diagnosis, the parents are at last enabled to make sense of their child's abstruse behaviour and irregular development which has puzzled them almost since his birth: 'Through this process the past was made to fit the present, so to speak'.[25]

Yet if the past becomes more accessible and easier to fathom after diagnosis, the future remains no less opaque and elusive. For the parents are in receipt of a label which testifies to the fact that their child will never be normal but which gives them no indication of how he will grow up; as one father said, 'It doesn't tell you what the child is going to be like'.

The problem now facing the parents is to translate the diagnosis of subnormality into terms that will vouchsafe its relevance in a social context. They were given little help by doctors, either family practitioners or hospital specialists, who were uniformly unwilling or unable to commit themselves to any sort of serious forecast of the likely effects of the child's handicap or his ability to look after himself in the future. Three types of prognosis were recollected by parents, all of which were typified by equivocation.

Some doctors were reported to have professed their ignorance and admitted to not knowing how the child's impairment might affect his competence: Mr Hammond remembers the specialist saying, 'He'll never grow up properly. We'll just have to see how he grows up – I've no idea. Only time will tell'. Others were said to have given a counsel of despair, cautioning the parents against an optimistic evaluation of their child's prospects: 'We were told not to hold out any hope at all for her to do anything.' Or, finally, parents recalled their doctor giving them an ambivalent and inconclusive estimate of how their child might develop which left them with no firm idea of what they might realistically expect him to achieve: 'We were told that sometimes they develop better, sometimes they're not as good.'

At this point then the parents are in possession of a diagnosis which describes their child's handicap in a way that affords little insight into how he will fare in the routine world of daily life. It depicts the loss of bodily functions and mental capacity without relating the effect on social performance. The parents are not told how the child will suffer as a result of his handicap or what penalties and sacrifices it will impose on them:

> Mrs McCloud says, '. . . not taking much interest in children like that; not knowing about children of that sort; not knowing anybody like that, we just didn't know what it was all about. We just took his (the doctor's) word and said we'd wait and see how things progress'.

> Mrs Duncan says, 'You can't look into the future. You don't know what it's going to grow into so you can't picture it.'

> Mrs Gant comments, 'We never did have any real idea of just how much he would develop or how much he wouldn't develop.'

These quotations document the origins of subnormality as a social state. From this point onwards it is left up to the parents to build the social meaning of mental handicap by making the link between the diagnosis of subnormality and the social world of everyday life. A mother of two severely mentally handicapped sons evoked clearly the personal and domestic focus in which this task is painstakingly accomplished:

> They say to you your child will be handicapped. It doesn't dawn on you really. The most difficult thing for me was, when he told me, neither of them were walking or talking or feeding themselves,

> or toilet-trained and I couldn't see how they were going to turn out. When they were both about seven – or when Tommy was about seven and Jeff was about five – you could gradually see. By that time they'd learnt to walk; they'd changed from their baby ways and you could see that they'd sort of become little boys. It gave you somehow more idea of them. But they were a totally unknown quantity when they were so small and doing nothing and I thought, 'Well, I don't even know what the handicap means.'

This link is forged in the course of the parents' efforts to reinstate the child into the family in a role which is compatible with the limitations imposed by his handicap and to establish predictable relationships with him based on their first-hand experience in practical affairs of his personal strength and weaknesses.[26]

Concluding remarks

In this chapter, I have tried to step outside the clinical perspective on mental handicap which has informed most research, and dominated professional practice, in this field. Without doubt most of the advances in the care and treatment of mentally handicapped people have been achieved within this tradition. But the medicalization of our thinking about mental handicap has been so complete that it has blinkered our vision as to how other approaches might help to further our understanding.

I have attempted to show how becoming a mentally handicapped person is an intricate social process which turns on a series of critical decisions initiating gradual but perceptible changes in a child's social status and leading ultimately to the elaboration of a social role which cannot be defined in clinical terms. I have argued that in order to develop this approach it is necessary to break with the view that mentally handicapped people present a set of characteristics and potentialities which can be identified and assessed by the tools of diagnosis and medical evaluation and to examine instead the nature of the process by which qualities and capacities are ascribed to or withheld from them. In other words, to work from the premise that subnormality is not a quality within the person but a status allocated to them.

Using parents' own accounts of their experiences I have traced the evolution of the idea of subnormality up to the point of its emergence as a distinct social state. I have shown that subnormality is not a fact which comes into the world fullblown, but rather that it is framed and shaped by social activity. Children are not born ready classified as subnormal. They are assigned to the class of people called subnormal as a result of a series of decisions, spanning a period of time, involving parents, professionals and other people. By limiting attention to the period leading up to diagnosis, I have illustrated how the idea of subnormality is brought into being by the imputation of social meanings to physical states.

In the final section I indicated how, following on the diagnosis, it was left up to the parents to elaborate the idea of subnormality into an organized social role. For these parents, their child bears witness to the social reality of subnormality. From this point onwards, the child's actions and behaviour are assessed as those of someone who is subnormal and thereby work back on themselves to define in turn what subnormality is. In this sense my argument implies that the content of the social state we call subnormality cannot be defined in advance of an understanding of the social context from which it borrows its identity.

Notes and references

1 In this paper I shall use the term 'subnormality' to mean 'severe subnormality' as defined in the Mental Health Act 1959 and to refer to the legal and clinical status of mentally handicapped people. I shall use the term 'mentally handicapped' to refer to the social status granted to people who have been ascertained 'severely subnormal'.

2 See, for example, FARBER, B. (1959). 'Effects of a severely mentally retarded child on family integration', *Monographs of the Society for Research in Child Development*, 24, 2. Also, FARBER, B. (1960). 'Family organisation and crisis: maintenance of integration in families with a severely retarded child', *op. cit.*, 25, 1.

3 See, for example, JAEHNIG, W. B. (1974). Mentally handicapped children and their families. Unpublished PhD thesis. Department of Sociology, University of Essex.

4 See, for example, BAYLEY, M. (1973). *Mental Handicap and Community Care*. London: Routledge and Kegan Paul.

5 See, for example, MORRIS, P. (1969). *Put Away*. London: Routledge and Kegan Paul, including Introduction by Peter Townsend.

6 MERCER, J. R. (1965). 'Social system perspective and clinical perspective: frames of reference for understanding career patterns of persons labelled as mentally retarded', *Social Problems*, 13, 18–34. There have been many criticisms of medical models of mental disorders for confusing diversity with pathology, being different with being abnormal, and for failing to relate behaviour and intention to the social context in which they arise. See, for example, SZASZ, T. S. (1962). *The Myth of Mental Illness*. London: Secker and Warburg; SCHOFF, T. (1966). *Being Mentally Ill*. London: Weidenfeld and Nicolson. The point I want to make here is simply that there is *another way* of looking at mental handicap, other than through the looking-glass of clinical theory, which though it might not contribute to the treatment of severe subnormality might help us to understand and appreciate how mentally handicapped people themselves are treated by others. On this, for a sustained critique of relations between 'professional technicians' and their 'clients', see PEARSON, G. (1975). *The Deviant Imagination*. London: Macmillan.

7 See, for example, KEW, S. (1975). *Handicap and Family Crisis*. London: Pitman.

8 For a discussion of this dilemma see HEWETT, S. (1970). *The Family and the Handicapped Child*. Ch. 4 and pp. 202–7. London: Allen and Unwin.

9 See KEW, *op. cit.*, p. 157; also SHERIDAN, M. (1965). *The Handicapped Child and his Home*. London: National Children's Home.

10 For a study of the different roles played and statuses held by mentally handicapped people in the community see MERCER, J. R. (1973). *Labelling the Mentally Retarded*. Berkeley: University of California Press.

11 See EDGERTON, R. B. (1967). *The Cloak of Competence: Stigma in the Lives of the Mentally Retarded*. Berkeley: University of California Press.

12 See FREIDSON, E. (1970). *Profession of Medicine: A Study in the Sociology of Applied Knowledge*. New York: Dodd Mead.

13 See DAVIS, F. (1963). *Passage Through Crisis*, p. 179. Indianapolis: Bobbs-Merrill.

14 The research was carried out from the Department of Sociology at the University of Essex and funded by the DHSS. The project was conducted by Walter B. Jaehnig, assisted by myself, under the direction of Professor Peter Townsend.

15 All names are, of course, pseudonyms. The same name is used to refer to the same family throughout.

16 It may be noted, nevertheless, that in the cases of three other mongol children in the survey a diagnosis was not made at the time of delivery but from four to sixteen months later. For a discussion of difficulties

and delays in the diagnosis of mongolism see KRAMM, E. R. (1963). *Families of Mongoloid Children*. HEW Children's Bureau Publication No. 401). Washington, D.C.: US Government Printing Office.

17 For the sense in which this concept is used here see GLAZER, B. and STRAUSS, A. (1971). *Status Passage*. London: Routledge and Kegan Paul. I have chosen to use the notion of status passage as a framework instead of the concept of the moral or deviant career because my intention is to focus solely on the sequence of changes, leading up to diagnosis, in the way mentally handicapped children are valued and judged by others, especially their parents. The concept of 'career' as it has been used in studies of 'adult socialization' and deviance refers also to the subjective changes in personal identity, in the person's image of his self, which accompany the changes in public status. This is an aspect that I shall not touch on here. See BECKER, H. S. and STRAUSS, A. (1956). 'Careers, personality and adult socialization', *American Journal of Sociology*, 62, 253–63.

18 For a detailed discussion of the temporal foundations of experience, and of the ways in which the past may be reinterpreted in the light of present experiences, see SCHUTZ, A. (1972). *The Phenomenology of the Social World*. London: Heinemann.

19 DAVIS, A. G. and STRONG, P. M. 'Aren't children wonderful – a study of the allocation of identity in development assessment'. In: STACEY, M. (ed) *The Sociology of the NHS*. Sociological Review Monograph 22, University of Keele, March 1976.

20 I use 'normalization' here in the same sense as LEMERT, E. M. (1967). *Human Deviance, Social Problems and Social Control*. Englewood Cliffs: Prentice-Hall, to mean 'the deviance is perceived as normal variation'. DAVIS, *Passage Through Crisis, op. cit.*, uses the notion in a similar context to refer to the ways 'those aspects of his person that distinguish him from and cause him to be viewed as different by "normals" are made light of, rationalized in a variety of ways, viewed from a less disadvantaged perspective, and denied to be of any importance'. The idea carries a different meaning in the professional literature where it is used to refer to programmes and policies based on the principle that mentally handicapped people should be offered 'patterns and conditions of everyday life which are as close as possible to those of the rest of society', see Campaign for the Mentally Handicapped, *Normalization?*, Discussion Paper No. 3, 96 Portland Place, London.

21 See DAVIS, F. (1960). 'Uncertainty in medical prognosis: clinical and functional', *American Journal of Sociology*, 66, 41–7.

22 BURTON, L. (1975). *The Family Life of Sick Children*. London: Routledge and Kegan Paul, also finds that in cases of cystic fibrosis

'diagnosis . . . required considerable parental effort to effect', p. 27.

23 CUMMING, E. and CUMMING, J. (1957). *Closed Ranks*. Cambridge, Massachusetts: Harvard University Press, observe that the cut-off between the mentally ill and the mentally well in the eyes of the lay population seems to occur as soon as behaviour becomes non-normative and unpredictable.

24 GARFINKEL, H. (1956). 'Conditions of successful degradation ceremonies', *American Journal of Sociology*, 61, pp. 420–4.

25 DAVIS, F. *Passage Through Crisis, op. cit.*, p. 11.

26 The analysis presented in this chapter and concluded in this section contrasts sharply with the point of view put forward by VOYSEY, M. (1975). *A Constant Burden*. Routledge and Kegan Paul. She writes that 'what parents say about their child may reflect less their own constructions than the imputations of others, notably doctors, and especially once a formal diagnosis has been made' (p. 36). And, she adds, 'definitions of his condition in terms of the three dimensions of onset, diagnosis and prognosis may be initially and ultimately those of doctors. It is they who act to provide the basic rules in terms of which parents' evaluations of their child's behaviour must then make sense' (p. 39). I have sought to show that subnormality, as a social status, is not foisted on children by the arbitrary decision of professional diagnosticians.

Both Intermediary and Beneficiary

John and Elizabeth Newson

> Long ago there lived a live leaf. But one day some water came and then mud then water then mud. Then at last it stopped and the leaf was changed and it was a stone leaf. It was a grey stone with the leaf in it. My dad found it in the pit. He brought it home. Then I brought it to school. Some have animals and some have a leaf all rocks are made in earth some are little and some are not. We have got a fossil Miss B brought it some rocks are shot up from a volcanoes. (Six-year-old girl quoted by David Ayerst, *Understanding Schools*)

'Did Miss B (the teacher) or the father get in first with the fossil?' asks David Ayerst: 'It does not matter: either way, home and school play into each other's hands; the interested child is both intermediary and beneficiary. Her world is one.'

The integration of the child's two worlds of home and school through the bringing together of contributions from teacher and father, moreover, has a third dimension here: the world of work, which is not in fact the child's world at all, but from which her father can bring his own special knowledge. A stone leaf, carried up in a father's hand from the deep mystery of 'the pit' where it had rested undisturbed from 'long ago' until now, makes accessible and vivid to the children notions of hardly imaginable time-perspectives, with an immediacy which any teacher might find hard to achieve, however well supplied with specimens from the Schools Museum Service. Some of our own children echo this child's experience.

Miner's wife:

> He's got two fossils that he's very proud of, which his Daddy brought out of the pit. And he's *very* fond of taking them to show his teacher. They've got leaves, branches of leaves. And he's got a very very old newspaper, about eighteen-ninety-something, which he likes to take. I'll tell you what he's very interested in – museums, castles – anything old he really likes. He will take an interest.

Yet fathers and mothers from far less remote workplaces than the pit have resources of experience which could enrich schools: both extending school horizons, and making explicit the points of contact and overlap between the too-separated domains of home, school and work.

From this point of view, what is striking when we look at the ways in which the home backs up the school's educative role is not so much what the school gains from the home as what it does not even try to gain. As we shall see, there were dozens of examples of parents helping with writing at home, 'hearing' a child's reading, overseeing spelling, setting sums; and schools themselves were often reported as taking the initiative in sending home reading books, asking for stage costumes to be made, inviting mothers to help escort a school trip, requesting jellies and cakes for the Christmas party, or goods for a stall at the summer fête, and generally using parents as a resource for old cartons, tins, toilet roll cores, egg-boxes, bottle-tops and other necessities of primary school life: but we did not have one example of either father's or mother's work experience being deliberately made use of. Considering that junior schools do think it relevant to have in their libraries rather pallid accounts of *The Nurse, The Merchant Seaman, The Miner* and so on, it seems strange that they do not attempt to tap the real-life experience of the coalface workers, lathe operators, lorry drivers and bricklayers who are their children's own fathers, many of whom work shifts which would allow them to bring their knowledge into school.

In this account, we shall be looking at how school interests are taken up, supported and supplemented at home, rather than the other way round, and will try to explore how parents see their home-based role as educative forces in the child's life. We shall be particularly concerned with the overlap between parent and teacher roles: how far do parents chiefly see themselves as providers of emotional and material support, or do they feel that they too may appropriately 'teach' in the formal sense? and what do they think that teachers think about overlapping roles?

An index of 'home–school concordance' was devised in an attempt to quantify these factors which seemed to us to have significance for the child's subjective experience of education. As usual, the meaning of the index is defined by the questions which contribute to it. These are as follows: the reader will note that they do not appear in direct sequence.

110. Does he often take things to school to show his teacher?
112. Does he ever come home and start doing something he's been shown at school?
113. Does he ever ask you questions about something he's heard of in class?
What sort of things?
115. Can you always answer his questions?
What do you do if you can't? [What would you do if you couldn't?]
128. Do you or his Daddy ever help him with other things [than reading], like sums or writing or any other school work?
134. Does he do any drawing or painting at home?

As with the previous index of general cultural interests, we will present analyses of the data from each of these questions in turn, and will then consider the index as a whole.

I encourage her to take things because he's a good little teacher, and I think it gives them more heart if somebody's interested . . .'

There are a number of ways in which 'taking things to school to show the teacher' can be interpreted; and how the mother perceives the intention of the act will inevitably influence whether she approves of and encourages it. She may simply regard it as a way of contributing to and enhancing the interest of the topic under discussion at school.

Caretaker's wife:

Well, he takes books; he's taken a bird's nest; ships, they had a display on ships and he took quite a few. [Do you encourage him in that – would you suggest that he should take something to school if he didn't think of it?] Oh yes, yes, I do. If they have a project or anything, you know, he'll take a book with the subject in, and he'll perhaps learn it at school or p'raps write something out from the book.

Electrician's wife:

Oh yes, oh yes, I mean if we find things, say at the seaside – if we found shells I'd say 'Oh, you ought to take these to school'; but he's not very bothered, he doesn't do, and yet I'd like him to – I think it's interesting, you know.

On the other hand, she may see the child's contribution as a hindrance to getting on with the proper business of school life – something which might cause an unnecessary distraction.

Foreman's wife:

Not a lot, because I haven't encouraged that, I don't believe in it, because while they're playing they can't be learning, can they? But he's got a guitar, you see, well it *is* a nice one, and Sir played – I don't know what the names are, you know, it's always 'Sir'! – played some tunes on it, and he said 'Sir said could I bring it again on another day'; so I said 'Yes', I said, 'but you tell Sir to tell you *what* day to take it, and whether it's morning or afternoon . . .'

Representative's wife:

Oh no! I think they go to school to learn, not to play with things.

'Sir' is clearly a positive influence here; other teachers are not, and mothers are bound to be inhibited by the thought of their child being seen as a nuisance.

Van salesman's wife:

Sometimes, but not often, because it's not encouraged there. She took this Koala bear when she had it. She would like to take things to show her teacher, but it isn't encouraged there at all, they get cross with them. [How do you feel about it?] Well, I think it forms a communion with the teacher. I would have thought it was perfectly all right.

The 'apple for the teacher' tradition is at the back of some mothers' minds: they worry that the child's offering might be seen as propitiatory, either by the teacher herself or by his peers.

Policeman's wife:

I would discourage that really, it draws too much attention to themselves. It gives the atmosphere to the other children that he's the teacher's pet.

Electrical engineer's wife:

[Would you suggest she should take something to school if she didn't think of it?] No. Sometimes if we'd got some roses in bloom, and she said could she take them, I'd let her take them. [You wouldn't yourself say 'Why don't you take them?'] No – 'cause I think she p'raps thinks we're getting round the teacher, you know.

These mothers find the 'giving and showing' relationship suspect, or are wary lest others might find it so; others again regard it as a natural and happy way in which a 'communion with the teacher' may be established, fostered and maintained.

Boiler cleaner's wife:

Yes, I like him to take things, because it does really help that little bit in getting used to the teachers, doesn't it?

Printer's wife:

Oh yes, she took three roses this morning, two white and one red; if she likes the teacher, she really likes to take her flowers on a Monday, and if I've any flowers in the garden I have to cut them for her.

University teacher's wife:

Anything new she has. She had a pair of plaits for dressing-up, which I made her. In this particular case, she had to go round all the forms in the school, showing them. This is in fact a sort of principle of the school, that all the forms are accessible – the headmistress likes the children to know the teachers of the other forms, and so she tries to get them sent on errands and to show things and so on; and I like this very much, and Polly absolutely loves it.

Doctor's wife:

> Yes, I think that's the beauty of it today – taking the little presents, and they're just like mother and daughter. 'Cause we were quite afraid of ours.

One further reason why mothers may be not altogether willing for things to be taken to school is that neither children nor teachers are always clear as to which contributions are for giving and which only for showing. Even fossils or seashells may be personally valued by the mother, so that she can be a little ambivalent about their removal to school; other articles have monetary value.

Hosiery presser's wife:

> Last week she wanted her father's football cups to show the teacher, she took them. Um . . . we had a pot of bulbs, she took those to show the teacher, but they didn't come back. [The teacher thought they were for her?] I suppose so.

Advertising manager's wife:

> Well no, I tend to try and discourage him; he's at the swapping stage, and he's lost several good books that have been swapped.

Table 1 shows the children who take things to show their teacher 'often' or 'never'; the middle category 'sometimes' is residual. It can be seen that nearly half the children take things 'often', with a detectable class trend but not a very marked one. More well-defined is the sex difference, girls being significantly more likely than boys in every class to take things 'often'.

Considering that only 12 per cent of children 'never' take things to school in this way, it is interesting to find that when the mothers were asked whether they actively encouraged the child to do so, only 21 per cent took a totally positive line. The majority (69 per cent) had some reservations of the kinds illustrated above, though only 10 per cent were definitely and actively discouraging. Class and sex differences are not significant in these terms, and it thus looks as if the class trend is a matter of *degree* of encouragement by the mother, rather than on an all-or-none basis. This presumably is also true of the sex divergence; in this case, it is likely to be contributed to by mothers' perception of boys as more heedless and careless of their property, and possibly also by a closer identity with school and

Table 1: Children who take things to show their teacher

	social class					*summary*		
	I&II	*IIIwc*	*III man*	*IV*	*V*	*I&II+ IIIwc*	*IIIman, IV, V*	*overall popn*
	%	%	%	%	%	%	%	%
'Often'								
boys	49	47	41	43	35	48	41	43
girls	65	57	52	57	44	61	52	54
both	57	52	46	50	39	55	46	49
Significance:	trend ↓ **					m.class/w.class *		
			between sexes ***					
'Never'								
boys	12	12	19	12	14	12	17	16
girls	3	6	10	7	21	5	11	9
both	7	9	15	10	17	8	14	12
Significance:	trend ↑ *					m.class/w.class *		
			between sexes ***					

teacher on the part of girls, which might make girls more highly motivated to insist on taking things to school.

'They come home from school and expect you to know everything about everything . . .'

We were interested in how far school activities were transferred bodily into the home setting, whether lines of inquiry initiated at school continued to be followed up at home by the child, and whether this was fostered by parental attitudes. The question 'Does he ever come home and start doing something he's been shown at school' was answered affirmatively by 83 per cent of mothers. Class differences were insignificant; a small sex difference in favour of girls was entirely attributable to skilled and semi-skilled class boys, 24 per cent of whom did *not* do this (compared with 12 per cent of middle-class boys). Among the children who did not transfer school activities to home there was very much the feeling that the school was dusted off their feet as they left the school gate: 'As I say, when he's been to school, that's it. In the summer when he's had his tea, he's out – he's a real outdoor child. He forgets school.'

Furnisher's wife:

> I don't really know what he enjoys. We can find out very little about school from Sam at all – very little. In fact I was shattered to hear from [another boy] yesterday that Sam is the best reader in the class! Now the impression he gives *me* is that he's, you know, pretty average – almost sort of bordering on the bottom of the class – but he said oh no, that without any doubt he's the best reader in the class; which annoyed me! And he said 'The teacher really does like him'. I said 'Why's that?' – 'Oh', he said, 'he's always so lively and happy'. Now I wouldn't have been able to give that impression of my own child – so obviously he must be responding at school, though we can't get anything out of *him* about it. He can never remember – that's the big phrase – 'I just can't remember, Mum'. He can't remember what he does.

A point made by the mother quoted next is apposite, remembering that both middle-class children generally and working-class girls are more likely to be collected from school by their mothers than working-class boys:

Administrative assistant's wife:

> If he's been writing at school and got interested, he may come in and get a book and copy writing . . . it depends on his train of thought – if he comes straight home with me, he comes home quicker, and he has that train of thought and carries on with it. If he comes home with schoolchildren, he may have lost that train of thought and carries on with something new.

The activities inspired by school are very various, even excluding for the moment reading and writing help given formally by parents. The following examples refer, as do the percentages given, solely to activities voluntarily followed up by the child, although some may have been deliberately suggested by the school.

Lorry driver's wife:

> Oh yes – in, um, well we used to call it art – I don't know what they call it now. They get all pieces of material now, and cut it into bits, and stick it on things. Ooh, she's always doing that, and she's got a vivid imagination as well for making things on her own, you know, at home – things you'd never think of, you know

– she'll get the toilet-roll cardboard, I couldn't do it myself, you know, and she made a beautiful rocket; the way she decorates things up, you know, oh yes, she's got a vivid imagination for making things.

Nylon winder's wife:

Yes, he showed my daughter of ten how to make a windmill – they'd been cutting them out at school. I said, 'Oh, you'll be able to do a trade down the road, sell them at sixpence each!'

Cook's wife:

When she learns something new at school, different types of sums and so forth: she comes straight home and asks me to write her some of these particular sums she's been doing.

Milk roundsman's wife:

She's always got a book and pencil. Well often it's something they've wrote at school, you know; they have these names what they call the news at school – she'll often write some news. Perhaps not what they've *done* at school, but perhaps something she would have liked to have wrote at school but doesn't get chance.

Miner's wife:

Well, such as – they'd been doing sewing, and the teacher must have showed them, like, and Karen said to me '*You* show me how to do it, and I'll tell you if it's the same'. So I said all right – but no, apparently I don't do it right. An then she wanted to know why have you got to put stitches in things – *why* have you? – can't you just stick it together? There's only one thing, when she starts with that, you must hide all your needles and cotton, 'cause she's sewing everything she can get her hands on – and there's nothing worse when you're trying to lift a towel off a chair, than it's sewn on to your back cover!

Tobacco worker's wife:

Oh yes, you know, painting – he sort of – I think they experiment with colours, you know, mixing things and colours.

A specific example of overlap of home and school experience is in fact in the area of drawing and painting, and we wanted to know what proportion of children were involved in this kind of activity at home as well as at school. In practice, school is likely to provide a wider range of art materials; and from the transcripts it was clear that much home drawing was done either in small drawing books or notepads, or using commercially-produced painting or crayoning books, which rely rather heavily on tracing, copying and 'colouring-in', and thus give rather limited scope to children's creative and imaginative ability. We wondered afterwards whether we should not have been more restrictive in our question and its coding. Forty per cent of children were said to draw or paint 'most days', and differences were not significant in this group. However, a class difference did appear among the children who hardly ever drew or painted, where the proportions ranged from 5 per cent of middle-class children, through 10 per cent of the skilled and semi-skilled groups, to 15 per cent in Class V.

Of greater interest, perhaps, is whether the child follows up school topics in the form of questions to his mother (Table 2); and we were interested both in the child's behaviour and in the mother's response to it. To some extent this is a circular matter: the child is

Table 2: Children who ask mother questions about school topics

	social class					*summary*		
	I&II	*IIIwc*	*III man*	*IV*	*V*	*I&II+ IIIwc*	*IIIman, IV, V*	*overall popn*
	%	%	%	%	%	%	%	%
boys	71	73	52	58	53	72	53	58
girls	75	54	62	61	46	65	60	61
both	73	64	57	59	49	69	56	60

Significance: trend ↓ **** m.class/w.class ***

between sexes n.s.

likely to ask questions about what he perceives as relevant, and his mother's encouraging response not only rewards this question and stimulates additional ones, but also confirms his perception of the relevance of investigation generally; conversely, a mother who fobs off questions not only negatively reinforces the act of questioning but also devalues the spirit of inquiry that prompted the act. Thus we must expect, and we do in fact find, some correlation between child's and mother's behaviour.

Administrative assistant's wife:

He does, usually because he doesn't quite know what the teacher's said; and then I've had to try and work out what she's thinking and what he's heard from his tale, and go on from there! Because he'll come out and ask a direct question, what do you know, do you believe so-and-so Mummy? And I'll say either yes or no, according to what . . . 'Well, my teacher says . . .' – the opposite, as a rule. And then I have to put her in the right as well, and I have to get a bit further just to see what she *has* said, and work it from there! [Would he tend to trust you rather than the teacher, or the teacher rather than you?] Well, when it was Mrs Lester, his first, it was the teacher all the time, I just didn't stand a chance! But now it's often fifty-fifty, according to what he thinks I'm capable of knowing!

Lorry driver's wife:

Oh yes, he likes to know the ins and outs of everything. He came home one day and said, 'M'am, you know that man that had his head cut off when he . . . this woman was dancing with him . . . he lost his head . . . there was a chapter in the Bible all about it . . . there's a very sad ending in the chapter, do you know it?' – he was going on in a garbled way. I said, 'Do you mean John the Baptist who had his head cut off?' – 'But Mr Field said there's a very sad ending to it – the chapter – do you know it?' So I read through this chapter and I thought, well, *I* can't find a sad ending to it, and the doves came down from Heaven and everything; and I thought, oh well, I can't go through the whole Bible, it'll take weeks. So in the end he nagged me about this, he wanted to know the sad ending; and I put my coat on and I went down to see the headmaster, and apparently it was just that he'd had his head cut off; well I *knew* that, but I was looking for the sad ending. But they come home from school and expect you to know everything about everything.

Joiner's wife:

I'm too busy really – I don't always listen. She jabbers on – I don't always know *what* she's on about.

We collected examples of questions that the child asked, both as a result of 'something he's heard of in class' and in general; and we went on to ask whether the mother could always answer the child's questions, and what she would do if she couldn't.

We had already learned in our earlier work (Newson, J. and Newson, E., 1968) that, when the children were four, there was a difference between *can* answer and *wants* to answer; at this point we were looking for mothers' strategies if they simply did not know the answer to the child's questions. It was not uncommon, however, for a mother to begin in terms of questions she did not wish to pursue with the child, usually involving sex information.

Maintenance worker's wife:

> Well, I don't really know . . . I'd have to try and get out of it . . . take her mind off it. There's quite a few things that other children tell her and really they never ought to know theirselves, and she asks us these questions, and we've got to get her on to something else.

Labourer's wife:

> Not all the time . . . I wouldn't like him to know the things he asks me [meaning look]. I make up something.

A rather more subtle interpretation of 'can't answer' involved meeting children's questions in terms of belief or faith rather than fact.

Teachers:

> The questions that I can't answer are about God and Heaven, you know – I'm just flummoxed. [Father:] Now that *is* difficult to cope with. [Mother:] I always say ask Daddy! [Father:] Now this is difficult, because I don't want to, er, make her mind up *for* her either way. In some respects I don't want her to just accept blindly that there is a God; but on the other hand I wouldn't like to sort of say to her, now look, this is superstitious nonsense or something, that would be the opposite extreme. When she's sort of telling me something which is sort of blind acceptance of what *she's* been told, I'm hedging; because – um – I don't want to sort of chop her down on what she's been told, but at the same time I can't go along with her and agree with it. But I think as time goes along I shall help her to sort of . . . well, to make up her own mind about it. [Mother:] Well, you usually say 'Well that's what some

people say'. [Father:] Yes, but it's a sort of feeblish . . . sort of . . . [Mother:] I can't answer that.

Postal worker's wife:

It is difficult on religion; because I don't always understand it myself . . . I mean – when you hear of these things happening to children – like it happened when all those children got killed [Aberfan disaster]. Well, that was an instance when he came in and he said 'Why did Jesus let it happen?' Well, I couldn't answer that. Well, I said 'He does these things to test us all – and he doesn't *mean* for this to happen to little children, you see'. But they do come out with things like that, don't they?

Having reiterated if necessary that we were interested in what happened when mothers merely did not have enough information to answer, we found that we could divide their responses into four categories: Mother consults books or newspaper, etc.; she asks someone else; she does nothing, but admits her ignorance; she attempts to conceal her ignorance from the child. These categories were regarded as an hierarchy in the sense that a mixed answer in the first two categories ('If we couldn't find it in the encyclopaedia, my neighbour might be able to tell us') would be counted as 'consults books'. Examples of responses in the four categories follow:

Consults books, newspapers, etc.

Teacher's wife:

We've got an encyclopaedia and we'd look it up in that, or in a book in the library. But usually between us we've got the book or the knowledge. We go on to the end to satisfy him – if only because *we* become interested! He might perhaps have lost interest, you know, on the way, but we still go on!

Tobacco worker's wife:

I would tell him I didn't know about it and we'll try and find out, and a lot of things he does want to know . . . my sister's got a terrible lot of encyclopaedias. I don't tell him that *he* should ask his Aunty. I tell him that *we* will find out.

University teacher's wife:

Very often his father can provide information, unless it's one of the biological sciences, in which case we have to make do with what I can manage. I haven't had to look something up so far; the exception to this is geology. He's very interested in these stones, and I've bought some books and I've read something, and have started to flog the subject for myself. It's difficult, this sort of thing, because it's really a bit advanced, and I don't want to make it boring by too much fact.

Asks someone else

Lorry driver's wife:

Oh no, if I'm really stumped I usually ask somebody else, I mean, if I was *really* stumped I should go down and see the headmaster or his teacher to find out, 'cause they set the tests in school and they're bound to know the answers [laughs] – at least I hope they do!

Machine operator's wife:

Well, the parents round here are pretty good; what we don't know they do. The boy next door comes here for certain things – English and maths – and Edgar goes down the street to a chap who's a Jehovah's witness for religion, and we sort of . . . I mean, this chap down the street, what he doesn't know about the Bible isn't worth knowing, and it's very handy. And the lady next door, she's very good as well, she'll answer pretty well everything that we can't, and we do the same for her children.

Representative's wife:

Well, I try and remember to get him to ask his Daddy while I'm there, so we both know about it.

Miner's wife:

Sometimes I can, other times I don't know how to word it, sort of; sometimes I manage quite well. [What do you do if you can't?] Say 'Tell you what, darling – I'll ask somebody, and tell you tomorrow'. [And do you?] Yes, quite often – maybe have a word with one of the teachers at her school.

Does nothing, but admits ignorance

Driver's wife:

I've always said 'When I find out the answer, I'll let you know' – and they've been satisfied with that. [Do you find out?] No.

Miner's wife:

I mostly find out how to [answer], I have to think it over carefully first. I say 'Oh well, wait a minute, Barbara, I'll tell you in a minute when I've done this', and I'll think about it first, which way I'm going to answer. [What do you do if you *don't* know the answer?] I say 'Well, I don't know the answer, Barbara'.

Display manager's wife:

Well, I try very hard to give *some* sort of answer; I don't like to say I don't know. [And if you really didn't know?] Oh well, I'd say 'I'm sorry, I don't know'.

Tries to conceal ignorance

Railwayman's wife:

I pretend I haven't heard her then. Say if she asks me if I can spell such-and-such a word, and I can't; then I say 'Oh, ask me a bit later, I'm busy'. I'll put her off if I can.

Electrician's wife:

Pass it off, or make a mild excuse.

Structural cleaner's wife:

I tell him his brain isn't big enough now to hold it all.

Depot manager's wife:

Well, I'm afraid I'd try to answer it in one way or another; I wouldn't exactly slide out of it, but try and pacify him . . . he gets a little bit annoyed because he's not got a proper answer.

Mothers' strategies when they are unable to answer their children's questions as summarized in Table 3.

Table 3: Mother's strategies when unable to answer their children's questions

	social class					*summary*		
	I&II	*IIIwc*	*III man*	*IV*	*V*	*I&II+ IIIwc*	*IIIman, IV, V*	*overall popn*
	%	%	%	%	%	%	%	%
Consults books								
boys	37	16	8	9	2	27	8	13
girls	39	25	14	9	3	32	12	17
both	38	21	11	9	3	30	10	15
Significance:	trend ↓ ****					m.class/w.class ****		
	between sexes n.s.							
Ask someone								
boys	39	38	42	36	19	38	38	38
girls	27	40	30	26	21	33	28	30
both	33	39	36	31	20	35	33	34
Significance:	trend ↓ *					m.class/w.class n.s.		
	between sexes *							
Nothing: admits ignorance								
boys	21	35	34	35	61	28	37	35
girls	25	25	41	45	63	25	44	39
both	23	29	37	40	62	27	41	37
Significance:	trend ↑ ****					m.class/w.class ****		
	between sexes n.s.							
Conceals ignorance								
boys	3	11	16	20	18	7	17	14
girls	9	10	15	20	13	10	16	14
both	6	11	16	20	15	8	16	14
Significance:	trend ↑ ***					m.class/w.class ***		
	between sexes n.s.							

Middle-class mothers, by virtue of their own educational advantages, are better equipped to answer their children's questions; this is likely to encourage their children to turn to them with questions more frequently, and no doubt contributes to the class difference in the actual asking of questions arising out of school which we have already seen in Table 2. The mother's attitude when her knowledge is not enough for the child takes the situation a step further, however. It can be assumed that the first two categories given are educationally supportive, since an effort is made to acquire the information asked for; that the third is neither supportive nor especially discouraging; and that the fourth, concealing ignorance, is frankly unsupportive, since the child is usually deliberately discouraged from persisting with these questions which diminish the mother's self-image.

Consulting books obviously comes more easily to middle-class mothers: more likely to have books at hand, to know their way around a library, to be able to pursue a topic through an index and cope with formal and elaborated prose, their whole white-collar or professional lifestyle imbues them with the expectation that the most authoritative information is obtainable from this source, and, moreover, that it is there to be used. The mother who consults books with her child, however, does more than induct him into an important subcultural expectation; she also immediately involves herself in the inquiring role in a particularly active way. This is much more marked in consulting books than in asking other people; although a mother may 'get him to ask his Daddy while I'm there, so we both know about it', her role tends to be active only in the initial stages, soon becoming passive as the informant takes over. The use of books, on the other hand, is likely to remain a co-operative effort throughout, since seven-year-olds are not yet very skilled at winkling the knowledge they need from a book without help in both scanning and actual reading. Additionally, because of this personal involvement, she thereby identifies his questions as being of interest to *her*, and worth giving *her* time and trouble to answer; whereas if she refers him on to some other person, she may not continue to be involved in any way at all. Thus, while we can hardly be surprised at the very clear class differences in turning to books to satisfy children's questions, the most significant feature of the act is its *implication*: that it defines to the child *the pursuit of knowledge via reading* as relevant for mothers as well as schoolchildren.

Looking at the second half of Table 3, we find ourselves with a rather large group (57 per cent) of mothers in the working class who are not educationally supportive of their children when they do not know the answers to the child's questions. Of some interest among these, although a small group, are those mothers who attempt to conceal their ignorance from the child by various 'fobbing-off' methods: twice as many in the working class as in the middle class. We can understand this class difference by looking at other attitudes which make up class styles. For instance the more authoritarian stance adopted further down the social scale depends upon the premise that mother knows best by virtue of her status: a demonstration of her ignorance is more difficult for her to tolerate and incorporate into that image than it would be for the more democratically-oriented mother, who has already conceded to the child that she can be wrong (a parallel to this is the class difference in mothers' willingness to apologise to the child) (Newson, J. and Newson, E., 1976). If middle-class mothers do feel that they have lost face by not knowing the answer to a question, they can easily regain it by showing their expertise in using resources; this course is less open to the lower-working-class mother, who may indeed feel it safer not to embark on a search which may still end in failure. Further up the social scale, educationally-oriented mothers may even welcome a situation which gives them the excuse to introduce the child to the use of dictionaries and encyclopaedias; further down the scale, mothers are less well equipped with such aids. Finally, we have indeed used mothers' attempts to conceal their ignorance from the child as one item in our index of 'bamboozlement' (Newson, J. and Newson, E., 1968), seeing it as one way in which the mother may try to maintain her authority at the expense of truthful dealing with the child; this index, like the index of 'evasion or distortion of truth' at age four (Newson, J. and Newson, E., 1976), shows major class differences.

The (minor) sex difference in the category 'Asks someone else' needs some comment, particularly as it unusually favours boys rather than girls. Reading the transcripts, it seems to be mainly due to the fact that many of the boys' questions are unanswerable by the mother but easily answerable by the father because they relate to conventional male interests – mechanical things, football, war and battles, space exploration, for example. In situations like this, where mother knows that her husband has the information needed, the obvious course is to 'ask Daddy when he comes in'.

For clarity, it is worth combining the first two sections of Table 3, in order to present in one scale the two categories judged to be educationally supportive. Table 4 makes it very plain that the whole issue of taking responsibility for extending children's information sources beyond the confines of the mother's own knowledge is closely class-linked; the child's sex is not a factor.

Table 4: Mothers who take responsibility for finding out the answers to children's questions if they cannot themselves provide them

	social class					*summary*		
	I&II	*IIIwc*	*III man*	*IV*	*V*	*I&II+ IIIwc*	*IIIman, IV, V*	*overall popn*
	%	%	%	%	%	%	%	%
boys	76	54	50	44	23	65	46	51
girls	66	66	44	35	23	65	40	47
both	71	60	47	40	23	65	48	49

Significance: trend ↓ **** m.class/w.class ****

between sexes n.s.

So far, we have considered items which we might expect to contribute to the concordance between home and school in ways which are somewhat peripheral to what parents see as the core purpose of school: to turn out a literate and numerate child. The most direct way in which they might back up this purpose (leaving aside for the moment whether either parents or teachers think them competent to do so) is by helping the child with reading and other school work at home. The question of help with reading is very dependent upon the child's actual reading competence, and raises many problems of how to measure the quantity and quality of such help. Help with other schoolwork tends to be of the more generally encouraging kind that the concordance index is concerned with: an environment is provided which is hospitable to ideas, inquiry, the following-through of initiatives, the sustaining and completion of projects. Sometimes parents will set and mark sums for the child; but this is usually at the child's request ('Do me some sums, Dad, dead hard ones!'), rather than stemming from the parents' anxiety that the child is not yet numerate; parents are wary of tangling with the mysterious processes of 'new maths', and all too often their doubts are reinforced by a scornful '*That's* not how we do it at school!' Help with writing is most often described in terms of spelling, but may also be largely a matter of taking thought to create a conducive environment – '. . . set the table out and a nice sheet of paper and sharp pencils – everything to invite him to write'.

Showroom foreman's wife:

He's doing a brief on water, and we've bought him a junior dictionary, and I've taught him to look words up – I have to help him to find out where the word is, but he knows it's water in the 'w's, you see. He's also got an encyclopaedia, and he looks at the pictures, you see; so if he wants to look at the boats of other years, I get him to look at that.

Foreman's wife:

Well, he brought some home about a fortnight ago, and we sat and went through it with him, you know how you do. Well it was adding up. Now – here's where you're up against it really, because we told him – like he says he's got to count. He says, 'I can't just add the two numbers'. So I says, 'Well, always *think* . . .' – it was a 6 and a 4 – '. . . always think of the biggest one, you see, the 6; then you've only got to add 4, you see'. So I said: 'Say 6 in your mind, and then get your fingers, and then go from there, that's 7, 8, 9, 10'. He says, 'We don't do it that road at school' – you see! So I says 'What *do* you do?' So he says, 'Well we get six blocks and we put them one side, and four blocks this side, then add 'em all together'. So you kinda – you think you're teaching them what you think is an easy way, but it's completely different to that, so . . . [And you haven't always *got* blocks, have you?] No – I says we shall finish up with blocks all round the house before we've done, when he gets on tens, units and hundreds!

Departmental manager's wife:

We help him with this arithmetic; and now, though the school doesn't approve, we're teaching him his tables. *They* say at school they're not *allowed* to teach them their tables. [Who doesn't allow?] The education, so they say. I happened to be talking to his teacher about how we taught Steven and Jennifer their tables – because Jennifer found that more help than anything when she got to Mundella [grammar school]. And I says 'Why don't you teach them here?' And she said 'We're not

> allowed to teach them tables. If the school inspector came and found us teaching tables, we'd be in trouble'. Well, I can't understand that. So we've taught them all, and Keith got interested when we were teaching Steven [eleven]; so I said well, if he is interested, we'll start him now. He thinks it's fun, you see; because one of us has Steven and the other has Keith, and he's *hoping* to get better than Steven at it!

Cotton winder's wife:

> When the weather's been bad, I've been learning him to play cards; I thought to myself, well, this'll help him with his numbers, it'll learn him them, it'll help him know how to exchange money, you know. And apart from that, it'll learn him *not* to gamble later on – they both start off with sixpence, and when he loses, like, when they've lost, they've lost – they can p'raps borrow, but they have got to pay it back when they win again . . . When we first started to play, he knew some of the numbers but he didn't know 'em all. Well, now he knows, and he knows which not to put down, and he can change his money. So we're helping him there on that. He thinks it's a game, but it's an education really.

Table 5 shows proportions of parents who have regularly or often tried to help with schoolwork other than reading, compared with those who have not attempted this at all; there is a residual middle category of parents who sometimes try to help. Class differences are similar to those found in other items of this index. Sex differences are not consistent: girls are favoured in the managerial/professional class in that only an eighth of them have *no* help, compared with twice as many boys, but equal numbers of boys and girls are given frequent help. Girls are favoured with frequent help in Class IV, but equal numbers are not helped at all. Once again Class V boys have the least favourable environment from an educational point of view.

The scoring of the home–school concordance index is shown in Table 6; as usual, we have then divided the sample into groups as nearly as possible equal in size, on the basis of their scores, and in Table 7 the low scorers and high scorers are shown in terms of social class and sex.

Table 5: Parents' help with schoolwork other than reading

	social class					*summary*		
	I&II	*IIIwc*	*III man*	*IV*	*V*	*I&II+ IIIwc*	*IIIman, IV, V*	*overall popn*
	%	%	%	%	%	%	%	%
Frequent help								
boys	35	23	19	7	12	29	16	19
girls	32	29	23	27	10	31	23	25
both	34	26	21	17	11	20	19	22

Significance: trend ↓ **** m.class/w.class ***

between sexes n.s.

	I&II	*IIIwc*	*III man*	*IV*	*V*	*I&II+ IIIwc*	*IIIman, IV, V*	*overall popn*
No help								
boys	25	12	20	21	35	19	22	21
girls	12	14	18	23	21	13	19	18
both	18	13	19	22	28	16	21	19

Significance: trend ↑ * m.class/w.class n.s.

between sexes n.s.

Table 6: An index of home–school concordance

Based on		*Response*	*Score*
Q.110	Child takes things to school to show his teacher	Often	2
		Occasionally	1
		Never	0
Q.112	Child continues school activities at home	Yes	1
		No	0
Q.134	Child draws/paints at home	Most days	2
		Sometimes	1
		Rarely	0
Q.113	Child asks about things he's heard of in class	Yes	1
		No	0
Q.115	Mother takes responsibility for finding answers she doesn't know	Yes	1
		No	0
Q.128	Parents try to help with school work	Regularly	2
		Occasionally	1
		Not at all	0

Possible score range 0–9, max. 9

Table 7: High and low scorers on the home–school concordance index

	social class					*summary*		
	I&II	*IIIwc*	*III man*	*IV*	*V*	*I&II+ IIIwc*	*IIIman, IV, V*	*overall popn*
	%	%	%	%	%	%	%	%
High scorers (7–9)								
boys	39	31	28	17	16	35	24	27
girls	55	43	37	37	20	49	34	38
both	47	37	32	27	13	42	29	33

Significance: trend ↓ **** m.class/w.class ****

between sexes ***

	I&II	*IIIwc*	*III man*	*IV*	*V*	*I&II+ IIIwc*	*IIIman, IV, V*	*overall popn*
Low scorers (0–4)								
boys	13	10	34	41	42	12	36	30
girls	11	14	24	21	31	12	24	21
both	12	12	29	31	36	12	30	25

Significance: trend ↑ **** m.class/w.class ****

between sexes ** interaction class/sex $p = 0.08$

The results given in Table 7 very clearly confirm marked social class trends in terms of both low scorers and high scorers on home–school concordance. In the working-class group as a whole, families are rather evenly spread across the score range, with just under a third appearing in each of the high and low categories and just over a third in the middle category; the unskilled group, however, is notably unlikely to score high (13 per cent) and unskilled-class boys in particular score low (42 per cent). In the middle class, families are not at all evenly spread through the score range: only 12 per cent show a low degree of concordance. Professional-class girls stand out as especially likely to score high (55 per cent).

The clear-cut sex difference deserves comment: it might not have been expected, since only one of the individual items (taking things to school) produced a sex difference of a similar magnitude. Of the other two results which showed sex differences of lesser significance, one favoured the girls, but the other the boys. This is an example of how an overall index measure of this kind can in fact tell us something over and above what we can learn from the individual items that make up the scale. In other words, the index allows us to draw conclusions about the *degree* of home–school concordance which is experienced by boys and girls; whereas the individual items strictly only allow us to make statements about the proportions of girls, as compared with boys, who behave in a certain way. The sex/class interaction found among the low scorers, though marginal, is of interest because it underlines an interaction effect to which we have previously drawn attention; in its clearest terms, lower-working-class boys are disadvantaged and upper-middle-class girls advantaged by virtue of both their class affiliation and the sex to which they belong.

An analysis of variance based on the index scores both confirms and extends these conclusions. Occupational class is the most important factor, followed by sex, and both these are significant at the 0.001 level. A less salient result, significant at the 0.02 level, is that children from small families have higher scores on home–school concordance than those from larger families. Over the full range of scores, however, the sex/class interaction fades and no longer reaches borderline significance.

We can bring together the two groups of findings which we have discussed here and in the previous chapter, and which we have presented as indices of 'general cultural interests' and 'home–school concordance'. In both cases we can see striking differences between social class groups. These can be summarized in terms of a number of tendencies: as we move down the social scale,

1 The range of cultural interests experienced by children as members of their family group becomes more narrow and restricted.
2 Although children in all classes sometimes carry over school activities into the home, further down the scale they are less inquiring at home on school-inspired topics.
3 Parents become less inclined to take up and expand children's questions, of whatever source, by whatever means.
4 Parents are, in particular, less likely to use books or newspapers to further the child's knowledge, and are more likely to attempt to conceal their own ignorance.

5 Children are less likely to receive help, direct or in the form of the encouragement of a 'hospitable environment', with school work other than reading.

The range of cultural interests, as expressed in the GCI index, is not apparently affected by the child's sex, whereas the concordance index scores are significantly higher for girls. This makes sense in terms of the mainly family-based nature of the first index compared with the child-based nature of the second: that is to say (leaving aside extra-curricular lessons), the trips and excursions of the GCI index will tend to be organized for the whole family, and therefore available to both sexes equally, whereas in the HSC index we are looking at parents' interactions with one particular child.

The factor of family size, on the other hand, is more consistently at work through both indices: families with four or more children are less likely to be taken out into the community by their parents and less likely to score high on the items which indicate a good concordance between home and school. Thus children from large families tend to be disadvantaged on both these counts. This is understandable in terms of a shortage of money, space, time, patience, energy; that it is understandable does not make it any less real as a disadvantage.

To sum up, when we consider circumstances of home background which fall broadly within the scope of the child's general education outside school, once again it is working-class boys, and in particular unskilled working-class boys, who seem most seriously disadvantaged; if they also come from large families with low incomes, the odds will be correspondingly more heavily weighted against them. In a variety of ways the interest of girls at this age tend to be home-centred, which also means that they tend naturally to be relevant to the educational process as it is conceived in school; boys' interests are less obviously relevant, and are often at loggerheads with school demands. Furthermore, there are a number of sex–class interactions in the data analysis which always point in the same direction, even when they do not reach significance level; taken together, they indicate an attempt by middle-class parents of boys to ensure home–school concordance as well as to introduce them to wider cultural events. In this respect, as well as in others which we have already mentioned, the difference between the sexes in their experience of socialization becomes markedly greater as we move down the social class scale.

'School doesn't like you to help him – their ways are different'

In this chapter we have been exploring the ways in which the school is or is not backed up at home by the parents' willingness to enlarge the child's cultural horizons and to provide an environment stimulating of and responsive to his ideas. It is, of course, also the concern of the school itself to provide such an environment. In a sense, however, the voluntary nature of home educational activities compared with the compulsory nature of school is paralleled by the voluntary nature of the school's cultural activities compared with the compulsory nature of its efforts towards literacy and numeracy: that is to say, parents, teachers and children all tend to subscribe to the belief that it is the business of junior schools to teach the three Rs, whatever else they may or may not teach. No parents are totally unconcerned as to whether their child will learn to read. At the same time, to say that literacy is important to all parents for their children does not imply that it is personally *relevant* to all parents' own lives. To what extent do parents regard it as their own ultimate responsibility to ensure the attainment of reading competence in their child, and how far are their attitudes in this respect defined by the relevance of literacy to their own lifestyles? Certainly what parents seem to have in common (and this includes parents who are teachers by profession) is doubt and uncertainty as to whether their role in helping the child should overlap with the teacher's.

The roles of teachers and of parents are fundamentally different. Parents have a clear duty to do their best for their own children; and that best includes a partiality for their own which has no 'reasonable' limits. Teachers, on the other hand, must be both reasonable and impartial; for although parents might be only too glad to see their own children preferred at school, they also realize that they would find it intolerable were other children given preferential treatment at the expense of theirs. 'Having favourites' is regarded as a major criticism by parents, teachers and children; fairness and impartiality is an important part of the 'good teacher's' role. To sustain this notion, a corollary is invoked: that teachers must be given a reasonably free hand to educate (and discipline) children without too much parental pressure and 'interference' in the classroom. In an era of educational thought which is more and more concerned to involve parents in their children's education, including classroom involvement, it was interesting to find how few parents were demanding any such thing: the prevailing attitude was that teachers have a difficult enough job, and could well need to be protected from particular parents who might have an overactive interest in the welfare of their own children. In this climate of thought, being a parent who was not 'always up and down to the school' was most often seen as a positive virtue. Even when children were clearly making rather poor progress, parents seemed to be leaning over backwards in an effort not to criticize the school and teachers directly – perhaps because they were acutely aware of the possibility of being branded as 'overprotective' or 'difficult' parents. The parental dilemma is, in fact, that intervention – even when it seems necessary and reasonable – might all too easily upset a delicate relationship, and in the longer run make matters worse for the child rather than better.

When children fail to make good progress, teachers also naturally feel concerned; but again their feelings are complex. They know that their classroom is not unobserved. Although parents still do not often spend time in classrooms during the working day, they are strongly motivated to discover what goes on there, and are fairly well placed to fill out the details of the picture they are given on Open Day: after all, their children and those of neighbours do talk at home about what they have been doing in school, and although some children are more reticent than others, and accounts given are not always very accurate, mothers are not socially isolated from one another; in talking among themselves, they can if they wish rapidly piece together a more-or-less consistent picture. A good deal of information is exchanged through the gossip chain around the school gates among parents waiting for their children, and (just as the conversation in the waitingroom of a group practice surgery endlessly compares the doctors' personalities and talents) much of this concerns the relative merits of different teachers. The teachers themselves can hardly fail to be aware that parents compare and evaluate them; they also know that, particularly with children of this age, the onus is very much upon them to ensure that their pupils acquire the basic skills of reading, writing and elementary mathematics.

At the same time, teachers are conscious that there is a certain amount of disagreement in the teaching profession about the best methods for teaching the three Rs or the most effective organizational framework in which to do so; it is also a matter for open professional debate whether teachers in training are adequately prepared in techniques for teaching these basic skills. There may be understandable reluctance to admit these professional uncertainties to parents. What often happens in practice, therefore, is that schools let it be known to parents that they use up-to-date educational methods, without being too explicit about the exact nature of these methods or their implications. Rather rarely, and usually where there is an active middle-class parent–teacher association, a school will put on a special workshop meeting to explain an innovation such as new maths; still more rarely does a school take parents into its confidence concerning techniques of teaching reading, let alone enlist direct parental help (other than 'hearing him read') in putting such techniques into practice. It is hardly surprising if to parents it seems that the teaching profession is closing its ranks behind the somewhat doubtful proposition that parents are not competent to help because the whole educational approach has changed too much since they themselves went to school – with the corollary that they cannot *learn* to help, either, because of the weight of expertise now required.

It is an advantage of a study such as this one that it provides an opportunity for parents to express their feelings about these problems more freely than they might to the teachers of their own children, who are likely to receive a muted version of any alarm parents may feel, if only for courtesy's sake.

References

AYERST, D. (1967). *Understanding Schools*. Harmondsworth: Penguin Books.

NEWSON, J. and NEWSON, E. (1968). *Four Years Old in an Urban Environment*. London: Allen and Unwin.

NEWSON, J. and NEWSON, E. (1976). *Seven Years Old in the Home Environment*. London: Allen and Unwin.

The Value of Parents to the ESN(S) School: An Examination

Len Barton and Susan Moody

Two of the most important institutions in our society are the family and school. Their interrelationship has been the topic of a great deal of research by social scientists from different disciplines; and the overriding conclusions from such investigations confirm the significance of the home's influence in the educational experience and performance of the child.

During the past decade in particular there has been an increasing demand, by a variety of bodies both outside and within the educational system, for closer, more meaningful and effectual links between the home and school. Illustrations of these types of demands are to be found in recent government reports. For example, the Green Paper on Education in Schools, a Consultative Document, maintains that:

> Until recently many parents played only a minor part in the educational system. The Government are of the view that parents should be given much more information about the schools, and should be consulted more widely. (1975, p. 5)

or the Taylor Report on the role of school governors contends that:

> Both individually and collectively the parents constitute a major source of support for the school. It is not a source which has been

> tapped fully in the past. We believe that governing bodies should encourage the widest and deepest parental commitment to their schools. (1977, p. 41)

Such directives raise questions about the actual running of schools and they are also a stimulant for encouraging schools to be more open, involving a re-examination of the role, rights and responsibilities of the major parties concerned as well as the establishment of, where necessary, a more evident democratization in the decision-making procedures of schools. To this end parental involvement is justified as being intrinsically valuable and/or instrumentally necessary, a vital means of assisting teachers to be both efficient and effectual in achieving important educational goals.

In this chapter we will seek to understand, discuss and explain some of the issues involved in home–school links, as they apply to ESN(S) schools. The approach of the writers is akin to that of Berger, who believed that:

> To ask sociological questions, then presupposes that one is interested in looking some distance beyond the commonly accepted or officially defined goals of human actions . . . It may even presuppose a measure of suspicion about the way in which human events are officially interpreted by the authorities . . . (Berger, 1966, p. 41)

An important feature of our analysis will be a critical reflection of taken-for-granted assumptions and practices, including the extent to which rhetoric either mystifies or supersedes practice, and how certain features of this topic are an illustration of conflicting and contradictory ideologies and expectations in the educational system generally.

The case of ESN(S) schools

Special education has been the subject of much debate in recent years and the Warnock Report confirms the importance of the role of parents in the education of such children:

> We have insisted throughout this report that the successful education of children with special educational needs is dependent upon the full involvement of their parents; indeed, unless the parents are seen as equal partners in the educational process the purpose of our report will be frustrated. (Warnock, 1978, p. 150)

This is by no means a novel idea, particularly as far as mentally handicapped pupils are concerned. Parent bodies like the National Society for Mentally Handicapped Children and Adults, in conjunction with their local branches, have been endeavouring for years to obtain a better deal for these people in all spheres of life, including education.

However, by contrasting the nature and organization of ESN(S) schools with those in mainstream education, we can identify certain characteristics that possibly provide more opportunities to establish and maintain home–school relations. Firstly, the nature of the curriculum is different because these special schools do not teach formal, abstract, examinable subjects and are thus not involved in competition for qualifications. Secondly, there are smaller numbers of pupils in the school, thus potentially allowing teachers to gain a more intimate and comprehensive knowledge of their pupils. Lastly, pupils remain in the same school for the duration of their school experience, thus giving the teachers and parents the time to get to know each other and establish working relationships.

Prevailing practices

One of the main themes to develop in this sphere of the educational system has been that of 'Parent–Teacher Partnership'. From the professionals' viewpoint the emphasis is on engaging parents in a much more teacher-oriented role in the home situation, in order to extend the time element and manpower available to the teaching profession.

The rationale on the teacher's side is based on certain fundamental features including the belief that the particular learning difficulties of these children call for much repetition and overlearning of new skills in different situations; the content of the teaching is frequently common to both home and school, particularly with regard to basic personal and social skills; the nature of teaching methods found to be successful calls for a very consistent approach by all those in contact with the child and who are concerned with his full development; the parents are a major source of information as regards their children, and this information is invaluable if an adequate assessment of the child's abilities and needs is to be made and maintained (Moody, 1980). These types of justification form the basis of such strong beliefs as those of Mittler who maintains that:

> No matter how successfully a child is taught at school, the effort is largely wasted unless systematic steps are taken to help the child to use and apply his learning in his own home and in other real-life settings in which he moves. The collaboration of parents is indispensable for this purpose. (Mittler, 1978, p. 248)

So parents, given the necessary advice and/or training, including support services, can become a vitally important means of extending the educational experience of these children, beyond the walls of the school.

Professional practices are treated as *non-problematic*, their work is maintained to be both good and necessary and what is required if it is to have a lasting effect in the lives of the pupils is for the teachers to gain the support of the parents who, under the guidance of the professionals' judgement, will seek to reinforce the necessary learning experiences within the home. The overall concern is to maximize opportunities for severely mentally handicapped children to progress in all aspects of their lives. The emphasis is upon a shared responsibility in which the needs of the individual child are paramount. The desired relationship between parents and teachers appears to be one requiring openness, trust and respect between the parties, through which parents may be directed into a more educative role (Butler, 1980).

The arguments presented and the desires expressed therewith for the development of parent–teacher partnership in the ESN(S) school are illustrated in practice by the growing number of 'parent participation projects'. Within this movement parent workshops constitute the commonest and most widespread form of parent participation. Workshops consist usually of short courses for parents on the art of handling their mentally handicapped child or children. They tend to be of around eight weeks' duration on one evening per week and include talks by various professionals, followed by discussion groups and the practice of behaviour management and development skills. Homework consists of trying out the suggestions derived from the workshop session with their child, attempting a recording of behaviour and carrying out short programmes they have designed. Many of these workshops are run by bodies *independent* of schools – child guidance centres, research centres, adult education centres, technical colleges, charity organizations – and the majority have been set up for issues relating to the preschool child.

Some schools are now beginning to incorporate this method into their home–school liaison programme and have extended the workshop approach into a continuing *structured* relationship between teacher and parents of children in the class (McCall and Thacker, 1977). Here the emphasis is upon regular communication: initially face-to-face contact, but later often by the written word between teacher and parent, particularly concerning what the teacher is attempting to do with the child, and the ways in which the parents may complement this at home. Specific problems the parent might be experiencing with the child might also be dealt with in this manner. Some schools have taken the initiative of using a specific programme of development with certain groups of children which involves a specific home-teaching element. One example is The Portage Early Education Programme (1987), and this method does make provision for regular communication between home and school.

The reports and research findings published on this topic suggest that parent participation projects over the last few years in ESN(S) education in England have been of the workshop or extended workshop type (Cunningham and Jeffree, 1975; Hewson, 1977). The emphasis is on the individual child, the criterion of success his or her development. However, there are some schools developing a *'multidimensional approach'* which attempts to involve the parents gradually as soon as the child enters school and to offer several areas of involvement including work with teachers on individual children's objectives, the use of school facilities purely on social grounds in the form of a family club and the development of a parent–teacher association. This approach is, at least on paper, significantly different from the parent workshop and extended workshop concept, in that it is offering a much wider basis for parent participation in schools including involvement in decision-making processes as regards the whole school and not just simply their own child. It is a much more flexible approach allowing for parents to be involved in different ways (Report of Working Party, 1980).

Impetus for parent–teacher school links has been derived from a number of sources, such as the material gathered from a whole spectrum of medical, social and educational research, from professional groups including teachers, from various directives in official government documents and from parents as individuals or through their national and local associations. An examination of the literature gives a strong *intended* message which crosses cultural, race and class boundaries, that is, parent participation or co-operation is absolutely vital and has benefits for the school, the home, the children and ultimately the community (Mittler, 1979; Chazan *et al*, 1980).

Points of contention

Despite such development, criticisms, expressions of bewilderment, frustration and anger from a number of sources are an indication that all is not what it is made out to be, or should be, and that rhetoric and good intentions are one thing, actually creating the conditions for their realization are quite another. It is quite clear that, for many, 'Often nobody asks the simple question, "What do the parents want?"' (Spencer, 1977, p. 30). Nor is this merely a question of a few isolated incidents, but rather it is symptomatic of a much wider problem, as Mittler notes:

> . . . there are *many* schools where such a partnership has hardly begun, where parents have played *no* part in helping to assess the strengths and weaknesses of the child, far less been involved in the design and implementation of a teaching programme. There are children whose parents have *no* knowledge of the objectives set by teachers for their child, if indeed any objectives have been set at all, schools where there is *no* system of communication, such as home school diaries, where there are *no* visits by teachers

> to the home and *only* yearly formal visits by parents to the school [our emphasis]. (Mittler, 1978, p. 245)

While home–school relations are often fraught with practical difficulties like parents having to work and not being able to get to the school, or they live too far away and have no transport or cannot afford the bus fares, or they cannot get a babysitter, these are clearly *not* the issues that have resulted in this serious indictment. The problems identified in the previous quotation are of a much deeper, fundamental sort, in which some schools and teachers are not beyond criticism.

The whole question of home–school links needs to be carefully re-examined and the taken-for-granted assumptions on which a great deal of the policies and practices are based must be critically evaluated. Analyses *must* go beyond the individual school or family and be located in the wider, but absolutely crucial, ideological, political and economic features of the social order.

Terms such as 'partnership', 'participation' and 'co-operation' are constantly being used by those who advocate the importance of home–school relations and this type of language contains assumptions about rights, respect for persons, equality and responsibility. While such language is appealing, clear definitions are notoriously difficult to find, because their meanings are ambiguous. Thus confusion arises at both an individual and group level over the nature of such practices and the extent of their effectiveness.

The frequency with which these terms are being used tends to generate a taken-for-granted attitude in which it is assumed that we all use these terms with the same basic understanding. However, upon closer reflection, a number of problems arise. First, 'partnership', for example, means different things to different people. Secondly, such rhetoric does not provide adequate directions with regard to how such ideals can be implemented and maintained. Thirdly, the ideology of individualism is apparent in that issues are seen largely in terms of the individual child and his parent(s), thus minimizing collective endeavour on the part of the participants. Fourthly, we have the situation in which a single rhetoric legitimates very different kinds of institutional arrangements and practices (Taylor, 1980). Lastly, very little concern is expressed over examining the inequalities of provision and practice of home–school links, within and across different geographical areas.

The political nature of schools

One of the most serious weaknesses of much of the literature dealing with this topic is its failure to provide an analysis of these schools that seeks to identify, understand and explain the *political* nature of education. Schools are institutions and, as Edgley reminds us:

> . . . any institution is a political institution, an institution with a particular constitution or political character: for any institution needs to make and implement decisions, and it therefore requires a procedure for doing so in accordance with which it distributes relations of power, authority and responsibility among the positions that form its structure. (Edgley, 1980, p. 12)

According to this view questions about the nature and consequences of parent participation are political, being taken up with who gets what and why. Historically, we have no legislation or agreed social norms or rules that give clear guidance as to the nature of the 'rights' of parents, so calls for more parental involvement within the school will involve varying degrees of struggle and conflict over power-sharing. For example, Pring (1980) notes that parents have a special responsibility for their children, therefore they have a right to have more information about what actually goes on in schools and the further right to act in the light of this knowledge. On the other hand, teachers as professionals claim the right to 'pursue their own judgement, often against that of others' because their judgement draws on their professional expertise and training. Thus, making schools more open and teachers more accountable to parents is an extremely complex and sensitive problem.

For some people parental involvement in school may seem to be potentially radical and a means to effect real changes, particularly in the democratization of the decision-making procedures. However, when we consider that there are varying possible degrees of participation, as well as to what extent parents are both able and willing to spend their energies, time and emotions in this task, coupled with the realization that the school is not situated in a vacuum but is related to and constrained by wider social and economic pressures, and reflects these in complex ways in its organization and workings in intended and unintended ways, it may well be that:

> Participation within a hierarchically structured organisation, such as a school or factory, will usually mean *consultation* rather than *sharing in the making of decisions* . . . (Hunter, 1980, p. 226)

It is possible to argue, therefore, that the actions of parents can often be accommodated within the existing procedures and structure of the school's organization. A great deal of participation is supportive of existing policies and practices, as Salisbury maintains:

> . . . it is undertaken with the intention of helping to sustain the school (or one's own child) *rather than to change it*. From the very beginning, parent–teacher associations and their equivalents have been organised primarily to provide public support for the schools [our emphasis]. (Salisbury, 1980, p. 8)

Giving information to parents about school policies and practices, enabling meetings to take place between teachers and parents, are undertaken with the desire for the more favourable support of the home, and teachers expect a positive identification with the school.

Certainly this is the case so far as ESN(S) schools are concerned, the vast majority of parent participation (where it takes place), far from questioning the policies and practices of the school, has been the means of legitimating them. Parent–teacher associations have three main functions. First, they provide a mutual supportive mechanism for parents to meet, share problems, gain from each other's experience or offer advice. Secondly, they provide opportunities for individual parents to meet their child's teacher and discuss factors relating to personal issues. Lastly, their major function is that of fundraising, offering additional financial support to the school, providing equipment, vans and even buildings (Barton and Hoskins, 1978). The extent of the school's control of these associations is to be seen in that often parents have *no real say* about why or how money is spent, nor the actual use that is made of that which is purchased. In this context, participation means passively responding to the demands of the school.

The role of the head

Any adequate analysis of the school cannot fail to acknowledge the extremely powerful figure of the head. It is very important to make a distinction between the teachers and head of a school.

Heads play an absolutely crucial role in the life of a school because it is their skills, understandings and decisions that powerfully influence in a myriad of ways the organization, curriculum, teaching methods, discipline and ethos of their schools. Part of their task is to protect their vested interests and when questioned by outsiders often give the impression that their school is 'one happy family' or a 'real community'. It is difficult to discuss the position of the head in the light of issues relating to accountability, because as the William Tyndale affair demonstrated, although various groups make demands, the power of the head to fail to take notice or resist such pressures is extensive.

It is a salutary point that while governments make recommendations and introduce new legislation or local authorities make demands on the schools under their jurisdiction, it is the head who is able to frustrate such policies from being realized or interpret them in a manner that suits his or her own purpose in terms of the functioning of their school. This is important when we consider home–school links, for, as Taylor reminds us:

> . . . in spite of all the evidence about the value of parent–teacher co-operation and the bland endorsements of official support *it is still up to the headteacher* to decide whether or not a school has any kind of parents' organisation [our emphasis]. (Taylor, 1979, p. 74)

Thus heads using various means will influence the nature, extent and consequences of home–school relations. Indeed, initial moves are often seen to be the prerogative of the school.

Rhetoric and practice

The contributions that parents can and should be making is often ignored by those in positions of power and their participation is limited to token decisions or rubber-stamping procedures. Even a government White Paper on special education purported to place parents in a position in which they will be able to exercise their rights and wishes over their children's education. Yet, as Kirp maintains:

> Here the appearance vastly surpasses reality. Parents can state a preference concerning the schooling of a special child to the Education Authority and, should they fail there, can bring their case to the appeals committee which will review all placement disagreements. But the parents will not be able to review all the information on which the LEA bases its decision; 'It would be wrong' notes the White Paper, 'to require full disclosure to parents of the professional reports lying behind the record', thus inviting the preparation of bare-bones official records. (Kirp, 1980, p. 4)

The very administrative machinery that the government will hope to establish will in itself frustrate the realization of the ideals it purports to be working for. That which is claimed to be established for the service of parents becomes another means of controlling them.

Various reasons can be offered as to why the potential for the real involvement of parents has not, in many cases, been fulfilled. One reason is that they have not had the necessary 'inside knowledge' about how various aspects of the system work, what their rights are, or how to go about getting their views expressed and taken seriously. In another chapter in this book, Sewell discusses the 'referral system' and the processes of interaction between the main parties involved. He seeks to identify the ways in which professional bodies deal with the parents of the children being assessed. He argues that:

> Parents who can be trusted to be 'intelligent' and 'not make a fuss' are offered 'performances' in the name of partnership. Those who are not to be trusted can often be persuaded. Those who object are subjected to visits from a succession of forceful and articulate members of the gatekeeping professions. (Sewell, 1981, p. 170)

The lesson to be drawn is that without such knowledge and the ability to act on the basis of it, parents are likely to be on the receiving end of both subtle and explicitly overt manipulative proceedings, experiencing frustration and even humiliation in the process. While an important distinction needs to be made between intended or unintended forms of behaviour or consequences on the part of the officials involved, the end-result will still be painful for the parents.

A further reason for the prevailing situation concerns the dominant perspectives or models that have historically informed theory, policy and practice in this sphere of special education. Medical and psychological ideas, legitimated by reference to informed professional judgement, created intentionally or unintentionally a powerful message system, the theme being that all important decisions about the child's welfare should be left in the capable hands of the *experts*. They have the necessary training and experience. These developments have taken their toll, on the willingness and/or ability of parents to challenge official judgements.

It cannot be assumed, therefore, that the interests of parents of children with special needs and those of the school are identical. Although both may argue that the goal of the school is to fit the child to take as responsible a role in society as possible, what the parents may feel are the actual capabilities or potential of their child, what they eventually hope he or she will achieve and the nature of the society in which the child will live, may be very different from that of the school's assessment. These differences of interpretation are often translated into conflicting expectations between home and school as to the type of teaching required and even some of the goals of the school.

The language that is used to encourage closer home–school ties is very appealing, but it tends to gloss over some crucial problems. These include the ambiguity of the directives, the relationship between these directives and other ideologies within the educational system, the problems of the inequalities of provision and opportunity, the realization that seeking to achieve these ideals involves the participants in some form of power struggle. There is no shortage of rhetoric; the major discrepancy is in the lack of conditions for ideals to be realized in practice.

Conclusion

It is necessary to make a number of important qualifications to the arguments that have been presented so far. First, it would be *quite wrong* to assume that there are no schools in which imaginative, exciting and radical changes have and are taking place in the area of home–school links. There clearly are many dedicated staff and heads who are committed to this task and they are clearly an example of what can be achieved. What is needed is more of these people. Secondly, many teachers may be sympathetic to the ideas advanced so far, but they need 'more open discussion and exchange of information' with their colleagues so that the teachers as a group do support each other and share responsibility in this venture. Within the context of the cut-backs, low morale among many teachers, coupled with the institutional and political nature of school relations, it must be remembered that it may:

> . . . leave individual professionals who want to practise differently in a very exposed position. (Robinson, 1978, p. 74)

This will be particularly so when those at the top of the authority structure within schools do not share their feelings, and may oppose the introduction of new ideas and practices. Thirdly, 'professional status' as far as teachers in ESN(S) schools are concerned, can be interpreted as 'more highly trained to care', and the energies and emotions that they spend on such children daily may drain them, and in these circumstances parents could be viewed as an uncontrolled force of additional worries. It may well be that the spirit is willing but the flesh is weak. Lastly, there are groups of parents who have little or no contact with the school and who, despite continued efforts on the part of the school, remain unresponsive. The school is not in a vacuum but needs to be viewed within a wider socio-economic framework, in order that we can begin to understand how social differences and divisions within the community may frustrate efforts by the school to communicate with certain parents.

Clearly there are costs to partnership for all the parties concerned, in terms of changing attitudes, organizational arrangements and practices, all of which demand effort, time, and persistence. Too much must not be expected of schools alone, and changes will be required in the wider social order, to which the struggles within schools will need to be related. It would therefore be naïve to suggest that no form of resistance or conflict will be involved because the changes required will so often, as Robinson notes:

> . . . threaten established ways of doing the job and because, generally, previous training and experience will not have provided a very adequate preparation for the different roles called for, those changes will be experienced as uncomfortable. (Robinson, 1978, pp. 73–74)

If by 'adequate preparation' is meant the extent to which parents themselves contribute to courses, or issues relating to parents are an important component of a course, then serious reconsideration needs to be given to the nature of many initial teacher education programmes. Ironically, the increased specialization and introduction of an all-degree body may exacerbate the differences between many parents and teachers as well as heads, in terms of their assumptions, knowledge and expectations, bringing further barriers to constructive relations.

Demands for a serious questioning of the assumptions and practices of home–school links in the ESN(S) sphere will not be without its critics or unsympathetic onlookers. One reason is because of the pervasive influence of the ideology of *individualism*. Hargreaves (1980) maintains that due to the 'excessively individualistic conceptions of the educational process' which he terms the 'cult of individualism', the 'social functions of education have become trivialised' (p. 187). Special education is excessively individualistic as can be seen from such working vocabulary as 'enhancing the aptitudes and abilities of the individual child', 'personal learning' and 'personal growth'. Depending on the degree of the handicap of the child, coupled with the related expectations of the parents, many parents may be content to gratefully accept any help they can get. Teachers become saints for they provide the opportunity for a hard-pressed parent to have a break from the demands of looking after their child. Or the interest in home–school relations for some parents is only considered within the context of meeting the needs of their child. The need to look beyond the individual family, their experiences and problems, thus becomes extremely difficult and a critical analysis that is directed towards the social, collective features of the school system may be interpreted as unnecessary or unhelpful. Yet it is the argument of this chapter that we need to consider the relationship between special education and the state, at both the central and local levels, and how these influence the way in which schools respond to parent participation.

This includes research on the way in which schools have historically related to parents.

Another point is that the ideology of *vocationalism* is particularly pervasive in special education generally, and the sphere of ESN(S) work in particular. Teachers are members of the 'caring profession', possessing those necessary qualities of devotion, love and patience. The penetration of such powerful ideologies makes the task of critical analysis difficult, especially where the demand is for the re-examination of the rights and responsibilities of *all* the major parties involved and where necessary in changes to be introduced.

In the end the realities of participation may result in cosmetic changes that make little impact on the structural and interactional aspects of school life. It will thus be a subtle, but additional, means of maintaining the status quo.

The final word is from a group of parents and it expresses their frustrations, anxieties and demands for change:

> We hope that there will be some who decide that we do not invariably misinterpret the explanations we are given and that on occasion we *have* been known to think . . . Whether or not the experts are ready to come out of their consulting rooms, committee rooms and staffrooms to communicate with us, we are publishing this book so that anyone who can recognise the reality of our position may join us as people *sharing* a responsibility for the care, treatment and progress of all handicapped. (Cooper and Henderson, 1973, p. 256, quoted in Robinson, 1978)

In times of austerity and cut-backs in government spending in all public sectors including education, affecting resources and the quality of the service provided, schools will become increasingly dependent upon parents for financial assistance. As parents are called upon to make more sacrifices in order to support the general running of the school system, issues about the nature of home–school relations become more pertinent, including the need for an understanding of the nature of those wider socioeconomic and political features of society and how they influence the out-workings of this vitally important relationship in the life of schools.

References

BARTON, I. and HOSKINS, K. (1978). 'The parent–teacher association – an instrument of change?', *Parents' Voice*, 28, 4, 21–2.

BERGER, P. (1966). *Invitation to Sociology: a Humanistic Perspective*. Harmondsworth: Penguin.

BUTLER, A. (1980). 'Parents as partners', *Parents' Voice*, 30, 1, 14–15.

CHAZAN, M., LAING, A. F., BAILEY, M. and JONES, B. (1980). *Some of Our Children*. Shepton Mallet: Open Books.

COOPER, I. and HENDERSON, R. (Eds) (1973). *Something Wrong?* London: Arrow.

CUNNINGHAM, C. C. and JEFFREE, D. M. (1975). 'The organisation and structure of workshops for parents of mentally handicapped children', *Bulletin of the British Psychological Society*, 28, 405–11.

EDGLEY, R. (1980). 'Education, work and politics', *Journal of Philosophy*, 14, 1, 3–16.

HARGREAVES, D. (1980). 'A sociological critique of individualism in education', *British Journal of Educational Studies*, 28, 3, 187–98.

HEWSON, S. (1977). School based parents' workshops – do they work? Paper given to annual conference of the British Psychological Society.

HUNTER, C. (1980). 'The politics of participation – with specific reference to teacher-pupil relationships'. In WOOD, P. (Ed) *Teacher Strategies*. London: Croom Helm.

KIRP, D. (1980). 'Opening the door to the gilded cage', *Times Educational Supplement*, 19 September, p. 4.

McCALL, C. and THACKER, J. (1977). 'A parent workshop in the school', *Special Education: Forward Trends*, 4, 4, 20–2.

MITTLER, P. (1978). 'Choices in partnership'. In: *Lebenshilfe für Behinderte*. The World Congress of the ILSMH on Medical Handicap, ILSMH, pp. 242–51.

MITTLER, P. (1979). 'Patterns of partnership between parents and professionals', *Parents' Voice*, 29, 2.

MITTLER, P. (1979). 'Learning together', *Parents' Voice*, 29, 2, 14–15.

MOODY, S. (1980). Teacher and parent: the new partnership in special education. Unpublished dissertation submitted as part of a BEd(Hons) degree, Westhill College, Birmingham.

PRING, R. (1980). Confidentiality and the right to know. Paper given at BERA Conference at Cardiff. Unpublished.

Report of the working party on the future of special education in Birmingham, 1980.

ROBINSON, T. (1978). *In Worlds Apart*. London: Bedford Square Press.

SALISBURY, R. (1980). *Citizen Participation in the Public Schools*. Lexington, Mass.: Lexington Books.

SEWELL, G. (1981). 'The microsociology of segregation'. In: BARTON, L. and MOODY, S. (Eds) *Special Education: Policy, Practice and Social Issues*. London: Harper and Row.

SPENCER, D. (1977). 'What do the parents want?', *Apex*, 4, 4, 30.

TAYLOR, F. (1979). 'What to do when a head doesn't want a PTA', *Where*, 146, 73–6.

TAYLOR REPORT. GREAT BRITAIN. DEPARTMENT OF EDUCATION AND SCIENCE/WELSH OFFICE (1977). *A New Partnership for Our Schools*. London: HMSO.

TAYLOR, W. (1980). 'Family, school and society'. In: CRAFT, M., RAYNOR, J. and COHEN, L. (Eds) *Linking Home and School*. 3rd edition. London: Harper and Row.

WARNOCK REPORT. GREAT BRITAIN. DEPARTMENT OF EDUCATION AND SCIENCE (1978). *Special Educational Needs*. A report of the committee of inquiry into the education of handicapped children and young people. Cmnd 7212. London: HMSO.

Part Three

Issues in Home–School Relations

The Management of Home–School Relations in the Secondary School

Leslie Sharpe

Parent–school relations is an area that has undergone a number of important changes at the level of both policy and research. In the early stages of state schooling, parents' exclusion from their children's schooling was often symbolized by white lines painted on the school playground.

In the post-Second World War period in Britain, with its concern for equality of opportunity and 'merit', the importance of 'parental interest' was discovered by educational researchers who argued, in effect, that parents provided the motivational element of the equation popularized by Michael Young – MERIT = IQ + EFFORT. The Plowden Report provided the policy implications for this discovery, arguing that teachers should hold out a hand in partnership to this hidden educational resource, and various schemes at the level of the school and the community sought to effect this. When it was rumoured that the educational system was failing to engineer the promised economic efficiency and social justice, yet another change occurred. Parents came to be seen as consumers with rights to hold teachers accountable, generally to improve standards, but more particularly to provide safeguards against the worst excesses of teacher autonomy as epitomized, for some, by the William Tyndale affair. Drawing on my research at a London comprehensive boys' school, I want to argue for another reconceptualization which shifts attention back to the level of the day-to-day business of parent–school relations.

My research (Sharpe, 1980) involved the collection of a wide range of quantitative and qualitative data, and its methodology is described in detail elsewhere. Much importance was attached to open-ended interviews with parents, and on the basis of these a number of 'ideal-type' parent figures were constructed as heuristic devices to clarify differences in parents' perceptions of the school and related strategies of involvement. These were the 'Agent', the 'Touchliner', and the 'Absentee'. Drawing from this approach, it was possible to construct an alternative to what I termed the 'hidden-hand' model of parent–school relations. This latter model conceptualized parent–school relations as a one-way process, with parents in the home providing the child with skills and attitudes important for success in the school. In contrast, my research was revealing a complex two-way process of interaction between parents and school, that I termed 'negotiation'.

My argument is that parent–school relations is centrally a process of negotiation by teachers and parents of pupil identities. The major condition for this negotiation is the process of differentiation, whereby schools attempt to confer stratified academic identities on to their pupils. This gives rise to a common problem for teachers, parents and pupils, namely the problem of continuity and change in pupil identities. This problem provides the common focus for their interaction and it is its management that forms the basis of parent–school relations. This management takes the form of parents and teachers bringing differing resources to bear in a negotiation of pupils' academic and social worth.

At Thameside certain conditions had to be met for negotiation to occur and for it to be carried through to a conclusion which was satisfactory to the parent. The most important condition was that there should be a discrepancy, or the possibility of there becoming a discrepancy between teachers' and parents' definitions of pupil identities. A second condition was the parents' conviction that their definition was correct. Thirdly, certain areas of negotiation, such as discussion of academic progress at anything more than a superficial level, required considerable knowledge and the confidence and experience to apply it. Fourthly, persistence and endurance was sometimes required, especially when negotiations were protracted. Fifthly, the ease with which parents might negotiate was related to their conception of norms thought to govern parent–school relations: everyday working concepts of 'interest' and 'interference' were particularly important here. Finally, the timing of an intervention could be crucial, as will be discussed later. These points may be brought together in the form of questions which became clearer and increased in significance as the research progressed, namely, 'How is it possible, and for how long, for parents to maintain high expectations in the face of correspondingly low professional expectations?', and further, 'How is it possible for parents to influence the expectations of teachers?'

Public relations activity and lobbying were the most highly developed forms of negotiation that I observed. These parents – the 'Agents' – began their 'campaigns' immediately on, or even before, their son's first day at the school. They did not wait for problems to occur, nor was their intervention restricted to a single negotiatory visit. Rather, it was a quite carefully staged strategy with the major purpose of ensuring that the child received 'appropriate' treatment. Initial lobbying gave way to public relations activity which in turn provided an excellent base from which to mount new lobbying strategies should these be required. Thus, in the lower school, Mr Tibble's concern was that his son should not carry over in to the new school the markedly antisocial characteristics he had developed at primary school, together with his 'fascination with fire'. The Hortons, Fawkners, Bennetts and Gouldings had 'discovered' their children to have severe reading problems which, they feared, might be misinterpreted as signs of 'slowness'. With the exception of the Gouldings, they had consulted child psychologists, who in two of the cases had diagnosed dyslexia, and in the case of Bennett, an untimely change from ITA to phonetic reading methods. They had been told what they had expected: that their children were of above average intelligence and suffering from temporary, but surmountable difficulties. Whether true or not, such evidence was an important resource in helping to sustain the parents' expectations.

Fundamental to the 'Agent' strategy was becoming known to the teachers. Mrs Deacon, the mother of a first-year boy in the bottom band put it this way:

> I ring up the headmaster, as I'm used to doing, and say, 'When is it convenient for you to see me?' He'll say, 'Oh! Mrs Deacon, so and so'. Fair enough, and I shall know that when I go along there he will be giving up half an hour of his time to help me with my problem. And this to me is right, because 60 per cent of children's lives is spent with teachers, so unless you work with the teachers how are you going to round out a child's future? And this is what I find. A lot of parents say, 'Let's leave it up to the teachers'.

> Or, if they go the teachers say to them, 'Oh! he's doing very nicely'. [Sarcasm.] So this is why I think it's right to belong to the PTA because you can get to know the teachers and get an objective report from them. Well, this is the first thing that I did and I found out that Mr Harris [the head of the lower school] was the main person connected with Charles, so I'm not really worried about Mr Anderson [the headmaster] [laughs]. So I made myself known to Mr Harris by introducing myself and saying that I was Charles' mother – that was before he started school. Then, this jumble sale came up so I immediately made myself known again, and this is what I will do until he will see me and he will think, 'Oh! That's Charles' mother, Mrs Deacon'. And then, you see, if I have any problems I can ring up the school and ask whether it is possible to speak with Mr Harris.

Successfully executed, the 'Agent' strategy set up a framework of mutual expectations which could be brought to bear on problems as they arose. Problems were less likely to be analysed by teachers in terms of general typifications. Knowing that parents like Mrs Deacon intended to get to know their children's teachers adds new meaning to the fact that they attended on average three times the number of parent–teacher activities at the school than did the largest group of parents – the 'Touchliners'. Personal taste was not of primary importance in selecting activities to attend: dances, fêtes, jumble sales, plays and so on were seen much more in terms of their latent than manifest possibilities. They provided an opportunity to 'show a face', to demonstrate 'interest' to the teachers, and generally to underline a favourable impression.

Mr Tibble was an accomplished lobbier. His son Keith was adopted, and his wife was a secretary. He was a civil engineer and the family owned their own home which was a large, detached house in a prosperous part of the area. I observed Keith over his first two years in the top band at Thameside. Keith was a difficult child. His parents found him lazy, introverted, desperately insecure and often deceitful. In class he was a loner, though a class leader, and chose his friends from the bottom band. School was anathema to him: only four boys in his year scored lower than his 46 points on an 'Attitude to School' test which I administered. Each of the teachers I formally interviewed had a lot to say about Keith. He was generally known among the staff and by the end of the second year his file was so thick that the headmaster remarked that he would soon need a box file for the lad. He was constantly in trouble. Over the two-year period he had variously been punished for lateness, missing homework, fighting, vandalism and extortion of money from other pupils. None of this, however, was mentioned on his record card, which simply stated that he 'came from a good family background', and that his father was a PTA member and Governor of a local school.

Keith's father took the major part in his schooling. He felt it 'essential to monitor what's happening in the early stages because there could be a very serious going off in the wrong direction at this stage'. He considered himself to be knowledgeable on educational matters, was a subscriber to *Where?* and would be seen circulating freely amongst the teachers and parents at various meetings that I attended.

There was, however, a mixed response by teaching staff to the Tibbles. The form teacher, Mrs Jewells, saw them as:

> Very interesting. The father 'runs' the PTA and has worked his way well in . . . I've met him a number of times at the PTA. He's on the committee. He's a professional man and very pushing. I could write a book about him. I have met him, about half a dozen times, and the mother about twice. She's a homely woman who doesn't like to fuss, and is overshadowed by her husband. He reckons to be on the ball about education, but he's a fair man. He does discipline the boy – he's fair. He's a deep man. You always feel that he's weighing you up.

Mr Dickson, the maths teacher, had been in correspondence with Mr Tibble:

> He's on the PTA. I expected him to be aggressive following my letter but he turned out to be reasonable. Obviously it's a good home . . . the father is some sort of civil engineer who wants the kid to do well, especially in maths.

In contrast, Mr Hedges, the English teacher, spoke sarcastically:

> Nosey, interfering so-and-so, a real nasty piece of work – that's the father. He's a civil engineer and tells you this to show his

> superiority. He once wrote a letter complaining about homework – he's always willing to run the school down. He knows everything about education and is a member of the PTA. It's a good home, though.

In fact, the letter brought an immediate directive to teaching staff from the Section Head:

> I have received a number of complaints about homework not being set. All the eyes are on our top band forms since reorganization and they must be stretched to the fullest limit. I would appreciate, therefore, a *dramatic* increase immediately in homework for this form. Really lay it on for a while. I will back you every time.

And Mrs Jewells thought that:

> He complained so much that this class must be the most well taught in the school. The kids here are fortunate. Everyone's scared of the consequences of not doing homework.

The effect of Mr Tibble's lobbying on individual teacher's views of Keith is difficult to measure with any precision. The three teachers interviewed certainly knew the 'facts' as recorded on the record card. But their interpretation had certainly been influenced to varying degrees by their having met Mr Tibble. Thus, Mrs Jewells felt she was 'nipping his delinquency in the bud' and that because he was adopted all the parents' 'expectations' fell on the child with the result that 'not doing homework is his way of rebelling'. She felt 'sorry for him because his father pushes a little too much and the kid lets off steam at school'.

Mr Dickson noted that he was 'probably the best known kid in the second year' and that he was 'a bit of a problem for women teachers. The fact that he was adopted with some trouble with his sister makes him feel apart and unwanted, and explains his conduct at school'. Likewise, Mr Hedges recognized the family difficulties:

> It's a good home but the boy resents the parents because they push. He's adopted. The class dislike him because of his parents. I heard him say the other day, 'My old man's been stirring it up

> again' and he said this to the class. He's a bright boy, smart, especially in dodging work. I feel a bit sorry for him really.

Of the three teachers, Mrs Jewells was perhaps the most influenced, or perhaps the most forthcoming. She confided:

> If we don't have some parents to wake us up we'd go to sleep, although I wouldn't say this to members of staff. Parents have this important role. I know it's wrong, and another aspect – I've noticed that with Tibble and with another couple of boys that I make sure that I spell correctly and put in the full stops . . . Mr Tibble cares and I suppose you feel that you must as well. I always put a comment on his work and then if I'm challenged I can prove that I've been conscientious. I do the same with Powell. I *always* put a comment on his work. Mrs Jones tipped me off very early on that the mother is a teacher. She said that at a progress evening that she didn't think much of teachers who just put a grade down and that she liked an assessment and a comment so I do this. I know it's wrong, but then I suppose everybody does it and keeps quiet about it.

At the end of his second year Keith achieved one 'D', two 'Bs' and a number of 'C' grades. The result was an average report for his class. He himself had mixed feelings about his parents. Generally, he preferred them to stay away from school, thinking it 'almost never a good idea for parents and teachers to meet'. But he felt that both his parents were 'very interested' in how he got on at school, and that the teachers recognized this.

Parents with low intellectual and social resources rarely took the initiative to attend the school to discuss their children's behaviour, and almost never to discuss their academic work. Faced with a discrepancy in academic evaluation, their response would typically be a quiet and private one, and discussion kept within the family. The pattern which emerged from the interviews was one of initial encouragement to the child to try harder, and if this failed to produce improvements, an accommodation of varying degrees to the teachers' definition. Without an account to explain why their children's problems were surmountable, 'high expectations' invariably became 'unrealistic expectations'. This process of accommodation was a gradual one of attrition, rather than an instant change, and reached its peaks with the issue of annual reports or letters of complaint received from the school.

Some parents had been convinced at the primary school stage that their children were not 'high-flyers' or 'professor brainstorms', to use two fairly common expressions. Mr and Mrs Redman were a case in point. Their son, Brian, was in 4W in the bottom band and had met with very unfavourable comments from early on, which the parents accounted for in terms of 'his birthday being against him':

Mother: When Brian was in the second class at the infant school and he was going in to the third class and I went to see the teacher as you usually do, she said to me that he was very slow in his educational ability, and he's never been particularly intelligent, but one of the things she said to me was, when I don't have any time for any of the children who are at the *bottom* of the class, and you felt straight away, goodness gracious what's going to happen? You know, and every time that I went into that school for an open day I would walk out *absolutely* depressed, and not knowing what to do, not knowing what was the best thing for him . . . and I think that each time you come home with a report and your report says your work is poor and there's nothing really good to say about them it's terribly depressing and it's terribly depressing for us as parents to read this.

Interviewer: Well, do you have to believe it?

Mother: Well, *this is it*, you do, don't you, if it's put down in black and white in a report book.

Later in this interview, after Mr Redman had confided that he had 'lost' his own opportunities, his wife gave some insight to the process of attrition, where one bad report followed another:

Interviewer: You say that while he was at the junior school he was in the bottom part of the class. But how did he get on generally?

Mother:	Not very well. As I said, each time I went up for an open day I don't think that I ever had a good report from any of the teachers there. In the end I just didn't feel like going up there, you know, you come home so depressed. And when he left school I spoke to the headmaster and I said, 'Well do you think that he's going to be a late developer?' and he says, 'Well if he is he'd better buck his ideas up' (hysterical laughter).
Father:	We haven't been pushing them, expecting them to do miracles.
Mother:	No, no. I think you *hope* for better things. You would like to see them achieve perhaps a little more than you've done yourselves but you accept, well, if it just isn't there it isn't there, and there's nothing you can do about it. I think the main thing is that they are happy.

Mr and Mrs Redman believed their child had had a fair chance and had failed primarily because of his own deficiencies. They appeared not to blame the school, the education system, nor the society at large for his failure. Although their child had been differentiated from others, they had not revolted and gave no indication of rejecting the central value of equal opportunity. When their son's identity was written down in 'black and white' it had become a social fact for them and one that was real, hard and indisputable.

Accommodation was not an all or nothing thing but was rather a complex mixture of acceptance and rejection of the school's definition. At one end of this continuum were families like the Redmans, but at the other there were parents like the Kirbys – who will be discussed shortly – who blamed the school for their child's failure. When parents reached the position of openly blaming and criticizing the school, invariably they had decided to 'write it off' and stay away. Although all parents had some criticism of the school to make, on balance they were prepared to make 'the best of a bad job'. When parents blamed the school for their children's failure such blame usually arose out of discrepancies in definitions of their children's identities. The most common discrepancy was where the teachers argued, for the most part privately, that a child's character was not suited to a particular kind of teaching, and where the parents argued that a particular kind of teaching was not suited to their child's character.

The Kirbys were a case in point which illustrates both the importance of adequate resources and the sorts of unintended consequences likely to follow from an unsuccessful attempt at negotiation. Their son John was in the low band of the third year during the first year of my fieldwork. The Kirby's first indication that his work was deteriorating came at the end of the first year at the progress evening, and the first indication that he was a 'discipline problem' in a letter from the Section Head during the spring term of the second year. Mr Kirby, an electrician, was on his own admission a fiery person. He visited the school to discuss the letter and although I did not attend this meeting I was able to inspect the record card and talk to Mr Kirby later. His son's record card was endorsed with the comment, 'Rather explosive parents'. Mr Kirby explained to me that he had in fact lost his temper because he could not persuade the Section Head to concede that firstly, the school should have alerted him about John's academic problems during the first year and not waited until its end; and secondly, that John was basically a 'good boy' but 'easily led'. Effectively, Mr Kirby was blaming the school and the school Mr Kirby. It was apparent that John was increasingly being pulled by two sets of opposing forces – on the one hand by his parents who were urging him to try hard for promotion, and on the other by friends who, like himself, were finding anti-school values more appropriate than academic ones. The pressures intensified when the Kirbys learnt that John would not be taking any 'O'-levels in his present band, and resulted in John's truanting during the early part of his fourth year. Once again, Mr Kirby visited the school and again offered his analysis of the problem, querying, as other parents did to me, why it was not possible to separate children like his own son who 'wanted to work' from the 'layabouts' who did not. Again, Mr Kirby's view that other boys' bad influence and lack of pressure from the teachers were the explanation for his son's decline was in sharp contrast to the school view that John was in fact one of the very same 'layabouts' his father was criticizing. During the interview I noted that Mr Kirby had tried to support his claim that his child was intelligent by referring to an architect acquaintance who had told him that this was so. Consequently, it was interesting to find another endorsement on the boy's record card:

> Father upset by progress. Some architect has said that the boy is very able! Father can be very forthright. Never happy about John. Visits school to complain.

Mr Kirby's attempt to supply 'evidence' was the source of some amusement, as the exclamation mark suggests. He had neither the resources nor the approach to negotiate a favourable identity for his son. Mr Kirby's case illustrates how easily good intentions can turn in to unfavourable unintended consequences. The best course for him to follow as far as the school was concerned was to accommodate to the school's view and co-operate with the teachers in encouraging John to shake off his anti-school values and work hard for his CSEs. Alternatively, he might have withdrawn his son, as other parents – the Bishops – had done.

From an analysis of teachers' comments on parents, which were recorded on the pupil record cards, it was clear that Mr Kirby was not the only parent to be labelled 'interfering'. What became apparent, however, was that neither this label nor the label of the 'absentee' parent had a clear and straightforward relationship with attendance at the school. With regard to 'Interference', it was quite clear that 'Agents' could interfere without being labelled in a derogatory way. Similarly, the label 'Absentee' was a misnomer. It was so because staying away was not a sufficient condition to become labelled an 'Absentee'. 'Touchliners' stayed away, but many of them were not identified by teachers to me as the parents who stayed away and they really wanted to see. Other variables were clearly important, notably the classroom behaviour of pupils. In general staffroom discussions, I noted that when teachers complained about 'Absentee' parents – as, for example, in discussions of progress evenings when the usual theme was 'the parents you don't want to see turn up, and those that you do want to see don't' – they usually did so with regard to pupils who were 'nuisances' in class. The feeling was that if such parents could be 'given a good talking to' they might 'pull their weight'. In other words, they, the parents, would begin to take their responsibilities seriously. In these sorts of arguments it is important to realize that the focus of interest is not the home or staying away parents per se. 'Absence', 'problem parents', and 'problem homes' may only come to be noticed by teachers in as much as they are perceived to 'cause' problems in the classroom. Thus the labels 'interfering' and 'Absentee' do not have a self-evident meaning. It was possible for parents to 'interfere' and 'stay away' and yet escape having a derogatory label attached to them, because they accorded with the teachers' ideal-parent typification.

The Broadmans are a good example of parents whose disillusionment had gone unnoticed by the teachers. Mr Broadman was a milkman and his wife a dinner lady at a local school. They lived in a council house with Cliff and his 17-year-old brother John. After two years in the bottom stream (prior to the banding system children were placed into one of five streams on entry), Cliff had entered the bottom band in the third year, remained there in the fourth year, and finished the year with 'C' and 'D' grades. At school he was a quiet boy whose attendance was excellent for the band.

Mr and Mrs Broadman's relations with Thameside had declined over the four-year period. They claimed to have attended not only progress evenings during the first and second years, but social events too – they saw themselves as quite sociable people and had some organizational skill, Jack being the Chairman of the local scout group. In the third year, when my observations began, their only visit was to the progress evening when they saw only one teacher, the English remedial teacher. In the fourth year they did not visit the school at all.

Of the two, Mrs Broadman had taken the leading role in her children's education over the years. Neither of her sons had achieved as much as she would have liked. She thought back to Cliff's preschool days when, 'he was so bright before he ever went to school. I mean the nursery rhymes he used to sing off. He used to sit down and write from one to ten. That was before even he went to school'. Over the years she had revised her expectations downwards, blaming in turn the 'overcrowded primary school [where] they packed them in like sardines and if you was clever, you got on but if not there was just too many in the class to concentrate' and the 'lack of discipline' and the 'lack of co-operation' of the teachers at Thameside. Whenever there was a need to contact Thameside she took the initiative. When I interviewed her in Cliff's third year, there was only one teacher who cared, she thought, and who didn't try to 'whitewash' her. This was Mrs Jones, the remedial teacher who left at the end of Cliff's third year. She was the only one to show any 'interest':

Mother: I always think that you get a true story from Mrs Jones, but the others when they say to me, 'He's getting on', I think to myself well you're telling lies because I can see that he's not, you know.
Interviewer: Why do you think they tell you that?
Mother: Because they've got so many kids that I think at times they don't know who you're talking about.
Interviewer: Do they know you?
Mother: Not really. As I say, apart from Mrs Jones seems to recognize you and she does seem to know the boys you know.
Interviewer: Does that upset you?
Mother: It does when they turn round and say he's getting on alright when I know jolly well that he's not, I mean.
Interviewer: How do you know?
Mother: Well if I get the paper and say, go on read me that and he can't, I mean I *know* he's not. And if I sit down with a book and he stumbles on his words at 14, I think it's not good enough.
Interviewer: And yet you do go down there and try.
Mother: You do *try* to get through to them. Yes I do try to get through to them.
Interviewer: Do you think that you fail?
Mother: I think at times that they don't know who they're talking about.
Interviewer: I mean if they say to you . . .
Mother: You *can't* turn round to them and say, 'Oh! no he's not', now *can* you, honestly?
Interviewer: So what do you do?
Mother: You can't. Well I just come away disgusted at times. I mean, that's all there is to it. I mean George (the husband) turns round and he thinks, 'Oh! he's getting on alright'. I mean, it *sinks* in to *you*. (She is not being malicious). 'He's getting on alright'. But I know he's not. It's lack of co-operation isn't it? It's all wrong really.

Interviewer: Why do you bother still going down?
Mother: Well, one day they might recognize you. One day you might get the truth. What else can you do?

At this point, half way through the third year, Mrs Broadman was still reasonably optimistic that Cliff might make some progress in his basic subjects, especially with his reading, even though he 'won't pass a thing'. There were signs, however, that she was increasingly being left alone in this view. Jack, the father, appeared to have given up. At one time he had been keen: there was a sad irony about the set of encyclopaedias and leather-bound Dickens in the display cabinet, and the half-literate boy standing next to them. Now, however, without bitterness, he described Cliff as 'thick as anything'. Neither did he blame the teachers entirely because, 'The teacher's entitled to take more time with the top ones because they are learning something. The likes of him is learning nothing. So why waste your time on him?'

A year later, any optimism there might have been earlier had gone. Mr Broadman felt that 'now that Mrs Jones has left I think it's a case of them doing what they like'. There was no enthusiasm even about the technical school course which Cliff had taken up on his own intiative: Jack felt that 'you don't need to do a course to be a painter and decorator'. For Mrs Broadman, the course too was counter-productive:

> Listen, all I ever wanted was for him to get the basics. I couldn't care less, really, about all this other stuff. All I've ever asked for is that they give him the basics, and I don't care what you say, there's no-one that can't learn to read and write. I've asked them for help and they don't care, and this is it.

And Mr Broadman added, 'We never thought we had a high-flyer. We just didn't know he was as thick as he is [Seriously]'.

Feeling that the teachers, her husband and Cliff had lost interest, she no longer saw any point in visiting the school: 'in the past I've thought that I owed it to Cliff to take an interest but he'd rather us not go.'

Indeed, Cliff did not want his parents to attend the school, and didn't mind if they stayed away. But although he saw his father as being only 'slightly interested' in his schooling, he still saw his mother as 'very interested'. Despite his failure at school, he reached the end of the fourth year with the desire to begin an apprenticeship, as his brother had done, after leaving school.

Though not an outstanding pupil, Cliff presumably qualified as a successful school product. Despite his great difficulties with academic work, he had not turned against the school and intended to continue his education in an apprenticeship. But this success could hardly be attributed even in part to good home–school relations as conventionally understood. Both parents had become disillusioned, the mother with the school and the father with his son's academic ability. Neither had been able to adapt successfully to what they perceived as the school's definition of Cliff. But, whereas Mr Broadman's was a negative and counter-productive adaptation, Mrs Broadman's perseverance and refusal to accept the school's definition somewhat ironically appeared to have been a major factor in the limited success that her son had achieved.

The Broadmans' case is interesting because it cautions against taking too deterministic a view. At Thameside, within the structural requirement to differentiate pupils, there was room for a variety of interpretations and responses from all the actors involved. Although the requirement to differentiate was a non-negotiable feature of school life, the manner in which pupils' official school identities were adjusted was not. There were no explicit rules, no bureaucratic procedures for the actors to follow. In their place there were a number of somewhat nebulous norms, open to considerable interpretation and reinterpretation, which gave certain pupils and their parents an advantage over others. A major consequence of this was that the management of pupil identities and school careers was not confined to pupils and teachers but centrally involved parents too.

Thameside was not so isolated and cut off from the home that changes occurring in the school were totally concealed from parents. In none of the cases that I observed were parents indifferent and oblivious to what was happening to their children. Where they differed was in their perceptions of the school and their role in relation to it, and in the resources that they could bring to bear on the problems occasioned by the differentiation process. But important as these differences were, it is clear that the different patterns of parental involvement with Thameside could not be explained exclusively in terms of the characteristics of individual parents. Aspects of the school's social structure were important too, especially the rapid change from openness to closure in the pupils' academic horizons that occurred during the first two years as a result of inter-band mobility. Whereas by the time that pupils had reached the third year approximately one quarter of them had changed band, thereafter instances of band mobility were rare. During the first two years there was a 'structural looseness' which both conferred on pupils an openness of identity and at the same time created those objective conditions under which parents could intervene to effect a closure of identity satisfactory to themselves. Taken together with the looseness of norms associated with parent–teacher interaction, this structural looseness effectively opened up the school and exposed teachers to parental influence. Early attempts to negotiate a child's identity with his teachers were more likely to succeed because teachers were working within a system that, both formally and informally, conferred provisional identities on pupils. After this time, however, during the third and fourth years, the virtual absence of band mobility and the rapid closure of pupils' formal and informal identities placed more rigid limitations on the kinds of changes that it was possible for either parents or teachers to make. When pupils became 'known' to the teachers there was less need for 'background information' about them, resulting in a more specific and limited set of expectations being applied to parents by teachers. Parents who were the most skilled and successful in influencing their children's treatment at school were those who brought to bear their high academic and social resources at a structurally opportune time. Whereas, conversely, parents who were the least successful were those who brought a low level of resources to bear at a structurally inopportune time.

There is a strong element of irony in this relationship between meaning and structure, which expresses itself in a telling correspondence between parental definitions and the hard reality of the differentiation process. Parents who defined the school as open to parental influence were those who took early steps to involve themselves and who thus experienced the differentiation process at its most flexible point. Their definition of openness was matched in fact by an openness of structure. Conversely, parents with low levels of resources were likely to intervene – if they did so at all – later and so experience the differentiation process at its most rigid point. Their definition of closure was matched in fact by a closure of structure. Thus, both definitions were confirmed in practice through confrontations with the school structure. A fairer competition might perhaps have matched the weakest parents with the 'softest' part of the structure, and the strongest with its 'hardest' part.

It is often said that conflict is endemic to home–school relations because of the universalism and particularism of teachers and parents respectively. Far from being endemic, however, at Thameside conflict was situationally specific and where it did arise could often be managed by the actors involved. The real significance of the teachers' application of universalistic criteria to pupils – through the mechanism of the differentiation process – was that it created the common problem of continuity and change in pupil identities. It was the management of this problem by teachers, pupils and parents that formed the basis of parent–school relations at Thameside. At its most dramatic level it resulted in conflict; at its most intriguing, in lobbying and public relations activity; and at its most mundane and unremarkable, in a long drawn out process of adjustment.

Reference

SHARPE, L. (1980). Home–school relations: a reconceptualisation. Unpublished PhD thesis, University of Sussex.

Home, School and Community

Sally Tomlinson

The successful education of minority pupils depends a great deal on co-operation, communication and mutual understanding between parents and teachers – on what are termed 'good home–school relations'. Indeed, home, school and community relations have emerged as a crucial area which must be improved if minority pupils are to be offered a fair and equal education alongside their indigenous peers. It is an area in which conflicts and misunderstandings were bound to arise. Parents who were immigrants into Britain and were educated in colonial education systems had high expectations of the education system their children were entering, but lacked information and knowledge about its workings. Little provision was made until very recently, to equip teachers with any real understanding of the home and cultural backgrounds of minority pupils, or the need of their parents for help in finding their way around an unfamiliar education system. Majority society parents were often hostile to the presence of minority pupils in what they regarded as 'their' schools, and minority home–school encounters have always taken place within a society marked by racial hostility and intercultural suspicion, rather than by harmony.

However, there are no easy answers to problems and tensions arising between home and school in a multicultural society. 'Improved home–school relations' is an often-repeated rhetorical phrase, but in fact minority home–school contact is the point at which basic values can clash and seemingly irreconcilable interests present themselves.

This chapter notes the difficulty of defining 'good' home–school relations, and documents some of the dissatisfactions which minority parents are currently expressing. Minority parents' views of schools and teachers' views of minority parents and pupils are reviewed, and the mismatch of expectations between parental and community desires and teachers' offerings is discussed. The chapter then examines contact and communication with minority homes, and suggests some policies to improve home, school and community relations.

Home–school relations

Home–school relations have never figured as a priority in education, and there is actually very little known about the purpose and effectiveness of home–school contact in general. Historically much of the available information suggests that 'normal' home–school relations have been marked by tensions and misunderstandings and sometimes by direct conflict (Grace, 1978). As Waller wrote in his classic study of teaching (1967), 'parents and teachers usually live in conditions of mutual mistrust and enmity'. However, major efforts have been made in Britain, particularly over the past 15 years, to improve home–school relations and to increase parental participation and involvement in the process of education. There is no general definition as to what constitutes 'good' home–school relations. Some schools may regard an absence of overt conflict and complaint as constituting good relations; others may seek the active support and involvement of as many parents as possible in school affairs before they are satisfied with their home–school relations.

Much of the literature on home and school, indicates that parental satisfaction with school and school satisfaction with home depend on children's progress and achievement. Good home–school relations are regarded by most teachers and parents as a means to the end of improving pupil attainment. Literature discussing the relationship between school achievement and home factors has tended to place some parents – particularly manual working-class parents – in an invidious position. Numerous studies have testified to the differences in achievement between the social classes; the influence of the 'good home' has been extensively documented (Douglas, 1964; Craft, 1970); the supposed linguistic deficiencies of the working class have attained folklore status

(Bernstein, 1971); and compensatory education for 'the disadvantaged' has usually included attempts to 'improve' homes and parents. The Plowden Report (1967) has been a significant influence on teachers' views of homes for the past 15 years. Plowden stressed that favourable parental attitudes towards, and interest in, education, were factors which strongly influenced children's school achievement. However, the report also stressed that parental interest did depend on the levels of knowledge parents held about education. In the 1960s levels of knowledge appeared to be low, and things may not have changed much during the 1970s. Schools and teachers do not seem to be very good at informing parents about the educational process, and find the idea of 'parents as partners' difficult to come to terms with.

The stereotyped dichotomy of the good middle-class home and the ineffective working-class home may have led many teachers to underestimate the ambitions of working-class parents to see their children succeed in education, and it may also have affected their views of minority pupils. It was unfortunate, in many ways, that the children of ethnic minority parents were entering British schools at a time when models of disadvantage and deprivation were so popular. Many teachers argued, and some still argue, that all inner city children, whether white indigenous or minority group, are equally disadvantaged. This is a simplistic view with which many minority parents disagree, and some schools are now beginning to see was mistaken.

Home–school contacts and communications have, however, improved enormously since the Plowden Committee recommended that all schools should develop special programmes for contact, including preschool contact. Many schools have sought to involve parents much more deliberately, and the Educational Priority Area action-research teams, set up in the early 1970s, pioneered some novel forms of home–school contacts and parental education (Halsey, 1972; Smith, 1974). Written reports, increasingly seen to be an unsatisfactory area of contact, have been studied at the National Foundation for Educational Research; and the expansion of school support services and home–school liaison workers over the past ten years has provided contact and communication with homes. Professionals engaged in home–school liaison go under a variety of labels: home–school liaison teachers, cultural liaison teachers, community education teachers, teacher social workers, educational home visitors, youth and community workers and educational welfare officers. The status of these professionals is ambiguous, and all of them face problems of professional recognition by home, school and community.

A further advance in home–school communication is the widespread discussion of parental rights and responsibilities, which is part of a general trend towards greater accountability in education. The increased participation by parents on school management and governing bodies, following the recommendations of the Taylor Report (1977) has meant that parental participation in decision-making processes about school has, to some extent, been increased.

Home, school and minority parents

Despite improvements in home–school contacts, minority home–school and community relations are, in the 1980s, in a critical phase. There is a crisis of confidence between minority homes and schools which takes the form of a questioning of the ability of schools to educate minority pupils in accordance with principles of equal opportunity and racial justice, and a questioning of the willingness of schools to genuinely accept cultural differences. There is mounting evidence to suggest that minority parents expect a good deal from the education system – far more, in many cases, than white parents. Parents of West Indian origin, in particular, are now more vocal in expressing their dissatisfactions with schools. The Rampton Committee wrote that a wide gulf in trust and understanding appeared to be growing between school and home; 'parents appear to be losing confidence in what schools are teaching their children, and schools seem to be having limited success in explaining their aims and practices' (1981, p. 41).

Minority parents have become increasingly anxious that schools are not equipping their children with the skills and credentials to compete for jobs with white pupils. These anxieties have been intensified as the economic recession has deepened, unemployment has escalated, and more qualifications are being demanded of school-leavers to compete in a shrinking job market or to go on to higher education. The issue of achievement has become a dominant concern, particularly for the West Indian community, and many parents are less willing to accept that home and family factors are primarily responsible for their children's poor school progress. Some black parents have lost faith in the ability of schools to improve things for their children; a black parent-governor recently asserted, 'we believe black underachievement can only be analysed and corrected by blacks themselves' (Neil, 1982), and there has been a sustained growth of black supplementary schools. Indeed, there has been sufficient criticism of schools, and enough initiatives taken by black educationalists, teachers and community workers to be able to speak of a black education movement in Britain. The participants in this movement are united by a belief that schools designed for white majority society pupils cannot offer equal opportunities to non-white children, unless they change considerably. The black parents' education movement has, over the past 15 years, taken the form of diverse parental and community groups which have campaigned against the overrepresentation of black pupils in ESN-M schools, and disruptive units (Tomlinson, 1982; Francis, 1979), and have organized additional and supplementary education (Chevannes, 1979; Clark, 1982). Haringey Black Pressure Group on education has gone so far as to send letters to Haringey headteachers, suggesting that they have failed to provide efficient education for black pupils (see Venning, 1983).

Minority parents are also increasingly expressing their desires that cultural diversity be genuinely respected and minority cultures taken seriously in schools. Muslim parents, in particular, are increasingly in conflict with a secularized co-educational Western system, and have become more assertive of their own community needs. There is much scope for misunderstanding here, as Islamic education is based on quite different values and principles to those of English education. Muslim parents question the materialist and competitive basis of English education, the education of girls, the predominance of Christian influence, and the separation of education from other aspects of life. These issues are allied with a major anxiety of many Muslim parents – that their British-born children will move away from their faith, culture and influence. The Union of Muslim Organizations wrote in 1975 that 'most Muslims acknowledge that Britain is a fair place to live . . . but it is hard to judge how possible it is to live as a Muslim in British society as a whole' (UMO, 1975, p. 10). Muslim organizations in Britain have spent some 20 years persuading schools to recognize the validity of at least some

Islamic ideas in education, but many schools have been unresponsive and have found great difficulty in reconciling Muslim and English values. It is only recently that some LEAs have begun to make genuine efforts to accommodate some Muslim needs and desires (see Bradford City Council, 1982).

The crisis of confidence expressed by the black education movement and Muslim anxieties that schools will not accept cultural and religious differences are illustrations of some of the difficulties to be faced when attempts are made to put into practice exhortations for closer contact and understanding between schools and minority homes. Such exhortations have been made by various committees and commissions over the past 15 years, for example, the Select Committee on Race and Immigration (1973), the DES, (1974, 1977), the Commission for Racial Equality (1978), the Home Affairs Committee (House of Commons, 1981), and the Rampton Committee (1981).

Minority parents' views of education

Minority parents' views of education in Britain are influenced by their own colonial and cultural backgrounds, and by the high expectations of education nurtured in their country of origin. As the Organization of Asian and African Women put it:

> the dream of a good education for their children has always had a particular significance for black people . . . the old colonialist equation of 'education equals power' explains why so many black parents passionately wanted for their children the education they never had (OWAAD, 1979).

Parental views are also affected by levels of education, social class, and knowledge and experience of schools and teachers in Britain. It is important to note, however, that although most minority parents in Britain are, in crude socioeconomic terms, 'working-class', their positive views and high expectations of education have always approximated more to 'middle-class' views; but they have lacked the detailed knowledge of the system which middle-class parents in Britain usually possess. In general, despite the different colonial and cultural backgrounds of minority parents in Britain, they mostly share high expectations about education and have high aspirations for their children, and they view schools as places where their children's life-chances should be enhanced. Many migrant parents, working in low-paid jobs, have felt that their lives in Britain might be justified if their children could acquire a more favourable position in society than they were able to achieve.

Despite disappointments engendered by encounters with schools and teachers, it still seems that most minority parents respect what they see as opportunities in education and expect a good deal from schools. This has been evident in research seeking the views of both Caribbean and Asian parents, although there has been considerable stereotyping of the supposed differences between these groups. Asian parents are popularly considered by teachers to be more interested in their children's education and more supportive of schools than Caribbean parents. There is, in fact, little evidence to support this notion. What is noticeable, in studying the research, is that there is a variety of studies, often carried out by Asian researchers, which have stressed the positive interests and characteristics of Asian families (Dosanjh, 1968; Gupta, 1977; Bhatti, 1978; Ghuman, 1980; Ghuman and Gallop, 1981); while white researchers, in the search for 'explanations' of West Indian underachievement in school, have often stressed the supposed negative characteristics of Caribbean parents (Rutter *et al.*, 1974; Jackson and Jackson, 1979). Caribbean parents may be, if anything, rather more likely to visit their children's schools than Asian parents (Rex and Tomlinson, 1979).

However, an important difference between the views and expectations of Asian and Caribbean parents does seem to be that from the early 1960s, Caribbean parents' expectations of school have centred on the belief that schools could offer equality of opportunity, and that this would be reflected in examination passes. Anxiety and frustration have resulted from the inability of schools to satisfy these expectations. Asian parents, expecting 'equal opportunities' have seen schools at least take their children's learning and language problems seriously, and have found their anxieties and frustrations centred more on schools' non-acceptance of cultural, religious and linguistic diversity. These differences are apparent in the research which has enquired into parental satisfaction and dissatisfaction with education.

In a study in Birmingham (Rex and Tomlinson, 1979), although over two-thirds of all minority parents expressed satisfaction with schools, Caribbean parents were more critical of what they saw as poor teaching, low standards of education, and inappropriate teaching methods. Asian (mainly Indian) parents expressed satisfaction that their children were getting regular schooling and good reports; were less likely to be critical of standards and methods; and were more interested in keeping their children in contact with religion, mother tongue and culture of origin. Caribbean parents were ambivalent about the idea of teaching 'black' cultural programmes in schools and these views have some support from black educationalists. It has been suggested that black parents want a traditional English curriculum for their children, and Woodford, a black headteacher, recently asserted that 'black parents don't want black studies or multicultural education for their children – that is for white children; black pupils need to be good at science, history, geography – at what society thinks of as things of worth' (Woodford, 1982).

The Birmingham study cited above indicated that all the parents were interested in their children's education, and there was little evidence of the 'parental apathy' that many teachers speak of. However, there were problems in home–school contact. Parents' evenings or open days were the times when most parents had visited the school – not the best time to establish much rapport with teachers. Caribbean and Asian parents were also more likely to be doing shift work and working longer hours than white parents, thus making it difficult for them to visit schools. It was also noticeable in this study that minority parents depended on teachers to inform them about the process of schooling, more so than white parents, and their understanding of the curriculum and examination was limited.

Ghuman's (1980, 1981) studies of 40 Jat Sikh families in the Midlands, and 30 Bengali families in Cardiff, indicated that these parents were generally satisfied with English education, valued education for its own sake, and expressed faith in teachers and their professional skills. However, issues such as single-sex schooling, dress, food, religious and mother tongue teaching were as important as issues concerning academic achievement. Muslim parents, in particular, felt their Islamic way of life was threatened if schools would not relax rules and regulations, and some parents were critical of lax discipline in schools and insufficiency of homework.

In these studies, too, parents demonstrated a lack of knowledge about school processes and curriculum. As one Bengali father said: 'because we do not know exactly what or how they teach in schools here, we cannot help our children'. More recent research[1] has indicated that, as in previous studies, minority parents do view English education as a potentially good education; but they believe strongly that it should allow for the possibility of passing examinations and acquiring skills, so that employment prospects or chances of further education are enhanced. West Indian parents also expect schools to teach their children in a disciplined and orderly manner and find it difficult to understand teachers' problems here. Asian parents expect that more of their cultural traditions will be incorporated into schools, and that schools will take more seriously the issues that concern them as parents.

Teachers' views

A review of teachers' views and expectations of minority parents and pupils does indicate that there is a serious mismatch of expectations between what schools think they can offer minority pupils, and what minority parents want and expect. This is likely to impede the development of good home–school relations and give rise to misunderstanding. Teachers in Britain still generally lack knowledge about minority groups and hold negative and inappropriate views, particularly about Caribbean parents. Teachers generally have no clear idea of their role in a multiracial, multicultural society, and little idea of how much minority parents depend on them for information about schools and for providing their children with credentials and skills.

During the 1960s and 1970s many teachers were committed to assimilationist views and perspectives, and at the time these perspectives may have seemed appropriate. They tied in with current liberal thinking that in order to provide equal opportunities, all pupils should be treated 'the same'; and they were compatible with professional beliefs that teachers' skills should be available to

---

[1] A study of 20 multiethnic schools undertaken by the Policy Studies Institute and the University of Lancaster has examined the views of parents.

all children equally. Although there is now an influential movement in education towards an acceptance of cultural diversity and alternative values, and towards combatting racism in education and society, there are undoubtedly many teachers in the 1980s still committed to assimilationist perspectives. These teachers feel genuine difficulty in responding to calls for cultural pluralism and anti-racism. A London headteacher has argued in the columns of *The Times Educational Supplement* that 'some teachers . . . would argue that the responsibility for the adaptations and adjustments of settling in a new country lies entirely with those who have come here to settle and raise families' (Honeyford, 1982).

However, other teachers would argue that the school system also has a responsibility to adapt and change. It is not surprising, however, that some teachers have come to hold inappropriate, stereotyped or negative beliefs about minorities, and some feel threatened or defensive in their contacts with minority parents. Teachers in Britain are mainly white, middle-class and educated into what the DES (1977) has referred to as a 'curriculum appropriate to our Imperial past'. During their training they have seldom received help or encouragement to develop more positive views about minorities, or to learn skills of contact and communication with minority parents. This aspect of teacher training has never been regarded as an urgent priority, and there has never been any co-ordinated national policy to ensure that intending teachers received any 'multicultural' training. This lack of preparation has been deplored at length in government reports and research (DES, 1977, 1981; House of Commons, Home Affairs Committee, 1981; Little and Willey, 1981). However, in the 1980s there are some signs that teacher training may be beginning to face up to 'multicultural' preparation, however fraught with difficulties.

It is certainly now possible to detail some of the inappropriate views of minority parents, pupils and communities which some teachers hold, and to consider their possible consequences. First, there is evidence of what Khan has called 'elaborate structures of myth making'. Lacking real knowledge of the cultural backgrounds of minorities or of their lives in Britain, teachers resort to stereotypes or half-truths which may be more of a barrier to home–school understanding than admitted ignorance. Khan uses the popular stereotypes of Muslim families – 'they don't want to mix – the father won't let the mother come to school – they spend hours at the mosque – the girls have to do all the domestic work', to show that crude beliefs can actually prevent contact between home and school. Similarly crude beliefs about Caribbean parents, particularly mothers – 'they all go out to work, the children are childminded, they have few toys or books in the home, they all believe in corporal punishment' – have probably prevented rather than assisted communication with parents.

A second inappropriate view of minorities may be teachers' popular belief that minority parents and pupils are all part of a group loosely labelled 'the disadvantaged'. The Birmingham study (Rex and Tomlinson, 1979) found that many teachers stressed material disadvantages – poor housing and environment, unskilled or unemployed parents – rather than disadvantages concerned with race, colour or migration; and that the 'disadvantaged' approach led some heads to view their schools in a social-pastoral context rather than as examination-oriented, academic places. Some teachers felt that lower standards and expectations were inevitable with a multiracial intake, and, although they tried to make schools a pleasant environment, did not expect high achievement. This, of course, was the antithesis of the expectations and understandings of minority parents as to what schools were all about. The one crucial way in which minority parents were disadvantaged in education – by not having sufficient knowledge and experience of the process – was not acknowledged by the schools in this study, nor, it seems, by other schools. Immigrant minority parents, who have needed more help than even white 'disadvantaged' parents, who at least have been through the school system, have never been the specific focus of teachers' attention.

A third, and perhaps the most extensively documented, inappropriate view held by many teachers, has been their persistent stereotyping of Caribbean parents and pupils as difficult and problematic. It has not been uncommon to hear this view expressed by teachers in 'white' schools who have never taught minority pupils. Stereotyped and negative views of West Indians have undoubtedly been translated into classroom action (Green, 1982), with effects on West Indian school performance.

It is not surprising that many teachers of pupils of West Indian origin have felt uncomfortable in discussing the low achievement of the pupils with their parents, and have preferred explanations for poor performance located in the home and family rather than in the school and the teaching.

A mismatch of expectations

There is undoubtedly a mismatch of expectations and basic value differences between what minority parents expect of education and what schools and teachers think they can offer. This makes good home–school relations more difficult to achieve. However, the basis for this mismatch does not necessarily lie in any deliberate obtuseness of teachers. The mismatch rests ultimately on the existing structures and functions of the education system and on it's cultural content, and it may not be in the interests of school to explain to any group of parents what structural limitations there are on access to 'equal opportunities'.

Minority parents' satisfactions with the education system – 'it's there for them to take advantage of' as one West Indian mother put it – rests on the post-war liberal notion that 'equal chances to be unequal' do prevail in education. But the ending of the tripartite system and moves to comprehensivization have not increased the possibility of equal opportunity for most children. The chances of children of manual working-class parentage being selected and prepared for an academically-oriented education which allows access to higher education have not improved, and most inner city schools – the ones attended by most minority pupils – are not geared to high-level academic work or a technical curriculum. Many such schools are now beginning to realize that they incorporate minority pupils of all levels of ability, but they do not have the resources or the skills to develop academic abilities, and it is unclear how far new developments in technical education will affect minority pupils. Confusion and difficulties are likely to persist unless schools can openly discuss with parents the kind of education they offer.

Explanations regarding schools' levels of acceptance of cultural diversity is another area where misunderstandings may be perpetuated. The areas where Asian parents would like to see most change – in the education of girls, mother tongue teaching, religious education, and less participation in extracurricular activities – are all areas which teachers may find difficulty in coming to terms with. The cultural content of the education system is based on particular beliefs and values which are distinctly at odds with some Asian cultural beliefs and values. This is not to deny the importance of curricular change, which will hopefully alter the ethnocentric nature of the curriculum, but it does mean that teachers will have to be very clear about the value base of their curriculum practice. A mismatch between school and community understandings of 'cultural diversity' may continue to be a source of home–school tension.

Contact and communication

Despite problems and tensions concerning contradictory expectations of parents and teachers, there is a variety of initiatives currently being undertaken by some LEAs and schools to improve minority home–school contact and communicate more clearly with parents. It is becoming clearer that although a good deal of the improved contact is along the familiar 'Plowden' lines of parents' days and evenings, PTAs, welcoming parents in school, preschool groups and visits and community school activity, there are also new-style links in the form of genuine discussion with community leaders and parents' representatives, debates on parental rights and duties, and the involvement of some parents, as school governors, in educational decision-making.

By 1981 some 28 LEAs had appointed multicultural education advisers and were giving serious consideration to minority home–school links, and about ten LEAs were in the process of producing written policy guidelines to assist schools in their dealings with minorities. In Berkshire, for example, an advisory committee for multicultural education – chaired by the Director of Education – was set up in 1981 to debate a variety of issues concerning 'education for equality', including the question: 'what should be done to increase mutual understanding between schools and parents, and how should issues to do with equality and racism be raised and handled?' (Berkshire, 1982, p. 14). It was noteworthy that representatives from 17 minority organizations were involved with this committee, including the Reading Asian Parents Group, the Pakistani Parents Society, the West Indian Peoples' Association, and the West Indian Women's Circle. The committee produced a discussion leaflet, translated into three minority languages, for all schools and parents in the area, and invited views and comments.

In Bradford the LEA produced guidelines for schools setting out a policy for education in a multicultural society. The importance of home–school contacts and parental rights were the first issues raised in these guidelines. Page 1 noted that:

> it is important that minority parents should – as should all parents – become familiar with the nature of the schooling their children are receiving, and be enabled to discuss difficulties that this may present for them. A clash of aims in the education of the child may undermine the opportunity for the child to take full advantage of the education system. (Bradford, 1982)

For most LEAs and schools who are taking minority home–school contacts seriously, the importance of actually bringing parents and teachers together to discuss educational issues and problems is certainly recognized, but there are problems with methods of implementation. While many schools recognize that there is insufficient time for educational discussion between parents and teachers, the solution of many local authorities has been to interpose an extra 'layer' of professionals in the form of liaison teachers. The idea of home–school liaison teachers dates back to a suggestion by the Plowden Committee in 1967, and during the 1970s many LEAs appointed such teachers. By 1980, some had been renamed 'cultural liaison' or 'community' teachers, and were seeking to consolidate a more autonomous professional status. Little and Willey, reporting their national survey of local education authorities in 1981, noted that while only 11 per cent of schools in the survey actually said they had home–school liaison teachers, one LEA reported appointing 20 home–school liaison officers with money from the Manpower Services Commission, and another LEA had appointed a group of 'cultural liaison' teachers specifically to work with minority parents (Little and Willey, 1981). Little and Willey also reported that several authorities claimed to discuss educational issues with local community leaders and with local community relations committees.

Improved home–school contact and communication is thus often regarded as a matter for 'liaison' by special professionals, or by consultation with community 'leaders' – who may or may not represent a full spectrum of parental views. There is little research providing information as to how parents perceive and react to community liaison or home–school teachers. On the positive side, minority parents in particular may appreciate discussion with a 'teacher' who not being involved in full-time teaching, actually has time to talk to parents and explain educational problems. Parents may also appreciate the use of extra professional skills in organizing pre-school groups, parents 'in the classroom', parental activities in school language classes for Asian parents, and so on. On the negative side, however, an extra 'layer' of professionals could mean that parents see even less of the teachers who actually teach their children than before. Liaison teachers may become the professionals who deal with 'difficult' or ill-informed parents, and they may not be in a position to discuss what many parents actually want to discuss – the performance of individual children and teaching strategies to improve individual performance.

However, if 'liaison' is dispensed with and contact and communication with parents encouraged at the individual teacher level, more school time will have to be made available for such activities. The Rampton Committee suggested that a senior member of staff in all schools take on the additional task of co-ordinating links between the school and the community, and that 'teachers should see home–school visiting as an integral part of their pastoral responsibilities (Rampton Report, 1981, p. 80). Taking time away from teaching activities may not, in fact, be assisting pupil achievement – the issue, as we have noted, that most concerns minority parents. There are particular problems concerning the professional definition of the teacher's role when improved contact and communication with minority homes is called for.

Improved practice

This chapter has attempted to show that current tensions and problems between minority homes and schools are based on clashes of values and mismatches in expectations, and that there is a lack of knowledge and misunderstanding on both sides. The achievement of improved home–school relations is thus no easy task. There is, as we have noted, no general feeling that parents, particularly working-class parents, should be involved in the state education of their children to any great extent; and despite major efforts to improve practice over the past 15 years, 'good home–school relations' are often more of a pious hope than a reality. Much of the improvement in home–school relations has been produced on an *ad hoc* basis by the initiative of individual schools and LEAs, and local authorities with large numbers of minority pupils may actually have been in the vanguard of the movement to improve home–school relations generally.

However, an important question remains as to how far policies to improve home–school relations should be specifically aimed at minority parents, and how far at all parents. Since there are no overall national home–school policies in Britain, suggestions for improved national practice must remain in the realm of speculation at the moment. However, one particular policy, adopted on a national scale for all parents, could be of particular benefit to minority parents. This is the policy suggested by Macbeth to the Commission of the European Communities at a conference on the school and family in Europe (see Wilce, 1983). Macbeth has suggested a 'School and Family Concordat', a contractual agreement between schools and parents, by which parental rights and duties and the duties of schools and teachers would be spelled out, so that each party would be clear about rights, responsibilities and expectations. Macbeth envisages that the school and family concordat would oblige schools and teachers to co-operate with parents, and would certainly benefit minority parents by ensuring parent–teacher contact, and improving teachers' knowledge about minorities. Spelling out the duties of schools would also help minority parents and communities understand more clearly the dilemmas inherent in attempting to provide equal opportunities and opportunities for cultural diversity.

There is also scope for specific policies aimed at minorities. Since minority parents expect a good deal, but lack information about the education system, community and liaison teachers could be given the specific brief of informing minority parents about the processes, possibilities and limitations of the education system. Schools with large numbers of minority parents could automatically adopt the policy of translating all home–school literature and reports, offer separate parents' meetings to different ethnic groups who may need to discuss their own problems, and have at least one minority parent governor. Ideally, also, special preschool education should be offered to all minority children, to prepare them for education in a system still largely designed to accommodate white majority society children.

Whatever new policies may be adopted, it is certain that unthinkingly offering more of the palliatives that have often passed for 'improved home–school contacts' will not solve the crisis of confidence between minority homes and schools. The issues at stake are the ability of schools to educate minority pupils in accordance with principles of social and racial justice – attempting to offer equal opportunities and respect cultural differences and diversity – and this demands new and more radical home–school policies than those previously offered.

References

BERKSHIRE DEPARTMENT OF EDUCATION (1982). *Education for Equality: a Paper for Discussion in Berkshire*. Advisory Committee on Multicultural Education, Reading, Berks.

BERNSTEIN, B. (1971). *Class, Codes and Control*. Vol. 1. London: Routledge and Kegan Paul.

BHATTI, E. M. (1978). 'Young Pakistanis in Britain, educational needs and problems', *New Community*, 6, 3.

BRADFORD CITY COUNCIL (1982). *Education for a Multicultural Society: Provision for Pupils of Ethnic Minorities in Schools*. Bradford.

CHEVANNES, M. (1979). 'The Black Arrow Supplementary Project', *The Social Science Teacher*, 8, 4.

CLARK, N. (1982). 'Dachwyng Saturday School'. In OHRI, A. *et al*. (Eds) *Community Work and Racism*. London: Routledge and Kegan Paul.

CRAFT, M. (Ed) (1970). *Family, Class and Education*. London: Longman.

DOSANJH, J. S. (1968). 'Punjabi immigrant children – their social and emotional problems', *Education Paper No. 10*, Institute of Education, University of Nottingham.

DOUGLAS, J. W. B. (1964). *The Home and the School*. London: McGibbon and Kee.

FRANCIS, M. (1979). 'Disruptive units – labelling a new generation', *New Approaches in Multi-Racial Education*, 8, 1.

GHUMAN, P. A. (1980). 'Punjabi parents and English education', *Educational Research*, 22, 2.

GHUMAN, P. A. and GALLOP, R. (1981). 'Educational attitudes of Bengali families in Cardiff', *Journal of Multi-Cultural and Multi-Lingual Development*, 2, 2.

GRACE, G. (1978). *Education, Ideology and Social Control*. London: Routledge and Kegan Paul.

GREAT BRITAIN. DEPARTMENT OF EDUCATION AND SCIENCE (1974). *Educational Disadvantage and the Needs of Immigrants*. London: HMSO.

GREAT BRITAIN. DEPARTMENT OF EDUCATION AND SCIENCE (1977). *Education in Schools – a Consultative Document*. London HMSO.

GREEN, P. (1982). Teachers' influence on the self concept of pupils of different ethnic origins. Unpublished PhD thesis. University of Durham.

GUPTA, P. (1977). 'Educational and vocational aspirations of Asian immigrants and English school leavers', *British Journal of Sociology*.

HALSEY, A. H. (1972). *Educational Priority, EPA Policies and Problems*. London: HMSO.

HONEYFORD, R. (1982). 'Multi-racial myths', *The Times Educational Supplement*, 19 November.

HOUSE OF COMMONS, HOME AFFAIRS COMMITTEE (1981). *Racial Disadvantage*. London: HMSO.

JACKSON, M. and JACKSON, S. (1979). *Child Minder*. London: Routledge and Kegan Paul.

LITTLE, A. and WILLEY, R. (1981). *Multi-ethnic Education – the Way Forward*. London: Schools Council.

NEIL, A. (1982). 'In loco parentis', *Issues in Race and Education*, 37, 6.

ORGANIZATION OF WOMEN OF ASIAN AND AFRICAN DESCENT (1979). 'Black education', *Forward*, Spring.

PLOWDEN REPORT. GREAT BRITAIN. DEPARTMENT OF EDUCATION AND SCIENCE. CENTRAL ADVISORY COUNCIL FOR EDUCATION (ENGLAND) (1967). *Children and Their Primary Schools*. London: HMSO.

RAMPTON REPORT. GREAT BRITAIN. DEPARTMENT OF EDUCATION AND SCIENCE (ENGLAND) (1981). *West Indian Children in Our Schools*. Report of the Committee of Inquiry into the Education of Children from Ethnic Minority Groups. London: HMSO.

REX, J. and TOMLINSON, S. (1979). *Colonial Immigrants in a British City: A Class Analysis*. London: Routledge and Kegan Paul.

RUTTER, M. *et al.* (1974). 'Children of West Indian immigrants. I. Rates of behavioural deviance and psychiatric disorder', *Journal of Child Psychology and Psychiatry*, 15.

SMITH, G. (Ed) (1974). *Educational Priority*, Vol. 4, The West Riding Project. London: HMSO.

TAYLOR REPORT. GREAT BRITAIN. DEPARTMENT OF EDUCATION AND SCIENCE/WELSH OFFICE (1977). *A New Partnership for our Schools*. London: HMSO.

TOMLINSON, S. (1982). *A Sociology of Special Education*. London: Routledge and Kegan Paul.

UNION OF MUSLIM ORGANIZATIONS OF THE UK AND EIRE (1975). *Islamic Education and Single-sex School*. London.

VENNING, P. (1983). 'Menacing warning sent to Haringey heads over exams', *The Times Educational Supplement*, 11 February.

WALLER, W. (1967). *The Sociology of Teaching*. 3rd edition. Chichester: John Wiley and Sons.

WILCE, H. (1983). 'Co-operation pledge plan drawn up for parents', *The Times Educational Supplement*, 25 March.

WOODFORD, O. (1982). Interview on *Ebony*, BBC TV, 17 November.

'It's the ones who never turn up that you really want to see': The 'Problem' of the Non-Attending Parent

David Bridges

To a group of schools which take seriously the business of communication with parents, those parents who are apparently unwilling, unable or reluctant to engage in this communication represent something of a problem or failure. Not surprisingly therefore a number of the Cambridge Accountability Project (CAP) schools asked us to explore this problem for them and help to explain the case of the non-communicating or non-attending parents.

Before going on to see what we have to offer towards such explanation, let me comment briefly on the nature of the 'problem' itself. To begin with, is it a problem? or why is it a problem? or what assumptions about the purpose or concerns underlying the school's commitment to strong lines of communication with parents are implied by defining the 'non-communicating parent' as a problem? The point is that if we simply see the information that the school provides as something to which the parent is entitled, then a parent's decision (if that is what it is) not to involve himself in the affairs of the school need not concern the school – the school will have acquitted itself of its own obligation. Alternatively, if the school sees the process of mutual communication as integral to the mutually supporting work of parents and school in the education of the child, then the school might feel that the non-communicating parent is not fulfilling his or her share of the joint obligation. Or, thirdly, the school might worry that the non-communication was somehow a reflection of its own failure to make itself accessible to parents who were perhaps inhibited practically or psychologically from communicating with the school.

The attitude of the staff of the school I was most directly concerned with, Robert Peel, was I think somewhere between the last two mentioned: a mixture of a feeling that parents owed it to their children to be in close communication with their teachers, combined with a desire to help those parents who for one reason or another found communication with the school difficult. Jennifer Nias' comment on Highstones suggests that she interprets that school's attitude in much the same terms:

> For those teachers who accept, as part of their moral accountability to parents, the responsibility for helping them to be effective partners in their children's education, the school's problem is *how to reach them* [her emphasis].

Increasingly perhaps these finer sentiments relating to duties, rights and responsibilities are supported by more prudential considerations. In contexts in which schools are effectively competing for pupils in a contracting market, or where schools are anxiously trying to establish a new reputation or change an old one (we had examples of all of these), the school's capacity to communicate its own view of itself to its parent 'clients' is crucial. The schools we worked with were especially alive to what they regarded as the misrepresentation of what they did or stood for through the informal network of communication and especially keen to provide their own accounts through the channels they had at their disposal:

> I think the more you inform them about what's going on the less likely gossip, rumours and misunderstandings will be to arise. (HI, 2B3)

Parents' non-participation in such channels had, among other consequences, the effect of weakening the school's capacity to present its own picture of its work and character.

Beyond this there was some, though never precisely articulated, awareness that the institution of compulsory schooling can be undermined if parents give it anything less than energetic and visible support. Indeed, as one education welfare officer explained, persistent non-attending pupils tend to absent themselves from schools with the connivance and support of parents who share their childrens' reluctance to submit themselves to its demands.

Some of the reasons CAP parents give for their reluctance to attend one kind of event or occasion are not necessarily generalizable to others. In a longer and more complex chapter I might have tried to discuss different kinds of occasions in turn. But we often elicited from parents fairly general explanations as to why they did or did not attend school functions and they do not always stand up to detailed analysis in relation to specific events. I shall therefore leave it to the reader to consider or explore which explanation would most probably apply to which kind of non-involvement.

1 Practical difficulties

A number of parents explained that their non-attendance at evening events reflected no lack of interest but rather some practical difficulties in getting there. They referred to the lack of public transport, not having a car, evening shift work, family ties and sheer exhaustion by that time of the evening:

> They might think we don't care because we don't go. We do care, but when you are out working all day and X [spouse] is on shifts you can't always get there and you feel so tired. (HO, 2)

Jennifer Nias reported that in response to her inquiries of non-attending parents at Highstones:

> Most replied and, overwhelmingly, they attributed their absences to lack of either transport or a babysitter. As one parent put it 'If I'm asked to work extra, that's four hours' overtime, say, and I feel, well I can do that for my family.' (HI, 2A4)

One of my own interviews was with a mother who on her own account had not been to a school event for a long time. This was a person who was trying to bring up a family on her own, working a full day, returning home to deal with household chores and preoccupied with other domestic worries. It is perhaps hardly surprising if at the end of the day she is left with relatively little energy or desire to face a parents' evening at school – especially if this is itself, as I shall go on to suggest, anxiety-inducing.

Some of the teachers we spoke to recognized that these practical difficulties can operate to the disadvantage of those already disadvantaged in terms of working hours and wealth. One teacher saw this as a problem associated with giving parents access to classrooms during the school day:

> In a way I think sometimes it's a little bit divisive in society to have your school open during the day for that sort of thing, because it tends to be those that have a kind of posh job who can negotiate some time off to come, whereas the ordinary working man really can't find the time to come, or it's the mum who doesn't need to work. (U, 15)

What we also observed was that in areas where there was a lot of night shift working it could be the same kind of people who were disadvantaged in terms of access to evening functions.

Without for one moment denying that parents, and some parents more than others, experienced practical problems which made it difficult for them to attend school events, it is worth noting that these did not always make it impossible. What they did was to face parents with a set of priorities and a decision which was not always made in favour of attendance at school.

2 Deference to teachers

We collected a good deal of evidence to the effect that parents were by and large perfectly happy to leave questions of broad educational policy to the teachers. The following comment is characteristic:

> I don't really know enough about education basically to feel that I have any right to comment on it. I think that if the school – that's their part of the thing. They do obviously know the right curriculum to set the children for what they are going to do. I don't think that parents really can comment on that. (RP, 1116)

This was supported for some parents by their satisfaction with what the schools were doing:

> We've been to no end of meetings with [the head] – he's a very nice chap – no doubt about it – but he goes on and on – and in the end you feel you know it and can't hear it over again. We could be more involved if we had time and were nearer. The school gives us plenty of opportunity to be involved but though one of us goes to [Y's reports] meetings we don't go to the others. They know best anyway and we are very satisfied.
>
> I leave it to X [spouse]. And X doesn't always go – but we like to know what's happening and we feel the school is doing a good job generally. You just can't go to everything. (HO, 2)

Now the point of all this in relation to the parent who, for example, does not attend an evening meeting on the curriculum, the teaching of maths or some other matter of educational policy, is that such a parent may simply regard these questions as ones best left to the teachers. Consequently he (or even more probably she) does not see much point in getting involved with occasions of this kind.

John Elliott illustrates this same point in the context of Upland PTA Committee discussions. He quotes one parent as explaining:

> I think in the last few months that only one point came up in the committee; that was about the sick children – and I discussed that – and that's the only thing – because there is a big gap really, they think it's not their business. Members are under the impression that the duty of the Parents' Committee is to raise money for a lot of things. (U, 15)

Parents' deference to teachers' expertise was if anything fed by the occasional evenings which were held on e.g. maths in the curriculum. (It is interesting to conjecture, in the absence of any evidence, whether parents would show the same deference to an evening on Home Economics or Motor Vehicle Maintenance.) Such evenings were very largely organized in a way which set up teachers as the source of information, the repository of educational wisdom, the people who could explain what parents did not understand and answer their questions. If teachers managed to avoid using language that parents did not understand then it was plainly only at the price of careful explanation. Even so a good number of parents would leave confirmed in their sense of their own inability to understand 'educational' arguments:

> The thing was, if there was something you didn't understand you didn't really like to attract him and ask him to explain. I think had you done that it would have taken another hour. (RP, 1115)

In some cases parents' deference to teachers is cheerful, based upon satisfaction with the school and a ready acknowledgement of the teachers' superior expertise; sometimes it is indifferent, based on apathy; in other cases it is grudging and feeds parents' cynicism in relation to the whole character of communication between the school and themselves.

3 Cynicism

A number of parents whom we interviewed, perhaps those with more personal confidence, might have taken part in more formal school–parent discussion had they not become cynical about the value of such discussion.

In her study of Highstones, Jennifer Nias suggests that 'a reluctance on the part of parents to participate more vigorously, and even critically, in their children's schooling may reflect upon their previous experience of local democracy'. She collected statements from a number of parents of which the following are representative:

> You see, I think that schools do what they want to do anyway, regardless of what parents think. That's why I don't bother [with school], because I think that. Regardless of what we think, they'd do as they want anyway.

> The teachers might listen [to parents] but not do anything . . . they all stick together. (HI, 3A11)

It was in fact a dinner lady who observed:

> One reason why parents don't get involved is because they know they can't alter the general policy of the school. They know they couldn't make an impact on the big things (like the changes in school dinner).

Another parent added:

> It's not because parents aren't interested. It's because they don't have a choice. If they did, they'd take more trouble to find out what the school is really like. (HI, 3A11)

John Elliott has I think something similar in mind, though he talks in terms of 'scepticism' rather than 'cynicism':

> Is it conceivable that some parents may not turn out to educational evenings not out of indifference or deference; but rather because they are sceptical about the school's capacity to have its practices questioned? . . . Parents seemed to be sensitive to what one at least called 'glossing over' responses to their questions. The phrase describes a response which fails to take into account the issues and doubts which motivate a parent's questions. It is interesting that, although they may ask teachers questions, parents do not always see themselves doing so from a position of ignorance. In 'asking a question' they are often tacitly 'questioning', and the teachers' responses are judged in terms of how they deal with this tacit content. (U, 15)

These comments throw revealing light on the nature of 'the problem of the non-communicating parent'. It is I believe only a minority of teachers who will be greatly concerned if parents are reluctant to offer their own opinions on a regular basis. The wider concern is that parents should be prepared to place themselves regularly in a position to receive and attend to the things that teachers want them to hear. As John Elliott argues:

> There is a kind of approachability which the expert may possess in relation to the lay person who is perceived to be in need of enlightenment. The experts are sympathetic to the concerns of the laymen and listen to their questions, but they are the ones who 'know best'. They see their role in terms of enlightening others but not being enlightened by others. Their 'knowledge' is not open to question. The communications of the 'approachable' expert, although responsive to lay persons' questions, are paternalistic. The exchange is not one of dialogue. (U, 15)

It will not be surprising, therefore, where communication is emphatically in one direction, that parents who do feel that they have something to contribute to discussion become disenchanted and in the end 'apathetic'.

4 Dominant parents

It is not only the dynamics of teacher–parent relationships which can discourage parents from participating in school meetings and other events. I have already begun to depict something of the different level of confidence in dealing with educational affairs that parents have. This in itself can add to the sense which some parents have of their own inadequacy in school and exclusion from the main hub of activity. Thus Jennifer Nias suggested on the basis of her study of Highstones that:

> Many parents feel inadequate when faced with curriculum and examination innovations, and this insecurity is compounded for some by educational differences between them. Many, especially in the isolated villages, themselves attended all-age village schools, or secondary moderns. They lack confidence when faced with other parents, the ones whom from their own childhood experience they described to me as 'the grammar-school snobs'. (HI, 2A4)

She illustrates one parent's acute sense of his own educational inadequacy:

> We could have our say at meetings, but you don't know if they'd listen, and anyway I can't speak out at meetings, because I am not educated. The ones who're educated go to the meetings, and do all the talking, and it'd sound funny to them if we spoke . . . Well, it's my Suffolk accent, I don't feel I can express myself properly . . . At parents' evenings, the forceful and educated ones push in; we might as well go home. (HI, 2A4)

Some parents expressed their sense of disqualification from active participation in school affairs in explicitly class terms:

> I'd quite like to be a parent governor but they don't want working class people – they wouldn't be interested in me. (HI, 3A11)

Some parents' ability to monopolize teachers' attention encouraged others to feel that the teachers were discriminating between those they wanted to talk to and those they did not:

> You *are* welcome . . . but you get the feeling, I don't know how to put it, that some are more welcome than others.

One consequence of this was distrust of any moves to give parent representatives more power in the school and a lack of confidence in the ability of one set of parents (e.g. parent governors) to represent the interests of others. Another consequence was to discourage less confident parents from participating in school events and institutions which would be dominated by the more confident, educated and articulate parents.

5 Alien social events

It is not only formal meetings and discussions about educational issues which discomfort the less confident parents. Even the kind of social evening devised particularly to allow a relaxed and informal meeting of parents and teachers can inhibit the participation of at least a certain section of parents. In any case not all parents are socially gregarious. As one parent explained, in commenting on a school newsletter:

> It paints a picture of a very active school from the point of view of parental involvement that makes us feel somewhat guilty – because we are not really the kind of people who are wanting to be involved socially. (U, 14)

Those of a generally more gregarious disposition may however be put off by the particular form of social event put an offer – especially if it is perceived as one located within a different social culture from that of the parents concerned:

Mother:	. . . there is nothing there. Even for the parents – you know – like dances and things for the parents. Not many – just once in a while, like Christmas time.
Child:	People would enjoy that sort of thing. It's one thing where all the teachers and parents can really get together and get to know each other. I think it would be a really great idea.
Mother:	Yes the parents would get to know the teachers more. Have an evening out with the teachers just to be one – do you know what I mean?
John Elliott:	There's not many of those at all?
Mother:	No, only near Christmas.
John Elliott:	There is one in a few weeks, at the end of term – cheese and wine.
Mother:	[looking doubtful] Yes.
John Elliott:	You don't think that cheese and wine is your sort of thing?
Child:	Not the sort of thing that Mum would go to.
Mother:	No, not really. A group or band or something like that.
John Elliott:	A dance?
Mother:	Yes. (U, 14)

But if, as John Elliott remarks, a wine and cheese evening had little appeal to a family from the Caribbean, the Calypso Evening which also featured on the programme was just as out of key with the real enthusiasms of a working-class West Indian family.

Perhaps it is an impossible task to devise social events at which all sections of the school community can feel equally at ease. However, if the PTA is dominated by one particular social/cultural group they may have little alternative but to risk the charge either of preferring the kind of events favoured by their own social set or of patronizing other social groups.

6 Dread of school

I have already made many references to the anxiety which parents feel about attending certain school events. This was a recurring theme in our interviews with parents who had not attended school events or had much to do with the schools, especially among parents who had little or no contact with the school at all. Jennifer Nias reported:

> Only two sets of parents claimed never to have been inside the school, and in one of these, both mother and father bluntly said, 'I hate schools . . .' Later each told a story of educational unhappiness, boredom and failure which would provide a reason, if not an excuse, for their confessed indifference to their children's schooling. (HI, 2A4)

I concluded on the basis of interviews with parents at Robert Peel that for a parent whose own memories of school are unpleasant – and especially one who learned to live in fear of teachers – the anxieties and inhibitions attached to re-entering the portals of a school can be quite overwhelming. Some teachers at least seemed sensitive to this:

> I think some of them are afraid. Particularly those that have memories of their school days which aren't very pleasant. Some of them I think are afraid because they know their child is failing and they don't want to be told so. (U, unpublished interview)

> When I get a parent on the 'phone, it was a very difficult situation – it has only happened . . . once – and I suddenly realized how nervous that parent was by the way they were behaving. I don't think we pay it enough attention perhaps. (HI, 2A4)

Parents' anxieties can be heightened when it comes to an interview with a teacher about a child who is not performing well, misbehaving, not doing homework, or truanting (perhaps with the connivance of the parent). The parents' expectation of the interview with the teacher may well be one of bleak prognosis and complaint together with some implicit criticism of the parent for failing to exercise proper responsibility. 'It's the ones who never come whom you really want to see', say the teachers – and 'the ones who never come' are alert to the note of recrimination.

Humiliation (or anticipated humiliation) at the hands of the teacher can be reinforced by the exhibitions of pride of the parents of more successful children. As one governor observed:

> Parents can be very hurtful when they are discussing the progress of their children. Every parent I think boasts or likes to boast, and that can be very hurtful to other parents. I have noticed this on open days, that the parents of the best children always manage to stay in the classroom examining the work much, much longer than parents of a child that works much harder but hasn't done so well. (HI, 2A4)

The extreme case of the non-communicating, non-attending parent almost amounts to 'parental truancy' – and we may usefully seek an understanding of this in the same sort of terms as pupils' truancy (with which I suspect it is commonly associated). In the course of our interviews we were offered a number of suggestions as to how this problem might be tackled.

One suggestion was to change the venue for the meeting between parents and teachers. Apart from anything else parents disliked the lack of privacy at meetings:

> I don't go as often as I should . . . you can communicate better by seeing someone on your own rather than going to an evening. I don't like big crowds. We all sit looking at each other. (U, 15)

Parents commented that meetings with individual teachers took place on the teachers' own 'territory' – a fact which some parents mentioned as an obstacle to the free expression of their views. As one said:

> There ought to be a place where you could talk to a teacher that isn't his place. (HI, 2A3)

Parents were often warmly appreciative of the conversations which they had with members of the CAP team in their (the parents') own homes. One commented approvingly on the practice of a friend of hers, a teacher, who visits the parents of her children once or twice during the course of a year in their own homes.

A second and rather interesting response to parental anxiety about coming to school was indicated in a wide variety of comments which pointed to the importance of having someone to support you on such visits:

> You don't go because you don't want to make a fool of yourself . . . It would be easier to go to some things if you had someone to go with. (HI, 2A4)

Our studies showed instances of people reluctant to go to school without the company of a *husband*. 'My husband is on night shift and I feel left out going on my own' (U, 15); a *neighbour* (as Jennifer Nias explained, in the scattered housing which made up her school's catchment area there may be only one child of a given age group in a single hamlet or group of houses); or a person of the same *colour or ethnic group*:

> I used to attend every meeting. Sometimes it's me alone. I don't know other parents attending. It embarrasses you. It makes you feel 'why don't coloured people turn out like the English do?' (U, 15)

It may even be a *child* who can provide the support:

> One thing I realized on these visits to 'non-attending' parents' houses was the closeness of the mother–daughter relationship (the latter often sitting through the conversation and chipping in). I was reminded of a sixth former's objection to children not being able to attend evenings with their parents below the fifth year. If this taboo was not enforced it might give these mothers the social support they needed to attend. (U, 15)

In the extreme case perhaps a parent needs the professional support of a *social worker*. One school's education welfare officer in trying to help parents of school refusers sometimes found it useful to offer to accompany them to school, giving them not only free transport but support in the interview with the headteacher (RP, 112). Perhaps similar support could help to overcome the anxieties of parents who were themselves in a sense school refusers.

It was a parent, not a teacher, who expressed the opinion:

> I think that those parents who are interested in their children's education will approach any school whatever it is like – and those that aren't won't. (RP, 112)

Our evidence suggests this is an over harsh judgement which underestimates the psychological complexity of parents' relations with teachers and ignores the ways in which the social and cultural character of those relations and their context can operate to the advantage of some parents and the disadvantage of others.

Reference

The references for the quoted material in this article are taken from the full version of published case study material, as follows:

ELLIOTT, J. *et al.* (1981). *Case Studies In School Accountability*. Vols. I–III. Cambridge: Institute of Education.

Educational Home-Visiting and the Teaching of Reading

Peter Hannon and Angela Jackson

Introduction

Educational home-visiting has developed over the last 20 years or so out of recognition of the importance of the home in the education of young children. Yet it has not been used much with young children who are at school. Here we would like to report a case of a school which set out to use home-visiting to increase parental involvement in a central part of the primary curriculum – the teaching of reading.

The home-visiting idea can be traced back to preschool intervention work in the United States. The Nashville Early Training Project (Gray and Klaus, 1970) and the Ypsilanti Perry Preschool Project (Weikart, Bond and McNeil, 1978) were notable examples. It was realized that preschool intervention with disadvantaged children had more lasting effects where home visitors had involved parents at home (Bronfenbrenner, 1974). In this country home-visiting was taken up by the EPA West Riding Project team (Smith, 1975). Later, there were cases of teachers working from nursery classes undertaking home visits (Evans and Hannon, 1977; Raven, 1980). Recently, home-visiting has been an integral part of various parental involvement programmes for handicapped children (Pugh, 1981; Cameron, 1984).

What is interesting about these initiatives is that they have not touched on the education of ordinary children of school age. But if home-visiting is valuable for young children before they start school, then why not afterwards too? Poulton (1983) listed objectives pursued by over 50 home-visiting schemes in England

and Scotland which were surveyed in 1981. Some of the objectives, such as 'to establish early contact between parents and school before children attend school', could only apply to the preschool years. But others such as 'to establish in parents an awareness of their own ability as the prime educators of their children' could apply equally well to children in school, at least during the early years.

Educational home-visiting was advocated in both the Plowden and Bullock Reports but there are very few signs of schools taking it up in any systematic way. An HMI survey of 80 first schools (DES, 1982) found a range of work with parents but no mention was made of home-visiting. A much wider survey by the NFER of almost 1,700 primary schools of all kinds found home visiting in one-fifth of them but mainly in nursery schools or classes (Cyster, Clift and Battle, 1980). It is likely that in certain community schools and schools with home–school liaison teachers some home-visiting for school-age children will have taken place (Bailey, 1980) but such cases have largely gone unreported. Macleod (1986) has described visits made by home–school liaison teachers operating in schools with ethnic minority populations in three local education authorities and Feeley and Karran (1983) have described an education visitor scheme in Coventry which extended to schoolchildren, but the emphasis in both cases appears to have been on preschool children or those children in school with particular problems. An exception to this pattern has been reported by Morris *et al.* (1985) who have described a New Zealand school in which all parents were offered a mid-year home visit from their child's class teacher instead of the more usual interview at school. About three-quarters of parents opted for a home visit. Their reactions, and those of the teachers who visited, were found to be very favourable.

There are possibly three main reasons why educational home-visiting has not developed for school-age children. First, there is a resources problem. Many schools would say they do not have sufficient teachers to spare any for visiting. This is a serious, and in some cases an insuperable, obstacle but in other cases a different pattern of teacher deployment within the school might provide the opportunity for visiting during the day or evening if it were a high enough priority. A second reason for not visiting homes is the widespread assumption that education is something which only happens in schools and therefore that parental involvement in children's education means bringing parents into school. From this perspective there may seem to be little point in venturing out of the school into children's homes to make contact with parents. Some teachers would also question the teaching competence of parents in central areas of the primary curriculum such as the teaching of reading. Thirdly, there may be some reasonably well-staffed schools, willing to be flexible in how teachers are used and aware of children's learning at home, who still prefer not to carry out educational home-visiting because they doubt its feasibility, its cost-effectiveness compared to other ways of working with parents, or they may be uneasy about possibly invading parents' privacy and wonder whether teachers would be welcome in homes. These views point to the need for evaluative studies of cases where schools have attempted to use home-visiting to support parental involvement in the curriculum.

The teaching of reading is one area of the primary curriculum where there has recently been interesting initiatives in parental involvement, some of which have included home-visiting. In the Haringey Reading Project (Tizard, Schofield, and Hewison, 1982) and in some of the work on paired reading (e.g. Bushell, Miller and Robson, 1982) home visits were carried out over the duration of the programmes. However in these cases visiting was researchers or educational psychologists so it is difficult for schools to judge their relevance to situations in which visiting would have to be undertaken by teachers without outside assistance.

A reading project

Educational home-visiting played an important part in a Reading Project carried out at a primary school in the north of England where all parents of five- to eight-year-old children were encouraged to hear their children read regularly at home. Details of the Project and data on the setting, implementation and take-up have been reported by Hannon, Jackson, and Page (1985). The school was in a social priority area and its catchment area, according to the 1981 Census, was overwhelmingly working-class with nearly three times the national unemployment rate. Most households were in council accommodation. The proportion of immigrant families was relatively low. The school, designated by the LEA as a community school, had been strongly committed to work with parents for some years previously. This had included a certain amount of home-visiting for preschool children (Evans and Hannon, 1977) and for some children of school age where there were particular problems. The Reading Project, which began in 1978, grew out of the desire of infant teachers to involve parents more directly in the teaching of young children and the desire to make their home-visiting wider and more purposeful.

The basic idea for the project was derived from the Haringey Project in that school reading books were sent home with children, and parents were systematically encouraged to hear children read at home several times a week. Reading cards were used by teachers to make suggestions about reading, and by parents to indicate what was done at home. The project, as a specially monitored innovation, continued for five years. No outside resources were available to the school for the project and any home-visiting required had to be carried out by school staff. The school's staffing was not unduly favourable by SPA standards. Over the five years of the project the average pupil:teacher ratio, after allowing for teachers engaged in non-school community activities, was 21.7:1 compared to the national average for all primary schools of 22.9:1 over the same period. However, the deployment of teachers within the school meant that certain teachers could be freed to work some half-day or evening sessions during the week outside the classroom. One of the authors, then an infants teacher at the school, had two such sessions per week to act as project co-ordinator.

Visiting to involve parents

Home-visiting for the project was undertaken mainly by the co-ordinator. She liaised closely with the teachers concerned and occasionally took classes to release them to make the visits themselves. Most visits took place during the day and lasted between half- and three-quarters of an hour. Working parents were visited in the evening but daytime visits were preferred if possible because it was generally easier to talk to parents without the child being present. On a few occasions the visitor found it useful to hear children read in front of their parents to lessen anxiety, to give encouragement to the parent or child, or to demonstrate a certain technique.

Preliminary visits were made before the Project began to discuss what was proposed and the important part parents could play in their child's reading development. A parents' meeting was arranged one evening in school and the visitor's first task was to call with personal invitations. The meeting was attended by just over a third of the families; the others received home visits or were seen in school before the project began.

Once the project was underway, visiting was undertaken on the basis of referral from class teachers or from information picked up from the reading cards for the following reasons: to respond to a specific comment or query from a parent or child; to give particular advice to a parent about what might be helpful for their child; to deal with any problems or anxiety a child was having; to praise the parent/child for any progress made; to encourage the parents to hear their child read more regularly; to discourage any unhelpful practice; to chase up a lost book or card; to make sure cards were marked. Parents were told that they could request a visit. None did this directly but many wrote questions on the reading cards and these were answered either in writing by the class teacher or during a home visit. The children themselves prompted visits by asking, for example, 'When are you going to my house again?'

The pattern of visiting was modified in later years. Parents who at first had needed frequent support and advice became more confident of their skills and convinced of the importance of what they were doing. Reading at home became a habit as children remembered to carry their books regularly between home and school. Children introduced to the project in the second and third years included brothers and sisters of those who were already taking their books home, so their parents were by then experienced in hearing their children read. The children's needs also changed during their three years in the project and parents usually wanted more information, and required more visits, when their children were in the early stages of learning to read. As children became fluent readers parents were less anxious about whether they were 'doing the right thing'. By this stage parents were usually only visited once a term unless there was a specific reason for more.

The content of visits

In order to study the nature of visiting more closely the co-ordinator's records for the first term of the project were examined. At that time 40 families were participating in the project and 100 visits, including preliminary ones, were made during the term. All but one family received at least two visits. Seven were visited three times, four families had four visits and two were visited five times. There were of course many teacher–parent contacts in this period other than home-visiting for the Reading Project. The co-ordinator's log showed three main types of visit: the *preliminary visits* to explain the project and seek parents' participation, *consultative visits*, and occasional *special visits*.

Preliminary visits

Each family was visited before reading books were sent home. The home visitor offered some general advice about hearing young children read, the nature of which can be conveyed by summarizing the points contained in a 'DOs and DON'Ts' sheet given to parents. When hearing their children read they were advised to make sure the atmosphere was happy and relaxed, to let the child sit close, to give lots of praise for effort, to allow the child plenty of time, to smooth out difficulties by telling children words they didn't know, and to repeat the whole sentence containing the word. For children at the beginning stages of reading parents were advised to talk about pictures in the books, to read the page to the child first, to emphasize and point to new words, to go back to pictures and discuss them again in relation to what had been read. They were advised *not* to make reading an unpleasant activity, not to threaten to tell the teacher if the child did not read, not to make children think they were in competition with others, not to show anxiety about lack of interest, not to have the television on, and not to be afraid to ask for help and advice from any of the teachers however trivial they might feel the trouble to be.

In the preliminary visits two parents expressed doubts about their child's co-operation in reading at home but there was no problem later when books and cards were sent home. A few parents were worried that their child was 'backward' and had been singled out for extra help; others were worried that they did not have the ability to help their child because they had not been successful at school themselves. Two families were concerned about books being brought home in case they were lost or damaged by younger children. Their fears were not realized in practice as this rarely happened. Almost all the children looked after their books carefully and younger children were often encouraged to use books positively as older brothers and sisters would sit and read to them. One working parent said that it would be her childminder who would have to hear her son read but in fact she herself did become involved. In another case there was some doubt about whether a child in a particularly large family was likely to be heard to read. A neighbouring parent offered to help but in the event the child's own mother heard him read almost every night, and later two of her other children as well. The general function of preliminary visits therefore was to iron out misunderstandings and practical difficulties which might have prevented the parents' involvement getting off to a good start.

Consultative visits

Subsequent visits began with a discussion about the child's reading with general advice again on the lines summarized above. The emphasis was on minimizing problems and reading for pleasure. Parents were reminded that they had a unique contribution to make and that their closeness with their child was something that teachers could not reproduce within a classroom. They were encouraged to relate the reading materials to their own child's experience and to give plenty of praise. Formal phonic teaching was included only once at the class teacher's request.

Some advice was given in response to parents' questions. They often noticed and asked about stages in their child's reading. Typical comments about *teaching points* in that first term were:

> She confuses words like 'it' and 'the', and 'what' and 'when'.
> He doesn't remember words from one page to the next.
> He doesn't know his alphabet.

The visitor dealt with these by reassuring the parents that the first two problems were common in children beginning to read and that they should continue to tell the child the words, or read the whole page again putting slight emphasis on the words which were causing difficulty. If the question of learning the alphabet or trying to 'spell the word out' was raised it was pointed out that these were of limited help in learning to read.

Parents asked about advice from teachers which they had received on *reading cards*, for example why a child had been asked to repeat pages either at home or at school. One asked why her child had been given a book with no words in it. Another frequent question concerned the amount given to read and whether the child could read more or less. The answers to these questions were given in relation to the individual child and with reference to the class teacher. Regarding the amount to read, the usual advice was that the parents should be guided by the child's interest.

Sometimes there was discussion about the *child's performance*. Four parents remarked that their child was bored with their book. The visitor was able to pass these comments on to class teacher and books were changed. Other remarks were about the tactics children used when they came across unfamiliar words:

> I've realized that she misses out the words she doesn't know.
>
> He used to skip bits when he read to himself – now I give him spot checks.

Advice was also given about teaching points which the class teacher wanted passing on. These were specific to each child and to the stage that he or she had reached. From time to time in the project parents were asked by class teachers to try various approaches: to talk through pre-reading books; to match words to those in the book; to play word lotto; to teach initial sounds; to read for meaning, not speed; to take a book more slowly; to encourage silent reading; and to talk about content. There were periods when parents of some two dozen older children who were poor readers were advised to play reading games with their children.

The advice was not only one-way from the teacher to the parents. Parents passed on many comments about their children's interests and reading behaviour. Home visits could be a time for detailed discussions leading to collaboration between teachers and parents in teaching children to read.

Special visits

These included visits to give books to children on prolonged absence or holiday reading for children who had been away on the last day of term. They also included visits to chase up lost books or cards. During the first term of the scheme the following problems were discussed.

OTHER CHILDREN IN THE FAMILY Eight families mentioned that their other children would have benefited from home help with their reading. Two parents said that the younger child who was being helped at home was now reading better than her sister and that this was causing problems. Three families talked about their preschool children. Two of these were referred to the nursery teacher and one was brought toys from the toy library when the co-ordinator visited about the older sister.

THE OTHER PARENT In three cases the mother expressed some concern about the father hearing the child read because he was too impatient. One mother said she only heard her child read when the father was out.

GENERAL PROBLEMS Very frequently difficulties with housing, money, unemployment or health would be mentioned during a visit and on three occasions the visitor became involved in quite lengthy discussion.

ADULT LITERACY AND LANGUAGE PROBLEMS One mother who said she could not read but who was unwilling to attend classes was found an adult education home tutor. There were only two families in this group where English was a second language but in both cases at least one parent spoke English and older brothers and sisters, who were able to read, regularly heard their younger sister or brother read.

Later developments

Over the years the number of children visited and the number of teachers in the project increased. By the second year of the project the original group was still being visited and a further 35 children were introduced to the project. By the third year over 100 children and seven class teachers were participating.

For various reasons the pattern of home-visiting became more complex. The children to be visited changed as some families left the area and others who moved in had to be introduced to the project. There was always some visiting to explain the project to new parents. Consequently it is difficult to generalize about the number of visits given to project children because, although the numbers in the year groups remained around 30 or 40, these were not necessarily the same 30 or 40 children. Class teachers, as well as the co-ordinator, undertook visits. In some cases the class teacher would have a special reason to see a project child's family herself or would not refer a reading problem to the co-ordinator because she had dealt with it herself during another visit. Also, with more class teachers involved it became difficult to keep records of the visits carried out by teachers other than the co-ordinator. Nevertheless, it is possible to identify some issues and developments which emerged over the years.

A significant feature of the home-visiting was its *continuity* throughout the three years the child was part of the project. This could be particularly valuable in the transition from one class teacher to another. Parents monitored and commented on their children's development, and any problems could be followed through and solved in subsequent visits. Although no parent actually requested a visit it was obvious that certain kinds of behaviour would initiate a response. One mother said, 'I thought you'd be coming round. He hasn't been reading and I can't do a thing with him'. Another parent wrote on the reading card that her child would not read to her but when visited she was more explicit about the problem and criticized the reading material which was changed with beneficial results.

Something else revealed through visits was *adult illiteracy*. No parent gave this as a reason for not wanting to join in the project but some did admit during a home visit that they could not read or had reading problems. Usually only one parent was illiterate so the other one, or older brothers or sisters, would help the child. In one case a father helped both his child and the mother to learn to read. Another parent said that she had learnt to read alongside her child from the beginning. During some of the time the project was running the co-ordinator and a class teacher ran an adult literacy class and one project parent attended this. In families where English was not the first language older children who could read English were often asked to hear the younger ones read. On occasions family members who were bilingual helped by accompanying the visitor and acting as interpreters.

As in many other educational home-visiting schemes, *non-educational problems* often emerged. One parent said she appreciated the contact she had with staff concerning her son's other behavioural problems; another said that talking to her son's teacher had helped them at the time of her husband's death. It was valuable to have the resources of a community school to deal with some problems. The visitor was able to recommend to parents various classes or groups that were running in the school including social groups like keep-fit, facilities for preschool children like the playgroup or toy library, and health services like the well-baby clinic, pregnancy testing and a well-woman course. Help with benefits and housing problems was also available from the full-time community worker based in the school.

Some reports on home-visiting schemes, for example in the West Riding (Smith, 1975) and in the Lothian region (Raven, 1980), have found that at certain times *family stress* from problems such as unemployment, lack of money, poor housing or crises in relationships make it difficult for parents to be involved in their child's education. Such problems were common in the project school area and the amount of help given by parents to children did vary at different times. Nevertheless only four families were ever lost from the project. In two cases teachers felt that reading at home had become one more cause of family tension and violence and substitute arrangements were made in school. There were two cases of single parents whose involvement eventually tailed off. The aim of the Reading Project was a specific, limited one of asking parents to spend a few minutes a night hearing their child read. The fact that this commitment was less than in other schemes where visitors worked with children in their homes for an hour or so each week, perhaps accounts for the comparatively low drop-out rate.

Parents' and teachers' views about home-visiting

It is difficult to separate the views parents have about being visited at home from their views about the Reading Project in general. One point however is clear – that many parents were glad to be able to talk about their child without having to come into school. One mother commented, 'Although I'm not always down at school I care about my kids'.

Parents often indicated that although they might see teachers regularly at school a home visit would be more helpful. One mother who had been seen almost daily in school worried for months about her child's reading before she was visited at home and could talk about it. She said, 'I don't think I've been visited enough. Because I'm always at school it's assumed that I don't need a visit'.

Parents in their own homes tended to make comments about the curriculum that perhaps they would not make at a formal parents' evening or in a full classroom. They readily criticized some reading scheme books because they were contrived and boring. They also felt able, perhaps because they were on home ground talking to the co-ordinator, to raise questions about class teachers which sometimes implied criticism. At times the co-ordinator's position became difficult as she had to take parents' views seriously and also represent the teachers' views. She encouraged the people concerned to sort out these difficulties directly, but it was not always easy. As one parent said, 'I don't like pestering them down at school'. This raises the question, to which we return, of who is best fitted to be the home visitor.

A survey was carried out after the project of parents of children who had completed three years in it. Some had finished two or three years previously. Parents of 60 out of 76 children were successfully traced and all agreed to be interviewed about a number of issues relating to the project. Most recalled that they had been visited more than once a term during the project. When asked directly if they thought the visits had been 'too often', 'about right', or 'not often enough' none of the parents replied that they had been too often and most (49) indicated that they had been about right. Interestingly, 11 out of 60 said that there had not been enough visits. Some reasons were given for liking visits:

> I'd rather be seen at home. You can talk better in private without kids around.

> She's come on since home visits. I found out she's stubborn in school – she's not like that at home. I should have been asked what she's like at home.

> I can see [the teacher] at school but it's different because the children are there. It's more intimate at home.

> It helps. The more frequent the communication, the better. When I was at school, home and school were different.

There was no evidence from the survey, or from any other source, that parents in this project regarded visits as an unwelcome intrusion. Instead the evidence suggests that visits were generally valued by parents. It is possible that the very fact of being visited about the curriculum – in itself a message from the school – was appreciated.

Teachers' views of home-visiting were not sought as systematically as those of the parents but there were some opportunities for them to volunteer those they held. All class teachers were invited to write down their views of the project for a report at the halfway stage (Jackson and Hannon, 1981). Included in what one teacher wrote was the following:

> A great help in the Project has been a teacher allocated time for home-visiting so that each set of parents can have individual help with any problems, especially if they have been poor readers themselves.

The project co-ordinator who had done most of the visiting wrote about how she had experienced it:

> Through home visits I have been freed, to some extent, from the role of teacher as someone who only contacts parents with complaints or problems. It's good to get a friendly welcome and a cup of tea while sharing concerns and exchanging advice. Perhaps most importantly, I often feel closer to the children whose houses I've visited or whom I have seen at home. They seem to feel this too; some have become friendlier and others more open and less tentative.

At the conclusion of the project all the class teachers were interviewed about their experience of the project and some views about home-visiting emerged. One teacher believed that parents had a 'better relationship with teachers' as a result of visits. Another had found visits valuable for resolving problems with parents:

> There were some confused as to what their role and job was, and they weren't sure it was their job. It would often be resolved in meeting with them in home visits. They were really helpful, home visits.

Two teachers noted the children's reaction:

> I was surprised how keen children were that we visited them at home. They like to think the teachers are going to talk to their mums.
>
> I find home visits amazing. Children's attitudes change when they realize you've been to their house. I wouldn't have expected five-year-olds to notice particularly.

One teacher regarded home-visiting as important in its effects on teachers:

> The success of the Project hinges on home-visiting. It's got to be backed up by home-visiting – a vital element. You've got to have staff in schools who are prepared to consider their own attitudes – in some schools you've got teachers who really think they're the only ones who can teach children anything.

Another teacher did feel that the experience of visiting parents had affected her:

> Yes, it's made me more aware of the home the children come from and affected my involvement with the children in school. I can be more sympathetic – know what difficulties they have to cope with at home.

In summary, the views of visiting expressed by both parents and teachers were entirely positive. A common view was that there were social and personal benefits for those concerned, including the children. This suggests that home-visiting in the early years at school need not be intrusive or uncongenial.

Implications for practice

What has emerged from this study is that home visits can be used to increase parents' involvement in a part of the primary curriculum which both they and teachers recognize as important. The educational content of the visits appeared to be high, and they were experienced positively by parents and teachers. It is probably a mistake therefore to think of visiting just for parents 'who you can't get into school' or just for children having special problems. From the parents' point of view, there may be advantages in having a teacher come to them, rather than in them visiting the teacher in school. However, in order to sort out the implications for practice in schools, some problems need to be considered.

First, there is the question of resources. How many schools have sufficient staffing for home-visiting to be a genuine option – especially at a time when local education authorities are under pressure to make staffing cuts? It must be accepted that for some schools releasing even one member of staff for occasional visiting might be too costly in terms of the poorer pupil:teacher ratio, or the enlarged teaching groups, which would result in the school. But there are many other schools whose staffing would allow some home-visiting if classes were reorganized to release some teachers for non-class teaching duties, or if they were prepared to rethink the role of any teacher or headteacher already free of full-time class responsibility. Findings from the Haringey Project have led Hewison (1981) to ask whether teachers in a school might be more productively employed working with parents rather than in remedial work. What matters here is a school's educational priorities, and its readiness to organize flexibly to meet them.

Another question concerns who is the best person in a school to carry out visits. Class teachers are obviously in a good position to discuss with parents the progress of children in their classes. At first, in the project reported here the co-ordinator's teaching duties gave her knowledge of the children but in later years this was not so and she often felt she could not answer detailed questions about a child's work as they moved up the school. On the other hand it was sometimes useful for the parents to be able to raise their problems with someone who was not their child's teacher. The overriding consideration when choosing a home visitor must be that he or she is convinced of the parents' valuable part in teaching their children and can communicate this to parents. An important problem here is that there is very little training for teachers who undertake home-visiting. It has to be recognized that teachers in all forms of early childhood education are now trying to work with parents or groups but this requires very different skills from those commonly valued in initial, or indeed in-service, training courses.

A possible objection to educational home-visiting might be that it is an unwarranted invasion by the school into the community. Home-visiting can mean working-class homes and middle-class visitors. Whatever the positive feelings of parents and teachers there is a danger of it becoming one-sided: visits are initiated by teachers and the resulting involvement of parents should not be mistaken for a partnership with them, although it might lead to this. Teachers could be seen merely as messengers from school, imposing their own values on parents. However, this kind of relationship would be hard to sustain over a number of years. Parents have a range of tactics for avoiding encounters that they feel will be unproductive. To make visiting possible the family has to allow the visitor over the doorstep. During home visits parents are on their own ground, and one parent can often be supported by their partner or other family members so they may feel confident to raise criticisms and give their own opinion. When there is mutual understanding, when teachers believe that parents have something to tell them as well as something to learn, then stereotypes on both sides can be challenged. Educational home-visiting may serve to change teachers and schools as well as parents and homes.

A final question to be considered is whether home-visiting is always necessary to secure parental involvement in the teaching of reading. The best way to answer this question would be to try to operate a similar reading project without home-visiting. This has in fact been attempted in a case reported by Ashton, Stoney and Hannon (1986) and a high level of take-up was obtained. However, the school in question was in a less disadvantaged area and the project ran for one year only so the comparison with the Reading

Project discussed above may not be entirely fair. Nevertheless it must be admitted as a possibility that for some families home-visiting may not be so important, at least for increasing the frequency of home reading, although the nature and intensity of the visiting may alter the quality of home–school collaboration.

It is tempting at this point to call for further research. But this would not necessarily help much if the hope was that research could ultimately specify the exact conditions in which home-visiting will have certain effects. Conditions in practice vary too much from one school to another for researchers to be able to anticipate all the possibilities and, furthermore, there can also be variations and shifts in people's perceptions about what is valuable in home-visiting. The answer is for schools to try to estimate the possible benefits for themselves and, if home-visiting seems appropriate in their situation, they should explore it in practice, and subsequently reflect on their experience. This of course is research too, but of a kind particularly appropriate for informing new practice in this field. The account given above may be of use as a resource for such school-based research.

References

ASHTON, C., STONEY, A. and HANNON, P. (1986). 'A reading at home project in a first school', *Support for Learning*, 1, 1, 43–9.

BAILEY, R. (1980). 'The home-school liaison teacher'. In: CRAFT, M., RAYNOR, J. and COHEN, L. (Eds) *Linking Home and School: a New Review*. 3rd edition. London: Harper and Row.

BRONFENBRENNER, U. (1974). *A Report on Longitudinal Evaluations of Preschool Programs. Vol. 2, Is Early Intervention Effective?* Washington, D.C.: DHEW Publication No. (OHD) 74–25.

BULLOCK REPORT. GREAT BRITAIN. DEPARTMENT OF EDUCATION AND SCIENCE. (1975). *A Language for Life*. London: HMSO.

BUSHELL, R., MILLER, A. and ROBSON, D. (1982). 'Parents as remedial teachers: an account of a paired reading project with junior school failing readers and their parents', *AEP Journal*, 5, 9, 7–13.

CAMERON, R. J. (1984). 'Portage in the UK: 1984', *Journal of Community Education*, 3, 3, 24–33.

CYSTER, R., CLIFT, P. S. and BATTLE, S. (1980). *Parental Involvement in Primary Schools*. Slough: NFER.

DEPARTMENT OF EDUCATION AND SCIENCE. (1982). *Education 5 to 9: an illustrative survey of 80 first schools in England*. London: HMSO.

EVANS, B. and HANNON, P. (1977). 'Catching them early', *Times Educational Supplement*, 27 May.

FEELEY, G. and KARRAN, S. (1983). 'The Coventry experience'. In: APLIN, G. and PUGH, G. (Eds) *Perspectives on Preschool Home-visiting*. London/Coventry: National Children's Bureau/Community Education Development Centre.

GRAY, S. W. and KLAUS, R. A. (1970). 'The early training project: a seventh year report', *Child Development*, 41, 909–24.

HANNON, P., JACKSON, A. and PAGE, B. (1985). 'Implementation and take-up of a project to involve parents in the teaching of reading'. In: TOPPING, K. and WOLFENDALE, S. (Eds) *Parental Involvement in Children's Reading*. London: Croom Helm.

HEWISON, J. (1981). 'Home is where the help is', *Times Educational Supplement*, 16 January.

JACKSON, A. and HANNON, P. (1981). *The Belfield Reading Project*. Rochdale: Belfield Community Council.

MACLEOD, F. (1986). 'What happens in the home–school liaison visits?', *Education 3–13*, 14, 1, 29–34.

MORRIS, J. AND THE STAFF OF BLUFF SCHOOL (1985). 'Home-visiting', *Set* (research information for teachers), 1, 13. Wellington, N.Z.: New Zealand Council for Educational Research.

PLOWDEN REPORT. GREAT BRITAIN. DEPARTMENT OF EDUCATION AND SCIENCE. CENTRAL ADVISORY COUNCIL FOR EDUCATION (ENGLAND) (1967). *Children and Their Primary Schools*. London: HMSO.

POULTON, G. (1983). 'Origins and development of pre-school home-visiting'. In: APLIN, G. and PUGH, G. (Eds) *Perspectives on Pre-school Home Visiting*. London/Coventry: National Children's Bureau/ Community Education Development Centre.

PUGH, G. (1981). *Parents as Partners*. London: National Children's Bureau.

RAVEN, J. (1980). *Parents, Teachers and Children: a Study of an Educational Home-visiting Scheme*. Sevenoaks: Hodder and Stoughton, for SCRE.

SMITH, G. (Ed) (1975). *Educational Priority. Vol. 4, The West Riding Project*. London: HMSO.

TIZARD, J., SCHOFIELD, W. N. and HEWISON, J. (1982). 'Collaboration between teachers and parents in assisting children's reading', *British Journal of Educational Psychology*, 52, 1–15.

WEIKART, D. P., BOND, J. T. and McNEIL, J. T. (1978). The Ypsilanti Perry Preschool Project: preschool years and longitudinal results. Monographs of the High/Scope Educational Research Foundation. No. 3.

Home and School at the Launch: Some Preliminary Observations

Robert N. Rapoport

Social scientists and educators tend to use a model of industrial society that emphasizes specialization of social institutions. According to this conception, which was expressed in Durkheim's metaphor of organic solidarity, modern societies cohere through the interdependent functioning of differentiated institutions, each, like organs of a body, contributing distinctively to the functioning of the whole. Families, schools, economic and governmental organizations, etc., pursue their special interests according to their distinctive modes of functioning. The society as a whole is integrated through such processes as co-operation and competition, exchange, and commitment to overarching values. Individuals become competent to function in complex settings through a socialization process which allows for the ordering of diverse experiences and values.

The prevailing conception has been that this ordering is facilitated through a linear progression of lifecycle phases according to which different social institutions hold sway serially. The individual is born into a family and in the earliest phases of his life it is the family and its values and modes of interaction that are dominant; then the individual goes to school and learns cognitive skills, during which period it is the school and its norms that dominate. Then the individual enters adult work roles, perhaps after a period of 'floundering' in the course of which a progression of learning experiences occur through which coping techniques are developed and firm occupational choices established (Super *et al.*, 1967; Butler, 1968). In the phase of adult maturity it is the normative system of the occupational world that dominates, with all other aspects of life falling into dependent, subordinate relationships.

This linear model has been extremely influential, in the society at large and in the academic disciplines. According to the model of serial dominance of social institutions, family influences were relegated to the periphery when a child entered school. The specialists in the educational institution tended to function with a 'closed door' policy, often viewing parents as providing noxious influences of one kind or another – by no means confined to those unfortunate families suffering from social disorganization and multiple deprivations. The formulations of Max Weber reinforced this viewpoint, and it is clear in Weber's writings that family influences were seen as antithetical to those of the world of work dominated by values of the Protestant Ethic. Weber felt that when family influences were too strong, they tended to undermine the development of rational bureaucracies based on individual merit (Weber, 1947, pp. 354–8). Educational policies emphasizing segregation of school and family, authoritative domination of school authorities and so on were legitimated in this framework.

While many empirical early studies seemed to indicate that family factors are important, it is only relatively recently that there has been a considerable effort to specify the aspects of family functioning that are specifically relevant to the educational experience. Although some of the new emphases may reflect fads and fashions in educational approaches (Howe, 1972), it seems that the issues of home and school relationships have followed an evolutionary sequence in which the familiar dialectical process has been at work. Initially, as societies which do not differentiate education from social life generally become modernized through urbanization and industrialization they give great emphasis to the role of specialists in the educational process and correspondingly de-emphasize the importance of the family. Inkeles describes this as follows:

> From a structural point of view, the central feature of this period is the gradual replacement of the family and adult kin by other agents and agencies of socialization: schools, teachers, peer groups, tribal or political authorities, local heroes, religious specialists, actors and other public figures, and so on. So far as the contents of socialization is concerned, problems of physical management, while far from irrelevant, become decidedly

secondary to others such as: the acquisition of values; learning specific adult relevant skills, especially those connected with earning a living; managing mature heterosexual relations, and manifesting increased readiness to accept responsibilities relevant to adult status such as marriage and parenthood. (Inkeles, 1969, p. 625)

The paradigm described by Inkeles has been prevalent in our own society until recently. Now, as the effectiveness of the specialist institutions comes to be reassessed, there is the reaction *against* the conception that they replace the family as effective influences, even in relation to the instrumental tasks outlined by Inkeles. And statements are made emphasizing the crucial nature of family influences and their continuing influence on the developing individual. Wiseman's weighting of the influence of early environment as twice that, pro-rata, of 'school' and 'neighbourhood' variables combined illustrates this, as does Moynihan's analysis of the place of family life in relation to problems of Negro participation in American life (Wiseman, 1964; Moynihan, 1965).

Midwinter writes, 'some research suggests that the home is more critical than the school in the ratio of four to one, in terms of influencing . . . the child's educational performance' (Midwinter, 1972), and Fraser writes, 'factors in the home environment . . . are more closely correlated with school progress than intelligence' (Fraser, 1973).

We are now in a phase of synthesis, in which different conceptions of the articulation of life-sectors are being explored.

One approach is to press schooling into the earlier years, formerly exclusively family territory. The appreciation of the crucial nature of early family experience is giving rise to a spate of new ventures in preschool education. This is illustrated by headstart programmes, educational priority programmes, parent-education programmes and other interventions by educators into life spheres and lifecycle phases formerly considered to be outside their specialist province (Bronfenbrenner, 1974; Halsey, 1972; Wall, 1955; Blackstone, 1971; Tizard, 1974).

The appreciation of *continuing* home influences on school performance has given rise to a spate of efforts to link parents' activities to those of teachers (Craft *et al.*, 1967; Green, 1968; McGeeney, 1969; Young, 1967; Miller, 1971). As well as inviting parents in, some teachers are advocating going out to the homes (Hudson, 1975). Musgrove suggests that 'home and school should merge, with home as the senior partner' (Musgrove, 1966), and many of the deschooling experiments urge much greater blurring of traditional lines of authority.

At the same time there is a recognition that no single conception of 'the family' or single policy as to the optimal type of linkage between school and home is universally valid. Families are increasingly seen in terms that allow for a more fine-grained appreciation of variation. Social class differences, which often in the past led to stereotyped conceptions, are among the analytic tools available, but so are concepts that cut across social class. It is recognized that there may be a tendency for tensions to exist between teachers and parents over issues concerning the child, who is of concern to both. But there is a greater tendency for each party to see their efforts as at least potentially constructive complements to those of the other (Sharrock, 1968).

Litwak and Meyer, noting the perils of too great a blurring of distinctive characteristics of families and schools as well as those of too great a differentiation, suggest a 'balance theory' of linkages. They suggest various devices, to be applied according to the situation, to enhance co-ordination of efforts between teachers and parents in the interests of the developing child (Litwak and Meyer, 1974).

Leichter, in her work on 'family as educator' has highlighted some of the parallel processes at home and school. The inculcation of language and communication skills, the organization of activity, of a sense of the past and one's part in a developmental process, the capacity to assess and evaluate experience and so on are elements in the growth process in which both home and school are crucially involved (Leichter, 1974).

School-leaving as a critical transition

Most of the attention to family influences as relevant to the educational and occupational career has been given to early influences. This has been consistently so, whether stemming from the wish to make predictions for selective cultivation of the more talented members of society or from the more recent preoccupation with detecting and compensating for early deficits before they become sufficiently ingrained to produce a cycle of deprivation (Porter, 1974). Recognition of early signs of developmental tendencies – whether gifted or anomalous in other ways – is important, as is the appreciation of familial constellations that impede or facilitate the educative process as it occurs at school. However, this does not necessarily imply that familial influences are no longer important later in the lifecycle, for example at the time of school leaving. And yet this is an area about which there is little information at the present time.

Douglas noted that school-entry and school-leaving are two of the most important of the critical transitions that punctuate the lifecycle. Our own exploratory data suggest that family influences are often of great significance in the school-leaving transition, though perhaps in different ways as compared with their earlier influences.

Why then, has the issue of family influence been neglected at this phase? A number of factors can explain the lack of attention given to family influences on the school-leaver. School-leavers themselves tend to de-emphasize the importance of family influences on their decision-making at this point because they are involved in a phase of their own development in which they are inclined to emphasize their individual autonomy. The schools tend to de-emphasize parental involvement at this point because for the most part parent–school contacts decrease with age of the pupil. Parents themselves tend to feel that their influence is declining, because they compare it with the earlier influence they wielded over the child. In addition, the parents themselves may, at this point, be undergoing critical lifecycle transitions which may distract them from involvement with their adolescent children's life decisions. Mothers may be re-entering work, if they have not already done so, and may be involved in coping with stressful transitions themselves. Fathers may be re-evaluating their own life situations as part of their mid-life preoccupations – or, among older parents, be anticipating changes in life style associated with retirement (Rapoport and Rapoport, 1975).

Characteristically, the school-leaving period is a phase of some turbulence, to which factors associated with adolescence as a lifecycle stage, factors associated with the parents' marital cycle and factors associated with the discontinuities between educational institutions and the occupational system all contribute. Research on school-leavers has concentrated on one or another of these dimensions.

Thus, signs of turbulence (personal disturbance, social maladjustment, intergenerational conflict, job instability or indecision) have been analysed as part of the adolescent phenomenon of 'identity diffusion' (Erikson, 1956), of disturbance associated with 'object loss' (the 'objects' being nurturing parents, teachers, the school, or the self as a child) (Laufer, 1966; Hansburg, 1972) or, as part of the family dynamics – reflecting the tendency for marital discord to rise to a peak at this phase (Rollins and Feldman, 1970) and for children's disturbances to reflect as well as exacerbate parental conflicts. The framework of analysing discontinuities between school and the labour force is partly related to assessing the utility of specialist bridging roles of various kinds, and partly it is associated with a critique of school and work as linked social institutions.

Maizels highlights the poor fit between school curricula and occupational life, particularly for those destined for less skilled occupations. But she queries the feasibility of schools preparing individuals for the realities of occupations which hold little intrinsic gratification without fundamental changes in one or the other or both systems (Maizels, 1970). Others recommend linking mechanisms of various kinds precisely for those sub-groups who experience the greatest discontinuity: youth employment specialists (Roberts, 1971), careers counsellors (Avent, 1974); the extension of educational participation into the community, and/or of industrial participation into the schools; the creation of special 'bridging institutions' (Hill, 1975), the cultivation of individual resourcefulness for *living*, in circumstances where occupation varies in importance (Rapoport and Rapoport, 1975). Except for the last-mentioned study, family factors are not prominent in formulations made about the school-leaving transition. When Roberts speaks of 'teamwork' in vocational guidance he means teamwork among specialists, though in a concluding section on the social context he cites research indicating that parental influences are likely to be greater than those of peers in matters of vocational decisions (Roberts, 1971, p. 143).

Our current explorations suggest that the understatement of

family influence at the school-leaving transition represents a phase of development in our thinking comparable to the earlier understatement of family influences in education at earlier phases. While there are powerful reasons for viewing family influences differently at this stage – where one of the individual's developmental tasks is to separate himself from infantile dependency on his parents – this should not imply the absence of influence. To imply this would be contrary to the facts, and counterproductive in relation to maximizing the use of available resources in facilitating the transition from school to work.

Observations of familial process at the launch from school

In our current research, which is an exploratory study in some depth of a series of 20 London school-leavers and their families as they experience the transition from school, a number of impressions are available though the analysis of the data is still under way. They can be presented as a series of conjectures, first about the patterns of parental influence which are 'enabling', as distinct from disabling for the school-leaver in decision-making at this point; and second about the possible implications for school-leavers, their families and educators.

(1) Our data suggest that fathers tend to play a different part at this point than in earlier transitions. In earlier phases, when the children are small and have to be managed physically, mothering receives greatest attention both in the culture generally and in the research literature. And, 'parenting' has tended to mean 'the mother' when it came to school visits, PTA and the like. At this later stage, however, though parents visit the schools less – and are often actively discouraged from visiting the careers officer by the young person himself (who wishes to sort out these things on his own) – the father is more important in the background than previously. This is true for girls as well as for boys, and seems to involve two components:

(a) Fathers are associated culturally and in the minds of most of the school-leavers as the knowledgeable ones about the world of work. They are not only the most likely ones to be employed in occupations that may serve as models (positive or negative) in the repertoire of the school-leaver, but they are considered to be experts on the world of work and its vicissitudes.

(b) Fathers are more likely to become involved in family dynamics as issues of social control increase in frequency and salience. Issues of enforcing rules of time, hours to be at home, friends to be allowed, dress and appearance, behaviour and the like may increasingly be thrown onto the father willy-nilly as mothers feel at a loss with the use of techniques that had been effective when the children were smaller.

This observation is consistent with our findings in an earlier national survey (sponsored by PEP and with the collaboration of the Oxford Department of Educational Studies) of social influences on sixth form boys' and girls' career aspirations. While the students indicated that their parents had little influence on choice of school subjects, they report that parental advice is the most useful to them when it comes to career decisions. As Table 1 shows, father is the more influential for boys and girls in all of the subject groups except for the arts students (Hutchings, 1971).

Table 1: Perceived sources of advice from family by subject group (percentages)*

	Arts		**Social sciences**		**Physical and biological sciences**	
	Boys	*Girls*	*Boys*	*Girls*	*Boys*	*Girls*
Mother	45	53	30	31	29	43
Father	58	34	40	51	52	44
Other family	28	57	50	49	58	60

*Total percentages include multiple choices.

The fact that such high proportions report help from other family members points to the second impression that we are deriving from our exploratory work.

(2) Our data suggest that siblings play a very important part in the decision process at school-leaving. Always a tantalizing, under-studied area of social research, the question of sibling relationships is

a most promising one in relation to occupational choice, and the development of meaningful lifestyles following school-leaving. Some of the earlier literature has concentrated on the implications of position in the birth order, or on the functions of sibling rivalry in teaching children to manage conflict and competition. Our data suggest that elder siblings often play a critical role in the transition particularly where the parental guidance is rejected by a younger sibling as unacceptable for any of a variety of reasons.

(3) Gender seems to be a more powerful determinant of turbulence at this stage than social class or social mobility. Nearly all of the boys from working-class families in our sample left school for work, and nearly all of the boys from middle-class families in our sample left school for further education – with relatively little sign of conflict about setting their levels of aspiration. In both subgroups, the main issues surround the specification of occupation within a band of occupational types, rather than which band to aim at. In both groups it tended to be the father who was the role model, or at least mentor, and mother considered pretty irrelevant. For the girls, in contrast, there is considerable turbulence and conflict about what level of occupation to aspire to, what place to give occupational aspiration in relation to the role of 'wife', and what weight to assign to mothers' vs. fathers' advice and experience (Henderson, 1975).

(4) Though it is possible to rationalize differentiated roles for teachers, careers officers and family members (the first emphasizing skill-training, the second assessment of 'fit' between the individual and the labour market, and the third informal supports for personal adjustment), in fact these roles may be taken in different ways by different parties in the transition. In one case that we studied it was the mother who gathered information about job opportunities and presented them more effectively to the school-leaver than the careers officer. In another family, it was a teacher who provided an occupational role model and moral support in making a job choice that allowed for further skill development through apprenticeship training. In this case it was the boys' peers and other teachers who were sceptical about his potentials.

Some implications

To draw implications on the basis of preliminary impressions about the pattern of findings in an exploratory study is perhaps presumptuous. However, a number of points seem worth bearing in mind as educationists.

First, it is important to recognize that family influences are operative at the launching point, even though sight of actual family members may have been lacking for some time. The influence of family members is usually indirect rather than direct at this stage, but should be kept in mind. This often includes siblings as well as parents.

Secondly, girls have a more difficult set of dilemmas at this point than boys, and they require special understanding if they are to come to grips with their problems of reconciling the newer egalitarian ideas with the conventional norms and models which are provided in their intimate environments and cultural experiences. This is not an issue involving them alone, but their family members, boys with whom they interact, and their teachers and employers. The schools might take a lead in efforts not only to understand the special dilemmas of girls in today's society, but to conduct consciousness-raising groups for boys and girls on issues of sex-roles. Thirdly, while specialist inputs are important to have available, it is important to recognize that the help which specialists seek to provide may be effectively applied by others as well – perhaps even more effectively in some cases. In the end it is the effectiveness of application of helping resources rather than the agent that is the crux of the matter. It may not be the specialist himself who makes the most effective use, for example, of job information, but a peer, a parent, a sibling, a teacher, or someone else. The aim, therefore, should be to make resources available, and orchestrating their use rather than husbanding them within specialist roles and organizations.

Finally, though our data are highly tentative and in their preliminary stages of analysis, we are impressed with the importance of reciprocal influences between parents and their children at this transition point. There has been a great deal of appreciation recently of the child's influence on his caretaker – concentrating particularly on infant interaction with parental figures. Obvious as it may seem to extend this framework to the adolescent's influence on his parent, this is relatively less explored. Jessie Bernard has noted how the life crisis experienced by middle-aged women has many characteristics in common with the identity crisis of her adolescent daughter (Bernard, 1975). Levi, Stierlin and Savard (1972) have noted a similar 'interlocking of crises' for fathers and sons. Our data suggest that there are not only various patterns of identification and interlocking of life decision processes as between parents and their adolescent children at this point, but that the ways in which they are managed are important to all concerned. The effects of a particular resolution may ramify to affect others; and, conversely, the failure of one individual at either generational level may impede the other's capacity to adapt. The school leaver in our series with the least satisfactory outcome a year after leaving school is a girl whose mother is highly identified with her and imposes very great expectations that the daughter will fulfil the mother's frustrated aspirations. This mother neither assesses the daughter's own needs and resources objectively, nor does she resolve her own unhappy marital and occupational situation satisfactorily – hanging on to her involvement with her daughter as a pseudo solution.

While these intricacies of family dynamics, of identifications and counter identifications, involvements and crisis resolutions may be felt to lie outside the sphere of competence of most teachers or careers officers, an appreciation of their existence may enhance the work of educators, whose participation in the launching process is also potentially more important than is generally appreciated.

References

AVENT, C. (1974). *Practical Approaches to Careers Education*. Cambridge: CRAC.

BERNARD, J. (1975). *Women, Wives, Mothers*. Chicago: Aldine.

BLACKSTONE, T. (1971). *A Fair Start: The Provision of Preschool Education*. London: Allen Lane.

BRONFENBRENNER, V. (1974). 'Children, families and social policy: an American perspective'. In: DHSS *The Family in Society, Dimensions of Parenthood*. London: HMSO.

BUTLER, J. R. (1968). *Occupational Choice*. London: HMSO.

CRAFT, M. *et al*. (1967). *Linking Home and School*. London: Longman.

ERIKSON, E. H. (1956). *Childhood and Society*. New York: Norton.

FRASER, E. D. (1973). *Home Environment and the School*. London: University of London Press.

GREEN, L. (1968). *Parents and Teachers – Partners or Rivals?* London: Allen and Unwin.

HALSEY, A. H. (1972). *Educational Priority*. London: HMSO.

HANSBURG, H. G. (1972). *Adolescent Separation Anxiety*. Springfield, Ill.: C. C. Thomas.

HENDERSON, E. (1975). 'Sex role dilemmas of modern adolescents'. In: MEYERSON, S. (Ed) *Adolescence: the Crises of Adjustment*. London: Allen and Unwin.

HILL, J. M. (1975). 'The transition from school to work', *Secondary Education*, 5, 1, 14.

HOWE, H. L. (1972). *Openness – The New Kick in Education*. New York: The Ford Foundation.

HUDSON, M. J. (1975). A consideration of the case for the systematic visiting of secondary school children's homes by their teachers. Manuscript, University of London, Institute of Education.

HUTCHINGS, D. (1971). The academic motivation and career perception of girls of high ability. Manuscript, Oxford Department of Educational Studies.

INKELES, A. (1969). 'Social structure and socialization'. In: GOSLIN, D. (Ed) *Handbook of Socialization Theory and Research*, pp. 619–32. Chicago: Rand McNally.

LAUFER, M. (1966). 'Object loss and mourning during adolescence', *Psychoanalytic Study of the Child*, 21, 269–93.

LEICHTER, H. J. (1974). 'Some perspectives on the family as educator', *Columbia University Teacher's College Record*, 76, 2, 175–217.

LEVI, STIERLIN and SAVARD. (1972). 'Fathers and sons: the interlocking crises of integrity and identity', *Psychiatry*, 35.

LITWAK, E. and MEYER, H. J. (1974). *School, Family and Neighbourhood*. New York and London: Columbia.

McGEENEY, P. (1969). *Parents are Welcome*. London: Longman

MAIZELS, J. (1970). *Adolescent Needs and the Transition from School to Work*. London: Athlone Press.

MIDWINTER, E. (1972). *Priority Education: an account of the Liverpool Project*. Harmondsworth: Penguin.

MILLER, G. W. (1971). *Educational Opportunity and the Home*. London: Longman.

MOYNIHAN, D. (1965). *The Negro Family: the case for national action*. Washington: US Federal Govt.

MUSGROVE, F. (1966). *The Family, Education and Society*. London: Routledge and Kegan Paul.

PORTER, J. F. (1974). 'Dimensions of parenthood and views of society'. In: DHSS *The Family in Society, Dimensions of Parenthood*. London: HMSO, pp. 44–55.

RAPOPORT, R. and RAPOPORT, R. N. (1975). *Leisure and the Family Life Cycle*. London: Routledge and Kegan Paul.

ROBERTS, K. (1971). *From School to Work.* Newton Abbot: David and Charles.

ROLLINS and FELDMAN (1970). 'Marital status over the family life cycle', *Journal of Marriage and the Family*, 32, 1.

RUTTER, M. (1972). *Maternal Deprivations Reassessed.* Harmondsworth: Penguin.

SHARROCK, A. (1968). 'Relations between home and school', *Educational Research*, 10, 3, 185–96.

SUPER, D. E. *et al.* (1967). *Floundering and Trial after High School.* New York: Columbia Teachers' College Press.

TIZARD, B. (1974). *Pre-school Education: a Research Review*. London: SSRC.

WALL (1955). *Education and Mental Health*. UNESCO. London: Harrap.

WEBER, M. (1947). *The Theory of Social and Economic Organisation*. (A. Henderson and T. Parsons, trans.) New York: Oxford University Press.

WISEMAN, S. (1964). *Education and Environment*. Manchester: Manchester University Press.

YOUNG, M. (1967). 'Parent–teacher cooperation'. In: CRAFT *et al.*, *supra*, pp. 136–42.